The Quiet Struggle

The Quiet Struggle

Information and Libraries for the People of Africa

Second Edition

Paul Sturges and Richard Neill

MANSELL

LONDON AND WASHINGTON

Mansell Publishing Limited, *A Cassell imprint*
Wellington House, 125 Strand, London WC2R 0BB, England
PO Box 605, Herndon, Virginia 20172, USA

First edition published 1990. Reprinted 1992, 1993
Second edition prepared by Paul Sturges and published 1998

British Library Cataloguing in Publication Data
A catalogue record for this book is available from the British Library.
ISBN 0 7201 2293 7

Library of Congress Cataloging-in-Publication Data
Sturges, R. P. (Rodney Paul)
    The quiet struggle: information and libraries for the people of Africa/Paul
Sturges and Richard Neill. – 2nd ed.
        p.   cm.
    Includes bibliographical references (p.   ) and index.
    ISBN 0–7201–2293–7
    1. Libraries–Africa.   2. Information services– Africa.
  I. Neill, Richard, 1953.   II. Title.
  Z857.A1S78 1997
  027.06–dc21   97–11831
                                                                                      CIP

Typeset by York House Typographic Ltd
Printed and bound in Great Britain by Biddles Ltd, Guildford and King's Lynn

Contents

Acknowledgements

We acknowledge with much gratitude the help of our employers, the University of Botswana and Loughborough University, for granting each of us study leave to work on projects including this new edition of *The Quiet Struggle*. Richard Neill's leave was during 1995 and Paul Sturges's was for the academic year 1996–7. Both of us owe a great deal to colleagues who, among other things, covered our responsibilities during study leave. Paul Sturges would particularly like to thank Eric Davies for taking on much of his teaching and Carolyn Pritchett for her invaluable assistance with teaching and research, which included the extensive bibliographical searches that were essential for this new edition.

Paul Sturges was a Visiting Fellow at the National University of Science and Technology, Bulawayo, Zimbabwe from September to December 1996, and is very grateful for the help and cooperation of all those with whom he was in contact at that institution. Both of us were helped and inspired on many occasions by academic colleagues and students, librarians and information professionals from all over Africa. Paul Sturges would like to make particular acknowledgement, however, to his friend and former student Diel Wele of the Senegalese Ministry of Culture, who made possible a fruitful research visit to Senegal in May 1996, and to George Chimseu of the Malawi National Library Service, his partner in field research in Malawi in July 1994. Their help and comradeship were invaluable.

Finally, Paul Sturges wishes to thank his cousin Sam and family Val, Dean, Tanya and James Peters, whose hospitality made his stay in Bulawayo so enjoyable as well as useful, and his own family Claire, Harriet, Isabel and Eleanor who supported him and put up with his regular absences (physical and mental).

Introduction

The first edition of this book began with the suggestion that the story of contemporary Africa is a story of struggles. Although much has changed since 1989 when that was written, it is still true. The struggle for political freedom has resulted in independence for Namibia and Eritrea and a new South Africa which grants full citizenship to all its people. At the same time Liberia, Somalia, Rwanda and Burundi have been wrecked by civil war. The struggle to create new political and administrative institutions continues, but the continent is still too frequently plagued by waste, corruption, electoral manipulation, coups and the subversion of constitutions. In extreme cases in the past the course of the struggle has been diverted by the murderous excesses of the personal rule of such as Bokassa, Macias Nguema and Amin. Today there are still massively corrupt and destructive regimes such as that of Abacha to remind us that there is much to be done.

There are also the long-running struggles for economic emancipation from a colonial legacy, from terrible burdens of debt, and from the activities of international corporations more rich and powerful than many sovereign states. The prescriptions of financial institutions such as the World Bank and the International Monetary Fund have sharpened the intensity of these struggles. All are often compounded by the involvement of an African elite more concerned with personal enrichment than the sufferings of their fellow citizens. At the same time there is the struggle to forge cultural identities, perhaps more successful because of the worldwide recognition of African music and art, but still a struggle in which the cultural imperialism of the great Northern economies threatens to

1

homogenize the cultural expression of the whole world. This, and others of Africa's struggles, have been intermittently observed by the world's media, in ways which seem to give substance to the common perception of Africa as a continent on the verge of disintegration.

There is, however, yet another struggle: a quiet struggle that rarely makes newspaper headlines, and that has failed to attract the attention of the cameras of press and television. Nor did this particular struggle, in the past, feature prominently in the considerable flow of books, articles, pamphlets, research papers and consultancy papers that discuss Africa in such depth and detail. This quiet struggle is a struggle of Africa's people, led by their writers, journalists, publishers, educationalists, broadcasters, media workers, computer and telecommunication specialists and, not to be forgotten, its information and library professionals. It is the struggle for information, the struggle for knowledge.

It is this quiet struggle which is the subject of this book. Although the book is primarily concerned with this issue as it directly affects the development of libraries and other information institutions, the authors believe very strongly that libraries, archives, documentation and information centres cannot meaningfully be discussed in isolation. They have to be considered within the context of a total information environment which encompasses issues from oral communication to virtual reality. Furthermore, this book embodies the conviction that much of the conventional thinking on information development in Africa needs to be turned on its head. Such an assertion can only be made on the basis of an extensive re-examination that goes back to the roots of information generation, transmission and use within the specific context of Africa.

This was obviously a major assignment when the authors began the first edition of this book and they did not then, and do not now, claim exclusive credit for the content of the re-examination. About 1980 the writings of commentators on the information scene in Africa such as Benge[1] and Amadi[2] began to suggest an approach, and the published research and comment of a talented few, led by Aboyade[3] and Mchombu,[4] gave it substance. While much of the literature on this subject continued to be conventional and repetitive, a steadily increasing number of contributions asked radical questions and suggested unconventional answers. By the time the first edition of this book appeared in 1990, the number of significant contributions towards developing a body of theory of information service for Africa was growing; there were plenty of outlets for such ideas; and a journal, *Information Development*, had been started, which was particularly hospitable. Since that time the number and quality of relevant contributions has continued to increase and now includes two major books by Ndiaye[5] and Olden.[6] All of this has convinced the authors that the time for a renewal of the synthesis which they first offered in 1990 has arrived.

The book still deals exclusively with sub-Saharan Africa. North Africa is omitted because the traditions and culture there are so distinctively different as to require a fundamentally different treatment. What has changed is that, with the ending of the system of apartheid in South Africa, the authors have begun to include South African examples and to attempt some comment on the impact that its powerful knowledge industries might have on the neighbouring regions. As in the first edition, the content of the book is derived mainly from the Anglophone parts of the continent. However, a much stronger attempt has been made to discuss those areas using other metropolitan languages, particularly French. It will still be necessary to look to writers with a firm base in these languages for detail on library and information work in those regions, but the authors believe that the generalizations in this edition are more solidly derived from the experience of the whole of sub-Saharan Africa than before. Fortunately, there is a real sense in which many generalizations do hold good for more than one African country, despite the rich social and cultural diversity that exists.

Perhaps the chief way in which this edition differs from the previous one is revealed in the subtitle which now refers to 'the people of Africa'. The decision to give the book an even more people-centred focus than before was made because the authors felt that there was not only rather more to be said on the role of information in African life and the ways in which community-based information services could be developed, but that there was also a need for a separate treatment of the strategic role of information in a developing continent. A companion volume to the present one, providing a strategic audit of information in Africa was planned at the same time as this new edition. The authors feel that a clearer focus and a better defined topic will make this book more helpful to its readers.

Those readers are, as with the first edition, primarily those directly and practically concerned with information service in

Africa. The intention is, as before, to present the arguments and proffer the solutions most likely to solve some of Africa's information problems. The book is intended to be of interest, not only to librarians, archivists, documentalists and other information providers, but also to writers, publishers, educators, communication workers and many others for whom information, whether they realize it or not, plays an important part in their professional lives. The evidence of the first edition is that, because of the intense and often committed interest in Africa to be found in many other parts of the world, some of the arguments presented here will also be of interest outside the continent itself.

References

1. Benge, R.C. *Cultural Crisis and Libraries in the Third World*. London, Bingley, 1979.
2. Amadi, A.O. *African Libraries: Western Tradition and Colonial Brainwashing*. Metuchen, NJ, Scarecrow Press, 1981.
3. Aboyade. B.O. Communications potentials of the library for non-literates: an experiment in providing information services in a rural setting. *Libri*, 34, 1984. 243–62.
4. Mchombu, K.J. On the librarianship of poverty. *Libri*, 32, 1982. 241–50.
5. Ndiaye, A.R. *Communication à la base: enraciner et épanouir*. Dakar, ENDA, 1994.
6. Olden, A. *Libraries in Africa: Pioneers, Policies, Problems*. Lanham, MD, Scarecrow Press, 1995.

Chapter One

Africa's Information Environment

Introduction

In 1986, at around the time when the world's attention was drawn to the horrific starvation taking place in Ethiopia, the historian Michael Crowder was presenting a paper at the Standing Conference on Library Materials on Africa (SCOLMA) Annual General Meeting which focused on Africa's other famine.[1] The famine he was referring to was the book famine, and the picture he painted was in its own way as dramatic as the scenes of starvation portrayed on the world's television screens. If not reversed, the famine Crowder so graphically described has been alleged to have implications as disastrous for Africa's long-term future as the catastrophic absence of food does for the short term.

This case was dramatically put by Kenneth Kaunda, then President of Zambia, when he warned Zambians that they were, as a people, heading for intellectual bankruptcy because of the impoverished and distressed state of the book trades. Calling the situation a national tragedy, Kaunda lamented the virtual absence of books from the nation's bookshops. By the 1990s the situation had deteriorated further, so that at

> Kingston's, Lusaka's foremost and only bookshop, potatoes, cabbages and exercise books are sold. On the first floor, a few dusty copies of Kenneth Kaunda's *Letter to my children* are waiting for customers, certainly no longer very popular after his downfall in 1991.[2]

Similar situations exist in other African countries, where the publishing industry and book trade have virtually collapsed so that major cities no longer claim a single well-stocked bookshop. In Tanzania, for instance, publishing is at a disastrously low ebb. Delays between receiving a manuscript and publication are long, because of shortage of materials, and even at the government-owned Tanzanian Publishing House such delays have taken years. International firms such as Oxford University Press and Longman withdrew from business in the country years ago. Small publishers are accused of habitually cheating authors of royalties, and many authors profess themselves too frustrated to continue writing for them. Imported books are scarce and prohibitively expensive, to the extent that the cost of a copy can easily equal a civil servant's minimum monthly salary. The shortage of textbooks is so serious that President Mwinyi ordered all those holding copies to surrender them to the nearest school or police station on pain of prosecution.[3]

In terms of books, this is certainly the context in which Africa's development is taking place and the future of her peoples is being shaped. It is a context which can be witnessed by a casual visit to almost any rural primary school class where it is not uncommon to see 40 or 50 children sharing three or four old and battered textbooks, with no additional reading material available. The convincing, though possibly apocryphal, story is told of the boy who could only read text upside-down because he had always seen it from the wrong side of the desk. This is a context in which the illiterate proportion of the population may be as much as, or even more than 60 per cent, but really trustworthy figures are seldom readily available. It is a context where an entire continent has over 11 per cent of the world's population, yet only 1 per cent of its book production, 1 per cent of its newspaper circulation and 1 per cent of its paper consumption.[4]

Africa's famine of published information, however, is not only due to the poverty which makes books unavailable but is also caused by the propensity of African governments to suppress information. The book famine could really be redefined as part of a more general information famine. Often information could be readily available but is withheld, and the fate of those seeking to expose it can sometimes involve the severest penalties. The example of the secrecy that frequently surrounds the subject of Acquired Immune Deficiency Syndrome (AIDS) is a continuing one. In East Africa during the mid-1980s, soon after AIDS first hit the headlines in Europe and North America, the condition was almost without exception characterized, by implication at least, as a 'gay plague'. However, another possible explanation for its spread was offered after a team of American researchers went to East and Central Africa and concluded not only that AIDS was endemic in the region but that its origins could be traced back to the local population. The fact that the tests the researchers had used later proved to be unreliable was lost in the combination of media hysteria and public ignorance which convinced many journalists and their readers that Africa was the source of an AIDS menace.

The response of many African governments, particularly in East Africa was, at the time and in the circumstances, quite understandable. They refused to allow subsequent researchers to publish their results and the medical profession even had difficulty acknowledging that they were indeed treating patients who were suffering from AIDS. In Kenya, for example, there was an immediate restriction on the reporting of AIDS in the media and it was made clear to Kenyan newspaper editors that there would be serious consequences if this embargo were to be broken. The result of these media restrictions was a burgeoning of rumour as to the cause and spread of AIDS, the frightening off of visitors and tourists, and a belief among the Western press corps that its initial fears were being confirmed. A spiral of further sensational reporting in the world's press was the consequence.[5]

It is also true that the control of information and repression of those who seek to disseminate it, is practised in many parts of the continent on a daily rather than an occasional basis. In the case of Cameroon, for instance, the pervasiveness of control in such regimes of censorship and repression is well illustrated.[6] The Cameroonian constitution protects freedom of expression and the freedom to form political parties. However, since 1982 the ruling Rassemblement Démocratique du Peuple Camerounais (RDPC) has run a one-party state with its main rival the Union des Populations du Camerounaises (UPC) banned. The police have used a 1962 Ordinance on Subversion which brings penalties of up to five years imprisonment for those who show 'lack of respect for authorities'. In February 1990 it was used against a group who were meeting to discuss the (constitutionally protected) formation of an opposition political party. Five people, from a group of eleven, were found guilty and one, the lawyer Yondo Black, was sentenced to three years in prison.

The constitutional protection of press freedom and freedom of expression is also bypassed by the government, using a Press Law which requires that publications should be given authorization in advance by the Ministry of the Interior. The government controls the only national daily newspaper, *Cameroon Tribune*, although there are a number of private publications which try to compete unsubsidized in an environment of high costs, particularly for newsprint. Official publishers are expected to practice a self-censorship, but private publishers must submit proof copies of what they intend to publish for approval by the official censor. Material with the stamp of approval can then be sent to the government company SOPECAM, which has a monopoly on printing and owns the official newsagency CAMNEWS. A second stamp is required after printing and then the publications are permitted to be sold. Even then a publication could still be seized, as in April 1989 when fully-censored copies of *Le Messager* were found to be offensive to the President. A new law on Social Communication was introduced in December 1990, by which:

> The distribution of any newspaper may be stopped if the administrative authorities consider that the said paper does not fulfil the necessary [unspecified] conditions.

In September 1991 seven publications were banned under this law, which had effectively given editors the option of choosing between the censorship procedure and facing seizures of copies and banning.

Radio and television are state-owned and controlled, although material which offends the government is still occasionally broadcast. A radio journalist, Sam Nuvala, was charged with defamation for calling members of parliament 'a bunch of monkeys, idiots and hand clappers', and in May 1990 a TV journalist, George Tanyi, was arrested and sacked for organizing a discussion programme on multi-party democracy.[7] The repression goes further. The innocuously titled Centre National de Recherche (CNR), working through its Brigade Mixte Mobile (BMM), controls the expression and dissemination of opinions which run counter to the government line. Raids involving the confiscation of books and papers, the detention of suspects and the torture of those detained are all practised by the BMM. The political activist and writer Albert Mukong also ran a small bookshop in his home town of Bamenda. Books were confiscated from his stock, customers were scared away from the shop, and he eventually had to go out of business.[8]

The effects of such policies filter down to the librarian too. An example from Malawi in the days of Kamuzu Banda illustrates how this can work.[9] In May 1983 three Government Ministers and another MP died, reputedly in a car accident, in one of the *causes célebrès* of recent Malawian history. Copies of three newspapers (the *Guardian* from the UK, and the *Times* and *Daily Mail* from Zambia) had entered the country, despite containing claims that the victims were murdered. What is more, the newspapers were displayed in the periodicals section of the library at Chancellor College, Zomba. Students discovering this and desperate to read uncensored views of Malawian affairs, virtually fought in the periodicals section to obtain a sight of the copies. The librarians were then placed in a dilemma, which they resolved by withdrawing the offending copies, and requiring students from then on to sign for access to those newspapers. The librarians also read each arriving copy to try to determine whether it could be seen as subversive. As a result of this some further copies were also kept in store, with student access forbidden. At the time, it was widely believed that plain clothes security personnel were entering the library to monitor what was read. In effect what happened was that the librarians' fear of this led to them voluntarily extending the censorship system down to the practical library administration level.

It is also possible to show the way in which the power structures of the Malawian regime affected information in ways that reached right back to its initial generation and expression. This was not merely relevant to overtly 'political' information, but included flows of 'neutral' information in both practical and imaginative publications. Literature, for instance, was viewed by those in power in just the same way as other types of communication and it was marginalized and suppressed in ways equally insidious. Many of the books banned by the Censorship Board were literary and, indeed, Albert Muwalo (formerly Secretary General of the Malawi Congress Party) was tried in 1976 for possession of books including Orwell's *Animal Farm.*

More sinister yet was the imprisonment in 1987 of Jack Mapanje, poet and head of the English Department at the University of Malawi. The reason for his arrest was not made public, and he had never been identified with any political organization or viewpoint. However, some of his more recent poems had criticized Banda and his entourage, and he was thought to be preparing further critical poems for publication. In prison Mapanje was denied writing materials, but kept his sanity and self-respect by composing poems in his head. Denied by his literate upbringing and schooling of the oral poet's exceptionally retentive memory, this method of composition virtually ensured that by his release in 1991, he had forgotten the content of what he had composed. The recall of titles and fragments of these poems enabled him to reconstruct them in freedom, but his work in its original form was gone. State power had thus effectively destroyed the information in Mapanje's poems at its source. The principle of this is important, because the same ability to influence whether information actually entered into public existence was exercised right through the system of government, through a pattern of non-censorship structural constraints. In other words, institutions with the power to collect and disseminate information often could not, or would not do so.[10]

Similar processes can be observed elsewhere – in the Sudan at the beginning of the 1990s, for instance. The government there chose not to admit what famine early warning systems were showing: that a major food crisis had developed.

> Such a position would have undermined their policy of food self-sufficiency and increased their dependence on western food aid donors from whom they were trying to distance themselves. Meanwhile, donor agencies were reluctant to provide resources to a government towards which they were ill-disposed and were suspicious about how relief resources would be used, or misused, if they did not have complete control over them, a condition unacceptable to a government which resented being dictated to by western donors.[11]

By the time that international journalists covered Sudan's food crisis in 1991, it was too late for relief to be sent in time. The problem need not be one, like this, of sheer government unwillingness to accept the significance of information which is supplied to it, but can be one of simple bureaucratic rigidities. Agencies, for instance, may simply not be geared up to making decisions about supplying relief until a full assessment of the data has been made. The process of reaching the point at which information that has been available for some time is actually recognized as pointing to the need for a decision to be made, may defer such a decision beyond the point when it could retrieve the situation. In such a climate of rigidities, it is hardly surprising that means of informing the average citizen about matters that may be of vital concern are also habitually neglected. There is no sense of public information policy as a priority.

The difficulty can be even more deeply embedded, with institutions adopting policies based on dominant theories which condition what should be accepted as fact, and what should be ignored or explained away. The case of policies towards the vegetation of the forest-savanna transition zone in Guinea provides a particularly striking example.[12] Kissidougou prefecture has a savanna landscape with scattered trees and some patches of forest which surround village sites. Since the beginning of the century it has been the orthodoxy that the area was once all heavily forested but has been degraded by local farming methods. The evidence of air photography and local tradition point in quite the opposite direction, however, showing that the areas of forest have been created by careful management, which has increased the tree cover on the savanna. As a result of the dominant view, forest reserves have been created by government; donor support for local projects has been linked to 'green' policies; and heavily funded environmental projects have been set up. All this and more has been perpetuated by studies by donor agencies and projects which have the environmental 'problem' built in to their terms of reference.

This process of the growth of patterns and structures which validate information in terms of a particular view of the world, is not merely a matter of academic or administrative interest in Kissidougou. The forestry services of francophone West Africa have drawn revenue from a system of the sale of permits and licences for exploiting timber and wildlife, and of fines for breaking environmental laws. The services thus have a vested interest in the acceptance of the environmental degradation theory. In effect they feed back to local residents the 'fact' that their activities are detrimental to the local environment, and reinforce this message with a system of penalties. The adversarial relationship this creates between foresters and villagers inhibits the passing on of more accurate information. Villagers when questioned by officials tend to agree with them because to argue may threaten their access to possible benefits such as new infrastructure projects. When asked in a non-adversarial context, they will describe their beliefs and practices, and their accounts are supported by the evidence of aerial photographs obtained over long sequences of years. At the same time, a whole interlocking intellectual, social, political and financial structure depends on fundamentally misleading information flowing both upwards and downwards through the channels of communication.

Yet as counterbalance to these examples of information deprivation, distortion and neglect, there are positive features in the
African scene. Viewed from a slightly different perspective, Africa
can be characterized as positively information-rich. Its citizens
possess an adaptable oral mode of information transfer which is
deeply embedded in the social and psychological make-up of the
people themselves. Little affected by the complexities and expense
of computer technology, or even by the messages conveyed by
books, this oral mode is a channel which enables the swift spread of
news, and which allows access to knowledge on a diversity of topics
preserved for use and enjoyment in the memories of the people.
The traveller on the African bus or informal taxi, the worker resting
in the shade at the end of the day, the women in the group
laboriously carrying water to their homes or pounding grain
together, will exchange details on subjects which could just as easily
include the potential victor in the American presidential elections,
the price of chickens by the roadside, or the possible influence of
witchcraft on the failure of a neighbour's crops. This is a phenomenon which forms a major theme in this book.

Distress over Africa's information famine or, somewhat less commonly, confidence in the resilience of traditional communication
are two dominant views that have in the 1990s been joined by
another sentiment. This is a definite tendency towards optimism
with regard to the general information scene, arising from a change
in the political climate. Freedom in South Africa and Malawi, and
less spectacular and more ambiguous events such as elections in
countries including Zambia and Kenya, have brought considerable
lessening of controls and rigidities in information flow.

This has brought many examples of media independence and
deregulation. In Zambia and Malawi, public broadcasting was being
brought under the control of independent boards in 1996. Legislation allowing for the operation of privately-owned or community
media had come into force in South Africa, Malawi, Mozambique,
Zambia, Namibia and Angola. It has to be admitted that this is not
wholly positive as licences for private broadcasting have sometimes
been granted to favoured individuals, and there is a temptation to
use media access irresponsibly. Radio-Télévision Libre des Mille
Collines in Rwanda, for instance, was implicated in broadcasting
material that incited communal violence. Nevertheless, taken in
conjunction with growing press freedom, media developments
contribute to a positive mood.

Relaxation of restrictions on the press has occurred in a number of countries. In Tanzania, which had only two daily newspapers under the one-party state, the reaction was to encourage the setting up of as many as 30 by 1996. The life cycle of such newspapers is hectic. In Niger, a young entrepreneur started up a newspaper called *Haske*, with borrowed capital of US$2800. Its lively content swiftly caused it to outsell its dull, government-controlled rival by a ratio of 3:1. Its cover price, however, was US$1, in a country with an average income of US$200 per annum. Advertising revenue, the means by which newspapers everywhere are sold at affordable prices, was unforthcoming for a newspaper with an anti-regime political stance. In this case, as with dozens of other similar under-capitalized ventures throughout the continent, we see the interface between a newly-unleashed enthusiasm and optimism on the one hand, and the old realities of economics and power on the other.

The excitement and bustle of the positive changes emerging in many parts of Africa is infectious, but the mechanism behind many of them is a surprise. Much follows from a democratization process promoted by major donor countries, principally the USA and the European Community.[13] This has effectively brought down unrepresentative governments and enabled their replacement with alternatives which at least begin with a mandate from the electorate. Open discussion in a range of media has been a natural part of this process. At the same time, the World Bank and the International Monetary Fund (IMF) have made aid conditional upon breaking up state control of economies and opening up to private enterprise. Because of their immediate deleterious effect on the masses of the population in countries where they have been applied, as subsidies of various kinds are removed, economic structural adjustment programmes (ESAPs) are widely regarded as yet another painful imposition from outside the continent. Yet paradoxically they too have promoted information openness in a variety of ways.

For many years the World Bank concentrated its financial help on projects for infrastructure, principally in areas such as electrification and transportation. Gradually projects to help people raise their productivity and gain access to clean water, health care, education and housing were added to the Bank's portfolio. The projects began to have an information element built into them, which might be a monitoring and evaluation system, a data gathering mechanism, or even a public information programme or a library. There is even a recognition that

> Libraries may be in a situation where they are information providers in a medium (written word) that may not be accessible to many of their constituents: in many places, people are not literate enough to deal easily with written publications. This may lead to a redefinition of information solutions, away from traditional libraries and documentation centres, and into alternative ways of information dissemination.[14]

Thus, sources of loan finance may actually be available to shift librarianship towards a more people-centred focus. This parallels a trend for NGOs generally to change their emphasis:

> NGOs do not like to think of themselves as capital transferrers, but as ideas transferrers. Almost without exception they downplay their capacities as service deliverers and emphasize instead their capabilities in innovation, model-building, experimentation and advocacy. NGO strengths, they argue, are non-financial: learning from the grassroots, channelling local knowledge upward, and creating lateral information linkages.[15]

The World Bank has also come to see itself increasingly as a knowledge-based institution, shifting its emphasis from projects to encouraging economic policy reforms. As part of this process it has promoted the gathering of data within recipient countries so that the decision-making capacity of the Bank and the countries themselves is drastically improved. The structural adjustment programmes themselves thus tend to contain major elements of information upgrading. The sidewash of this tide has been to benefit the community of information providers. It has been an irony of policies that impoverish countless families, and reduce funds for government welfare expenditure, that they have put resources into certain aspects of information provision, with heartening effects for the professionals concerned.

What is presented in the following sections of this chapter is a survey of the main spectrum of the 'modern' information environment of Africa. In Chapter 2 the analysis turns to the ancient, but enduring roots of information activity which answer so much of the people's needs. As already suggested, what is described in both chapters reflects a struggle in progress. If the mood of many of those involved has become a little more positive in the 1990s, there are still many negative and disturbing long-term trends to report. Africa is a difficult continent for all types of information service providers, be they information officers, librarians, documentalists, database managers or archivists, and any account of the environment in which they are players must, sadly, reflect the negative features unflinchingly. Yet a comprehension of the total information environment is essential before directions for a professional future can realistically be sought.

Radio

In a survey of the political information received by Ghanaians it was found that about 30 per cent credited people (politicians, chiefs, elders and travellers) as their usual source of information, while over 40 per cent said that the radio represented their principal source of information.[16] This is a fairly typical finding from such surveys. Yet, while the significance of radio is undeniable, the extent of the significance is a matter for caution. It is sometimes argued that radio and, to a lesser extent, television, have extended the scope of the oral tradition and are even enabling Africa to 'leap-frog' the literate stage to develop a more modern media-based society. Closer investigation tends to suggest that this is facile and unconvincing, but, such is the significance of the medium, it deserves to be discussed first in this overview of Africa's information environment.

The importance of radio can be seen very clearly by the speed and extent of its spread. The proliferation of radio was made possible largely by the invention and increasingly cheap availability of transistorized models. By interesting coincidence the advent of the transistor radio and the political independence of much of the African continent occurred at roughly the same time. Precise figures for the number of receivers are not really available, but the best estimates for sub-Saharan Africa suggest that from a few hundreds of thousands of sets in 1955 there has been a steeply rising curve of increase, through 16,500,000 in 1975, to over 80,000,000 in 1995 (of which about 12,000,000 are in South Africa).

Governments have not been slow to appreciate that radio is the most significant mass medium available to them, nor for that matter have their opponents. It is no coincidence that in the event of a coup, the nation's radio station is always a key point of conflict between the current regime and its opponents. In more peaceful times it has been a priority of governments to extend transmission to as many people as possible and to use the radio not only to entertain but also as an instrument of policy. Often this has been in the form of outright propaganda and exhortation but it is not uncommon at the same time for radio to be used fairly extensively to communicate development-oriented information.

Positive views of this type of programming, dull as it often sounds to the outsider, are not too hard to find. For example, in Mali during the 1960s the Keta government turned to radio as a means of building a sense of nationhood, since the medium seemed quite appropriate for the pre-literate context in which it was going to deliver its message.[17] Political information supporting the policies of the ruling party did form an important element in news and current affairs programming, but what is interesting is how the folk tradition was also used for the same purpose. Baba Sissoko, one of Mali's most famous *griots* had a weekly programme called *Tales of Baba Sissoko*. His stories were reputedly much loved by the listeners and valued not only for their moral lessons but also for the glorious vision of the Malian past they inspired. This was done mainly through tales of the deeds of local heroes which were well calculated to encourage strong sensations of national pride. Families listened to the radio together and no doubt actively participated in the shared experience of this continuation and enhancement of the oral tradition. Examples like this of the ways in which radio has proved to be an effective medium for the dissemination of government policy, however unpopular the policy, could be multiplied from all over the continent.

Despite the generally optimistic and positive way in which radio is often described, scepticism about its potency as a medium for communicating information to support national development is not uncommon. The sceptical view begins by drawing attention to the misleading tendency to talk of radio as though it were universally available. Remote areas may receive no signal, or only a weak one, despite various efforts to improve transmission. Radio receivers, although undoubtedly cheaper today than ten or twenty years ago, are still an imported product for many countries which are already starved of the necessary foreign exchange. Mains power supply is still confined to the relatively well-off urban enclaves and even the cost of batteries can prove almost impossible for the rural dweller struggling to survive on a meagre subsistence wage. In addition to the problems of reception and cost, transmissions frequently fall below the standards required for the successful use of radio as an instructional medium. Under-funded services with too few trained staff are all too common and they are forced to take the easily available options for programming; a heavy diet of Western popular music, intermingled with the monotony of unedited political speeches and commentary.

When governments have planned to use media for development communication it has been to radio that they have usually turned. However, as Kwame Boafo has said of many such projects, they tend to be:

> short-lived, ad-hocish, limited in time and scope, and have not been sustained or built into a permanent national and comprehensive communication planning for development.[18]

Boafo has also suggested that in fact the political elite pay lip-service to the use of radio for development, while actually seeking to use it for their own preservation and aggrandizement. Despite this, the present status of radio is that it obviously plays a very effective role in providing entertainment. This makes it a familiar and acceptable part of people's lives. Because of this familiarity, radio clearly does have a potential to contribute significantly to Africa's development. Nevertheless, that potential has not yet been fully exploited and radio remains a medium with only a limited effect in passing on development information.

Television

The spread of television, has been very much smaller in scope, and some countries, notably Malawi, do not have their own television *NB* service. Videos and satellite dishes are used in those countries by the few who can afford them, as is the case in parts of countries not reached by a national service's transmissions. The numbers of receivers have risen from zero in 1955, to something like 1,000,000 in 1975 (with 100,000 of them in South Africa) and about *14 m.* 14,000,000 in 1995 (with about 4,000,000 in South Africa). Compared to radio, however, television is only narrowly available, being entirely the preserve of a comparatively rich urban elite. In addition, the expense and technical difficulty of creating sufficient programmes has led to an almost total dependence on the cheaper products of American television companies which dominate the *+ Australian (eg Zimbabwe)* screens of television viewers throughout Africa. The fictional adventures of characters in popular US soap operas like *Santa Barbara* are as familiar to African viewers as they are to their counterparts in Europe and North America. Entertaining as these programmes no doubt are, they have nevertheless become yet another powerful instrument of cultural imperialism.

Indigenous content on African television stations tends to be of variable quality, although at its best it can be highly informative and entertaining. For example, news output in many countries is governed by the natural principle that, to be broadcast, an item must be backed up with visuals. As a consequence, the majority of news departments, with limited news gathering facilities, become embarrassingly reliant on material available via satellite. The effect of this is compounded when local stations pick up the transmissions of news networks like CNN and BBC Worldwide, which guarantee consistent, smooth news programming, but which present an unrelentingly Northern perspective on the world.

Locally produced entertainment material is limited by the technical capacity of the stations, with music programmes usually being the most straightforward. As a result these are often of a very high standard, and extremely enjoyable to watch. Stations do sometimes grapple with the complexities of broadcast drama. Some of the most interesting attempts can be witnessed on Nigerian television, which has captured (as far as this is possible) the exuberant improvization of Yoruba traditional drama. It has also experimented with drama series, with *Cock Crow at Dawn* a well-publicized example. Unfortunately, such examples are the exception rather than the rule. The Afrikaans productions of SABC are reputedly of very good standard and popular beyond the white community, but even then their potential audience is only a few million. In contrast, SABC English-language drama and entertainment is not particularly successful with its potentially much larger audience in South Africa and further afield, viewers seeming to prefer the Anglo/US product.

This is significant, because it is to the South African media industries which the continent might look for a challenge to the influence of the North. Multi Choice provides a pan-African satellite service using the South African-developed Irtedo decoder system to carry MNet to up to one million subscribers in 42 other countries. However, even though the digital transmissions of MNet are widely watched outside the borders of South Africa, they reinforce the status quo in fact, rather than challenge it, providing a flow of undemanding entertainment largely bought on the world (that is, Northern) market. Francophone countries also have access to satellite broadcasting. Canal Horizon is broadcast from France, using the Intelsat satellite, by Canal Plus. A chain of local companies has been established to market the channel in North and West African countries including Gabon, Senegal, Cameroon, Ivory Coast. For a monthly subscription the viewer obtains programming that includes sport, films, current affairs and even some local programming. However, in general, these are fine services for those who want to watch material including cartoons, old episodes of entertainment series and soap operas, but there is really very little about their content that is African.

Film

Films also confirm the hold of American entertainment corporations on African markets and the African consciousness. Films are expensive to produce, yet while India and other Asian countries have managed to develop massive film industries, creating entertainment in their own languages and cultural traditions, the story in Africa is comparatively bleak. True, South Africa has in some years produced as many as 100 films, but many were actually American productions exploiting South African opportunities, and other films were made with little interest other than exploiting the state subsidy system. South African output tended to be either mainstream entertainment of a poor quality, going straight to video distribution, or the occasional excellent political film which would be suppressed by the apartheid regime.

Only in the francophone countries of West Africa has cinema production had a good hold for any length of time, but even there financial and artistic problems have meant that major directors have not been able to make films on a regular basis. World-renowned directors such as Ousmane Sembene of Senegal and Souleymane Cisse of Mali do not have *oeuvre* in proportion to their talents, and younger directors from these and other countries like Burkina Faso find artistic life offers its rewards grudgingly. Ouagadougou, Burkina Faso, holds Africa's most important film festival. The festival gives some indication of the temperature of African film-making. The 1993 festival was opened in front of 30,000 spectators, and the showings filled thirteen cinemas with audiences watching nearly two hundred different films from Africa and the African diaspora. The main prize was won by Roger Mbala's *Au Nom du Christ*, which was later shown in Europe and North America to great critical acclaim. The sad and significant thing is that it has since been shown very little in Africa, and that this tends to be true of most of the output of the best African directors.

Most African countries have reasonable numbers of cinema theatres, but even a comparatively well-off country like the Ivory Coast is a market for films rather than a producer of them, and relies heavily on the output of the North. The dearth of African film is largely to do with money. Raising finance to make a film is difficult anywhere and in Africa it can be impossibly difficult. French sources have tended to be the most useful, because of the continuing interest of France, and the French business world, in exercising influence in the former colonies. The situation in the anglophone countries is much less positive.

Only Zimbabwe shows some fairly strong signs of developing a viable industry. Before independence there was some propagandist film-making, and independent Zimbabwe was used as a backdrop for films which had South African settings but could not be shot there for political reasons. The effect of these productions, even including a *King Solomon's Mines* which travestied Africa and its people, was to give experience to significant numbers of potential film-makers. The first wholly Zimbabwean feature was *Jit*, a musical comedy, and other productions dealing with authentic African themes have followed. Training courses and workshops have been organized, local film-makers have taken on projects for overseas television stations, and Zimbabwe has begun its own film festival. All of this is fairly small scale, but at least it is a positive beginning.

The Press

The history of the press in Africa can be traced back well into the early days of the missionary, colonial period, where, almost from the outset, successful newspapers were created by Africans to express the views of Africans. True, the circumstances in which this took place were not easy, for resistance to such efforts came from missionary, trader, settler and colonial civil servant alike. Nevertheless, against considerable odds an indigenous newspaper industry did develop. For example, the *Nigerian Times*, a nationalist newspaper founded in 1908, was the beginning of the extremely lively, highly politicized and largely privately-owned newspaper sector in Nigeria, which is still strongly in evidence today. While most other countries had to wait a little longer for the emergence of similar enterprises, in all of them newspapers played an important part in the struggle for independence. Political parties and the trade unions often founded newspapers which could frequently boast contributions from future national leaders such as Julius Nyerere who was the *de facto* editor-in-chief for the pre-independence *Mwaafrika* (which subsequently became the Swahili daily *Uhuru*), or Quett Masire, who started his career as a journalist for the now defunct *Naledi ya Batswana*.

The tradition of a press which was highly involved in politics and at least partly owned by political groups was also present in South Africa, where the apartheid regime covertly subsidized ostensibly independent newspapers, deployed a formidable propaganda apparatus and pursued genuinely independent journalists with terrifying zeal. A similar tendency towards politicization of the press continued in the rest of Africa after independence. Since the press had played its part in winning political independence, it was perhaps natural that its role should subsequently be seen in the context of nation-building. African leaders recognized the potential of the press as a means of rallying the people towards a call for national unity and national development. The creation of government newspapers which could put across this message better was a natural consequence, and as a result although many countries still retain some semblance of a privately-owned press, in almost all cases it is the state-owned, government-controlled press that predominates.

The results have been disastrous, with the press now being almost exclusively used as a mouthpiece for the information which governments think the people ought to hear. The resulting tensions that exist between African governments and the press are too obvious and too well documented to be ignored. Journalists in Africa are often the first to be proscribed, interdicted and detained at the first hint of unrest and instability. Self-censorship appears to be the key to survival in Africa and the journalists of a 'free' press express criticism in a coded manner difficult for the outsider to unravel.

Among commentators on the press it is common to argue that the African news environment is, and should be, different from that which operates in Europe and North America. A philosophy of 'development journalism' has been evolved to guide the efforts of those involved with the news. This philosophy, is based on the idea that the press is too important to be allowed to follow the allegedly free, but frequently frivolous, course of newspaper publishing in the North. Unesco's 'New World Information and Communication Order' (NWICO) was a call for not only a free but also a balanced flow of information between countries.[19] There has been a strong feeling in the North that this merely represented a ploy to further endorse government control of the press, reinforcing press censorship. The spectre has been raised of Northern journalists being denied their accustomed freedom to move around and report what they want in the way they choose.

This issue of how Africa is reported by the rest of the world is important. Reporters and cameramen fly in to cover an issue, usually a disaster like a famine, drought or flood, or one of Africa's periodic coups, provide dramatic stories for a few days or perhaps weeks, and then move on to the next global trouble spot. Stories for which dramatic pictures are not available or which fail to confirm the prejudices of the newsmen's intended audience, are conveniently ignored. The way in which Ethiopia ceased to be headline news in the Western media almost overnight, despite the continuation of the drought and the resultant catastrophe that it caused, is perhaps sufficient to illustrate the point. It is as if news does not exist where it cannot be backed up by dramatic film footage.

The creation and development of better sources of news on Africa, by Africans, is the best response to this. The Pan African News Agency (PANA), founded in 1983, was intended to supply the world with a consistent and reliable flow of information on Africa. It sought to use modern satellite communication to provide editors with material that was less oriented towards dramatic events and more concerned with chronicling the development struggle. Although satellite systems such as Intelsat enable agencies like PANA to reach the news desks of the world, Northern editors tend to ignore agency material which cannot be edited on-line and incorporated directly into their electronically produced newspapers. The low capacity telex channels often used for material from Africa produce only hard copy, which unfortunately does not meet this requirement. The stories coming out of Africa have thus been consigned to that great volume of material which is received by newspapers but never used for publication.

By 1990 PANA was in crisis, with enormous debts and a pathetically small output of stories, many of which sycophantically reported the doings of the regimes that gave financial support to the agency. Fears about the tendency of NWICO seemed to be confirmed. Between 1992 and 1995, the fortunes of the agency have been turned around. It acquired a staff of professional journalists and obtained editorial independence. Its output increased and distribution of its stories was widened to 35 different countries. Once again it seemed like a genuine contribution to improved reporting of African stories outside their immediate area of origin.

This problem of the reporting of Africa both within and outside the continent has proved thoroughly intractable. Surveys of the content of African newspapers have tended to show that their reporting of news from other African countries is slow and limited in scope. There is a sharp divide between anglophone and francophone Africa as far as the passage of news is concerned, and stories from countries in the immediate region outnumber those from further afield. An analysis of the content of some Nigerian newspapers showed that between a quarter and a third of their stories consisted of foreign news and only about half of this was from other parts of Africa.[20] Since Nigerian newspapers and the News Agency for Nigeria had no reporters based in other African countries largely for financial reasons, these stories were obviously derived from other news agencies. This meant that the vast majority were obtained from the very Northern agencies that Africa accuses of misreporting the continent. This is still typical of newspapers continent-wide.

Despite problems of government ownership, control and censorship, the press, in particular the private press, is flourishing in a number of African countries such as Nigeria, Kenya and Botswana and is managing, at least in part, to tell the news. There are problems, however, even when this is possible. The private press in particular suffers from a lack of finance for equipment, and a dearth of newsprint. If, as is usually the case, newsprint is imported by the government, supplies can be restricted in such a way that newspapers are forced to conform or close down. This is clearly an indirect form of censorship. The price of newsprint, when it can be obtained, is so high that it results in the sad paradox of newspapers being unable to produce sufficient copies to satisfy demand, because the revenue from the increased sales would not cover the cost of additional newsprint. Even when newspapers have managed to overcome these considerable hurdles, and the paper has been produced, circulation is restricted mostly to the cities and towns. In the rural areas distribution is usually unreliable and often only occurs when a traveller or migrant worker returns to the home village. The common practice of an individual reading the news to a group who may not themselves be able to read, multiplies the effective use of each copy. The listeners are quite capable of absorbing the content and passing it on even further through subsequent conversation.

Although the existence of the press is definitely a constant struggle, improvements in technology (desktop publishing, colour printing, etc.) are gradually making more attractive, up-to-date and locally-focused newspapers more common. The successful future of this important medium of communication is vital to Africa, and signs of progress such as this are very welcome.

Books and Publishing

The poverty of book resources in Africa has been mentioned already. The weakness of the book trades has been variously attributed to massive illiteracy, the lack of a reading culture (even among the present generation of educated Africans), lack of book production skills and equipment, poor library and distribution networks, trade barriers and closed markets and the economic dependence of the book trade, as well as to the political, cultural and linguistic divisions of the African continent. It is perhaps not too surprising, therefore, that when confronted with this formidable list of obstacles, the book has failed to play a significant role in the social and cultural development of the continent and its people. Only in South Africa has there been a significant publishing industry, aimed primarily at its white population, and supplying other South African languages and communities rather poorly.

In an attempt to quantify Africa's acute shortage of books, Robert Escarpit came to the conclusion that the figures that are available are so low that any form of comparison or quantitative analysis is virtually impossible.[21] This judgement was subsequently confirmed by Unesco when during the course of an international survey of book production it was noted that, of the 55 countries and territories included under Africa, a few only produce books. And of those, a smaller number report their statistics to Unesco. Many of the countries do not have a depository system and would be at pains to produce statistics on book production, even if there was any.[22]

This is, then, an unrelievedly gloomy picture of a continent apparently uninterested in publishing and not having books in sufficient numbers and presumably of sufficient quality for the needs which are apparent.

Low levels of literacy underlie most of the other problems. Illiteracy has been condemned by African librarians as the

> scourge, menace, humiliation, enemy number one, the worst evil of the human race and other dismal but apt phrases.[23]

Precise estimates of the numbers who are literate are difficult to obtain. Those that are available are unreliable, and mask extreme variations between town and village, between different generations, and between different geographical regions. Even a simple definition of what constitutes literacy can rarely be agreed. However, great efforts have been put into adult literacy programmes in most African countries. In fact, only Equatorial Guinea, where Macias Nguema is said to have sought to eliminate the literate part of the population, who were considered dangerously well-informed, has followed a radically different direction. In Ethiopia under the revolutionary regime of the 1970s and 1980s, for instance, the literacy programmes were massive. At the time of the revolution in 1974 which saw the overthrow of the Emperor Haile Selassie, only 1.38 million adults (defined as the 10–45 age group) in urban areas, and 1.05 million adults in rural areas, were estimated to be literate. This was from a total population then in excess of 20 million, and in a country almost unique in sub-Saharan Africa for its ancient literary culture.

The National Literacy Campaign, launched in 1979, set out with the aim of providing permanent literacy for every Ethiopian. The campaign was organized with a military-sounding terminology of attacks (programmes of classes) and mop-up operations (remedial classes). Fourteen such campaigns had been completed by 1986, with each attack catering for 1 to 1.5 million people, and the mop-ups for 0.5 million. By that time it was claimed that 13.5 million people, over 60 per cent of the population, were literate, as opposed to only 7 per cent before the revolution. The aim was to make the entire population literate, and in that the hopes and aspirations of this campaign are typical of programmes elsewhere in the developing world. The primary objective was to have

> an impact on productivity and organisational capacity which will contribute to a rise in GDP per capita and a higher degree of self reliance.[24]

As might be expected, such enormous expectations are usually doomed to disappointment. However, literacy campaigns generally have had at least some impact on the problem, and new readers do exist. Their particular literature needs, which centre on the availability of easy but interesting writing for adults, create both a market and a problem for publishers. Because new literates are frequently readers only in their mother tongue, their needs emphasize the problem of language, which has always plagued African publishing.

Put quite simply, a continent with an estimated 1000 languages or more is never going to be an easy publishing environment. Major languages do manage to achieve comparatively reasonable levels of publication. This, however, is only achieved in an international language such as Kiswahili (which has about 20 per cent of all the new titles published in African languages), or the language of the major population group in Nigeria, Yoruba (with about 12 per cent of the new African language titles). The majority of the continent's languages have at the best a tiny published literature. Some have none at all, and indeed may not even have a written form or an established orthography. The missionary presses which were usually the first to publish in African languages often devised a clumsy orthography which led to many disputes not only among Africans, but also among the various missions. The legacy of this still lingers today.

The prestige of the old colonial languages, particularly English and French, has encouraged many writers to continue to use them. About 80 per cent of new titles from Africa are in these languages, despite the fact that less than 5 per cent of the continent's population is regarded as being really fluent in either of them. English is the more successful of the two languages, with approximately twice the number of publishers producing double the volume of new titles. This is perhaps not surprising as it serves the more populous areas and enjoys a worldwide currency. The majority of popular imaginative literature is produced in English and the number of titles produced in African languages is discouragingly small. This problem of a dearth of material in the people's own languages has worried most commentators on African publishing. Encouraging signs, such as Amos Tutuola's decision to rewrite his *The Palm-wine Drinkard*, originally in English, in his mother tongue, Yoruba, are few and far between. It has been suggested that the use of a foreign language makes it difficult for individuals to learn to read and to develop a reading habit. Yet when someone aspires to be an author they tend to want to write in one of the metropolitan languages. The Ndebele novelist Ndabezinhle Sigogo, with thirteen books to his credit, puts this down to frustration with the small market for most African languages. 'If I was writing in English I could have built a mansion in Matopo by now' he has claimed.[25]

Many solutions to the problem have been suggested and some have been tested in practice. For example, in the 1940s the East African Literature Bureau and the Publications Bureau of Northern Rhodesia and Nyasaland both set out to foster the publication of vernacular literature, textbooks and periodicals. The latter's intention was not to undertake the publishing itself, but to place manuscripts with suitable publishers and then assist with the distribution of the publications through 'libraries, bookstalls, and colporteurs'.[26] It had some modest success over the years, as did sister organizations such as that in Southern Rhodesia, for which Sigogo's first novel entered print as the winner of a prize for new manuscripts. Successor organizations have carried on their work, but none of them have succeeded in promoting mass publication of African language books.

Setting aside these earlier initiatives, and examining the origins of African publishing generally, we find that it was originally a means for producing and distributing educational and missionary texts written by non-African authors. The publishing of books by African writers can only really be traced back to the 1950s when a number of aspiring young authors with manuscripts in the metropolitan languages began to be published with some frequency. In the francophone countries this was welcomed and indeed encouraged by an organization specifically devoted to that purpose, the Institut Francais de l'Afrique Noir. This effort was complemented by the setting up of a publishing house in Paris, Presence Africaine, which was largely responsible for bringing to public attention the writings of the poet, and later national leader of Senegal, Leopold

Senghor and the novelists Camara Laye, of Guinea, and Mongo Beti, of Cameroon.

The system in the anglophone countries was not nearly so supportive, with the local branches of British publishers showing little interest in publishing non-textbook material written by Africans. Undeterred, a number of these writers bypassed this obstacle and were able to attract the attention of a few publishers in London who fortunately recognized their talents. The initial breakthrough was made by West African writers, notably with Amos Tutuola's, already mentioned, *The Palm-wine Drinkard* in 1952, and Chinua Achebe's *Things Fall Apart* in 1953. In the 1960s it was the turn of East Africa, with the works of Ngugi wa Thiongo, David Rubadiri and Okot p'Bitek appearing in print. In bringing the work of these writers to a world readership, publishers such as Faber, Oxford University Press, Andre Deutsch and Heinemann undoubtedly performed an important service in nurturing and developing Africa's creative writers. At the same time though, as a consequence of their efforts, they effectively detached some of the best talent from its roots, which in turn probably did a disservice to the prospects for a strong, commercially sound African publishing industry.

The patterns of publishing now to be found around the continent are still broadly similar, with the international publishing houses maintaining the upper hand. They retain considerable ability to determine what and who ought to be published, and ultimately what should be read about Africa. At the advent of independence local branches of publishers such as Longmans, Nelson, Evans and Heinemann registered as companies in the countries in which they were operating while at the same time increasing the level of local participation in their activities. For instance, by 1963 the Nigerian branch of Oxford University Press was able to handle the whole publication process of locally-written books and publish its own titles under its own imprint. The only element which could not be said to have been localized was the resultant profit from these titles, which continued to be exported back to the parent company.

Some international companies set up new local operations in which they maintained a minority holding, with the most notable examples being African Universities Press based in Lagos, and the East African Publishing House with its headquarters in Nairobi. Both were initiated by Andre Deutsch, with the latter managing fairly quickly to dispense with any outside involvement to pursue a highly creative policy as an indigenous publishing house. State publishing houses developed along similar lines, with Macmillan in particular playing an important role in Ghana, Uganda, Tanzania and Zambia. Similar arrangements developed in the francophone countries, where, for example, Ivory Coast and Senegal shared a controlling interest in Nouvelles Editions Africaines, with a group of French publishers making up the minority stockholding.

State publishing houses were conceived of originally as being similar in their role to the government-controlled newspaper press, with the overt aim of fostering unity and national development. Many formed agreements with international publishers, providing them with closed markets in the countries with whose state publishing houses they were cooperating.[27] The tenacity of international publishers to hold on to what is a comparatively unimportant market on the world scale is particularly notable in the francophone countries, where the direct French influence is institutionalized in the financial structures of the states themselves. Such arrangements ensure that Africa remains a captive market for their products, while at the same time stifling attempts at local publishing initiatives.

Books by the most successful writers have no doubt gained from their publication by international publishers, some of whom specifically promote African writers, as Heinemann have done with their African Writers Series. But the main purpose of such efforts is to identify and promote a limited number of 'outstanding' titles for the convenience of book buyers in the developed countries. The African market tends not to be a major priority in determining what shall or shall not be published and the limited outlet provided by international publishers for Africa's creative talent is no substitute for the broad development of African writing that is necessary to alleviate the endemic book hunger. Indeed, major publishers find it difficult to judge how to market books in Africa with a mass audience in mind. Oxford University Press in South Africa has experimented with low-priced titles produced to good quality standards, aimed at a wider market in South Africa and other countries. Sales were very disappointing and clearly, outside the predictable textbook market, understanding market needs is a problem.

If we look for alternatives to the approaches of the international firms, there are actually plenty of encouraging signs in the informal sector of publishing. This sector is best known in Nigeria, where the once famous 'Onitsha market literature' gained, quite a few years ago, some attention from the book world. This publishing phenomenon consisted of simply printed and bound, locally-written books. Their content was lively, racy and topical, and they were written in vigorous local English or local languages. They were sold outside the conventional book trade, from pavement stalls and kiosks, in shopping malls and traditional markets, in buses and along the streets, in Onitsha as well as other major towns and cities such as Ibadan, Lagos, Aba, Port Harcourt and Enugu. While the Onitsha market literature did at one time arouse a certain level of attention, it has received little detailed study.[28]

The informal sector is, in business terms, chaotic and unreliable. The actual level of book sales is therefore more or less impossible to assess. Writers often sell the copyright of their books to the publisher for a single payment only to find that the publisher proceeds to reprint the book, possibly under a new title, without acknowledging the author and almost certainly with no royalties being paid. To the publisher the stories are merely a product to be sold for a quick profit and the stories' refreshing lack of literary pretension obviously helps in achieving this objective.

Further spontaneous publishing initiatives take such forms as 'photoplay' magazines, known as *romans photos* in the francophone countries. In Nigeria these tend to be serialized versions of the prolific Yoruba popular drama, using still photographs of the characters with captions telling the story. The magazines do have a small amount of other content including pages of fiction, humorous commentary and penpal pages. These pages have the picture as well as a brief biography and address of the aspiring penpal. A study of them in a large number of these magazines would give a fascinating sample of their readership, but at a glance, students and semi-skilled workers, mainly lorry drivers, seem to predominate. In the francophone countries, new copies of the *romans photo* can be found on sale alongside cartoon books, or *bandes dessinées*, some of local origin, in bookshops and market stalls. They are also sold secondhand in the pavement *librairies par terre*. The equivalent of these humblest of all booksellers are to be seen spread out on the street corners of many African cities, often selling copies of textbooks, alongside more popular material.

Street traders operate with a minimum of capital, and African entrepreneur publishing is also very undercapitalized. It has low profit margins and fails with great frequency. In these circumstances, bank credit is hard to obtain. In addition to the obvious financial difficulties, aspiring publishers find themselves involved in a multiplicity of tasks such as composition, presswork and binding, diverting their attention away from the actual business of publishing. Machinery, spare parts and materials such as paper, ink and offset plates are all in short supply and skilled workers are at a premium.

All these difficulties have produced an unstable and bibliographically problematic local publishing industry, with the less established sector being graphically described by Obasi in the following way,

> In general the printers are slow or even reluctant to give any information about their existence or origin. Some of them go into liquidation after a very short history of operation. The young entrepreneurs who own them appear to be nomadic moving from one shop or city to another within a few years. This is often due to financial reasons, to meet increased rates and electricity bills. Often they do not leave any contacting addresses and in circumstances where these are known, the omission of the post office box numbers makes them impossible to locate.[29]

This is a librarian's point of view, but one can imagine the difficulties these fluctuating circumstances must cause for the writer, publisher, book buyer, materials supplier and, no doubt, for a list of creditors too.

However, out of the uncomfortable area between the power of the international publishing houses on one side and the chaotic but exciting stirrings of popular publishing initiative on the other, a more solid indigenous publishing industry can be seen emerging in some countries. Zimbabwe is certainly the most encouraging of all of these. Right from independence in 1980 there was a very strong interest in the literary expression of feelings about the struggle which had just ended and the new nation which was being built. The government, by encouraging the localization of the writing and publishing of textbooks and other educational books, gave a certain commercial security to publishers which freed them to experiment with literary publishing, if they so chose. Companies like Baobab, Zimbabwe Publishing House, College Press and Mambo Press have brought out the works of local writers like Chenjerai Hove and Shimmer Chinodya, although it is also true that other writers like Tsitsi Dangarembga and Jon Eppel had to look for a publisher outside the country. The volume of writing from which publishers have to choose is high: for instance, by 1990 Zimbabwe Publishing House was receiving as many as 50 unsolicited manuscripts per month. Most of this type of material is not of publishable standard, but the urge to communicate is strong.

What is not so strong is the level of sales once books have been published. These are simply not sufficient to support even a successful writer from royalties, unless he or she has some other form of income. Part of this is specifically because of the price of books to the country's admirably high proportion of literate people, part because outside Harare and Bulawayo bookshops and other distributors are not well developed, but part is quite simply because publishing facilities generally are not strong enough. As is the case in most of the continent, shortages of paper and other materials are paralleled by a lack of trained personnel. In addition, the type of network of agreements for export, co-publication and licensing which can make the difference between publishing viability and failure are not well established. These problems are, however, closer to solution in Zimbabwe than in many other countries.

Much of the favourable aspect of Zimbabwean publishing is owed to the remarkable Zimbabwe International Book Fair. First held in 1983 under the auspices of the Ministry of Information and Zimbabwe Publishing House, it has since become a regular event. Zimbabwe Writers Union took over the role of second partner in 1989 and it is now run by the Zimbabwe International Book Fair Trust. Despite some difficult years, the Fair has grown in strength to the point where publishers from inside and outside the continent see it as a venue to make deals on co-publishing, joint ventures, sales and distribution agencies. These deals now include major agreements between organizations from countries which do not necessarily include Zimbabwe itself, and, remarkably, even deals between buyers and sellers who are both from within South Africa. The value of such a business forum to Zimbabwe and its publishers is obvious enough, but the stimulus to the industry in the whole of sub-Saharan Africa is considerable. Companies from countries which have a book market barely sufficient to support a developing industry use the Fair to look for the wider markets which will make expansion viable. What has inhibited such deals in the past is the policies of governments which treat books like any other commodity in relation to tariffs and non-tariff entry restrictions. The Fair is beginning to provide an important forum for the persuasion of governments that they need to stimulate publishing by breaking down such restrictions. In the 1990s, the Trust has staged an *indaba*, or conference, in association with the Fair, and in 1996 the theme was precisely that of National Book Policy.

Another theme that the Fair has tackled in the past is children's literature. This is arguably both the most important and the most neglected form of publishing for Africa with its overwhelmingly youthful population. According to *African Books in Print*, the publication of literature for children in Africa rarely exceeds more than a few hundred titles a year. This quantity of children's material is nowhere near enough to satisfy the demand placed on it by young readers. Ideally the bulk of the material available for children should be written by African writers and at least some of it should bear a close relation to the conditions that the African child is likely to experience. The first few books of reasonable quality for young adults started to appear in the 1960s trying to emulate the success of Cyprian Ekwensi's *The Drummer Boy*. Unfortunately, writing for children has not gained a particularly high prestige among African authors, with only a few of the famous like Chinua Achebe, who (with John Iroaganchi) wrote *How the Leopard got his Claws*, and Ngugi wa Thiongo, whose *Njanba na mbaathi i mathagu* is written in Gikuyu, producing books suitable for children.

Some books for young people have tended to take a rather obviously didactic line and, as has been pointed out in the case of Nigeria, 'These novels reflect what Nigerian society wants Nigerian youths to be or what it does not want them to be'.[30] This is a reassuringly familiar complaint from the youth of every generation and from every continent. The important thing is that there are attempts to develop a much needed market in books for young adults. A major proportion of this market has been taken up by international publishers, such as Macmillan with their inexpensive *Pacesetters* series of lively and appropriate stories written by African authors.

Unfortunately, there have not been a great number of African publishers with a strong interest in children's books. A few indigenous publishers such as Nouvelles Editions Africaines of Dakar, East African Publishing House of Nairobi, Baobab Press in Zimbabwe, and the Mazenod Centre in Lesotho are producing some good material, but the majority seem to have retreated from the inherent difficulties of producing children's literature and have abandoned the market to the international publishers. The problem is so grave that the Nigerian writer Flora Nwapa had to set up her own Tana Press to specialize in children's books. Initiatives like this, however, are few and far between and are unlikely to provide a proper solution to the lack of suitable reading material for children and young adults.

Money is once again the major problem, for publishing children's books is an expensive business, made difficult by the fact that the cover price should not be so exorbitant as to inhibit children or their parents from purchasing the book. Publishing at a low enough price can be achieved either by producing a long print run with the intention of selling large numbers of copies, or by saving money on the actual production of the book. The first option is extremely risky and it is to the second that most of the local publishers will be tempted to turn, resulting in an unattractive and easily damaged product. Children's book publishing in Africa needs to be well capitalized if local publishers are to compete with the richly endowed international publishers who presently dominate the market. The Children's Book Project, launched in Tanzania in 1991 with international aid agency finance, is an example of help to achieve this.

The Noma Award for Publishing in Africa has been won by several books for children since it was first offered in 1973, but again, this can never be enough. The market for children's books is potentially enormous in Africa, the creative talent to write and illustrate the books is not lacking, nor is the expertise and even the capital to produce and publish them. What is lacking at the moment is the incentive and the will, and until a more assertive approach is adopted by African publishers, African children, who represent the continent's future, will continue to be denied sufficient good material to read.

Computers

The computer has been present in Africa since the 1960s and anyone spending time in urban Africa will find it more or less everywhere – particularly in the offices of businesses and government organizations. Shops and agencies for computer companies are visible in the business districts of the cities; educational institutions, homes and even libraries also have computers. It might seem that there is really no difficulty here and that everything is moving along quite nicely. This is indeed the case in some places. Urban

South Africa, in particular, has the capacity to acquire and indeed assemble, install, use and maintain computers, and train and educate computer personnel and users at all the necessary levels. They clearly make an essential contribution to the thriving industrial and business base of the country. This strength spills over into the neighbouring economies, such as those of Botswana and Zimbabwe. Pockets of similar strength are also established in cities such as Lagos and Nairobi. The kind of critical mass of skilled personnel, well-informed and discriminating users, and manufacturing, programming and maintenance capacity is growing.

The other side of this is whole countries without worthwhile computer capacity, and there are great rural and urban swathes, even of those countries where the computer has a solid foothold, where the computer is almost unknown. In practice, Africa pretty certainly has less than 1 per cent of the world's computers. Just as from the rural perspective literacy and the written word can seem an urban aberration, so information technology can also seem too rare and utterly marginal°to real concerns to be worth a thought. This urban–rural dichotomy is not the whole of the problem, however. The presence of computer machinery is not actually an indication of the existence of computer activity. Much more depressing than the absence of computers is the presence of unused computers. Reliable accounts of equipment, usually provided by donors, that has never been unpacked from its boxes are not uncommon.[31] Equipment of a high technical specification that has been acquired 'because Africa should not lag behind the North', is too often found woefully underexploited, used for a little tentative wordprocessing only, for instance, because there is no one trained to do anything more. Equipment rendered inactive by a small technical fault, or lack of some minor piece of hardware like a cable or a connector, is also frequently found. The proud assurance of some African professionals that their organization has computers should not necessarily be taken at face value.

Literature on the reasons why the computer has so often been a disappointment in Africa has tended to lay stress on a list of difficulties summarized by Zulu.[32] Two genuine problems which surface in most such lists are electricity supply and environmental difficulties. Electrical supply which is frequently interrupted, and which suffers surges and weak spells used to be devastating for computer use. Systems are now much more robust, so that, while files insufficiently backed up may be lost, wholesale damage to data is less of a problem. Again, while it is true that computers operate best in a cool environment, low in humidity and free of dust and airborne detritus, the hardware is now much less likely to react violently to such conditions. Much more crucial are inadequacies of the human support systems for computer use. The idea that acquiring systems is enough should be rejected whenever it appears: computer systems only operate usefully when set in human systems that can cope with them. While this does mean people with programming skills to a certain extent, it is much more important that people who have a good generic grasp of hardware and software are on constant call. Problem solving and trouble shooting are crucial. A strong grasp of systems – how one machine interlinks with another, and how to make all the little adjustments that are necessary to achieve what in principle is straightforward – is essential if a system which will work, and continue to work is to be put in place. The requisite mix of know-how, from the most up-to-date cyberskills to the comparatively simple screwdriver-wielding technician level, are at a premium in Africa.

An earlier prerequisite is at the planning level. Selection of systems too frequently fails to relate to well-identified and clearly articulated organizational priorities, but rather to a series of pragmatic imperatives. The sales forces of computer companies are renowned for their willingness to sell unsuitable equipment to underprepared buyers. In particular, the big American corporations have placed a great reliance on maintaining growth through the export of information goods and services. Similarly, the export-minded Japanese have aggressively pursued world markets in order to ensure that their information technology products maintain their position as market leaders. It is in such a climate of pressure salesmanship that African governments have to make investment decisions of the most sensitive kind. It is little wonder that mistakes have been made.

The priorities of donors are also frequently too apparent in the provision of systems. The issue for a donor may be more that its own domestic IT industry is prepared to supply at low cost, than what is most needed by the recipient. For instance, one African university library found itself the recipient of a computer system for which it was subsequently discovered that virtually no library applications software existed. The whole issue of dependence on donors is crucial: it is arguably better to have no computers than donations which vary from the unnecessarily powerful and expensive to maintain, down to the nearly obsolescent and hard to keep in spare parts.

Smaller local suppliers are not necessarily the whole answer to such difficulties. True, the presence of a local office and storefront, with the guarantee of aftersales service that this implies, is very important. Maintenance contracts, ongoing dialogue with sales personnel and technicians do make an enormous difference. There can be a minus side to smaller suppliers too. One of these may seem to be an advantage at first glance: it is the availability of any up-to-date software that the purchaser wants, free or at minimal cost with the hardware purchase. It may not seem like a problem that this will certainly be unlicensed software supplied, in many cases, in defiance of national statutes and international agreements on copyright in force in the country. The argument goes that the major software companies and their highly expensive products are marketed and protected in developing countries with little or no regard to the urgent needs and low incomes of those countries. It is very easy, and sometimes fair, to portray the companies as insensitive and exploitative. Yet this does not get over the problems caused by unlicensed software. A disk with a program on it which is not supported by the manual, helpline, automatic updates and add-ons that come with the licensed product can often seem almost as useless as no disk at all.

The answer surely lies in government-level pressure on the companies to negotiate appropriate rates for weaker economies, not in an illegal free-for-all. This only becomes apparent when the frustrations and hindrances of software anarchy are experienced. On a broader stage, the effective supply of computers and programs in African countries depends on the building of local manufacturing capacity for both hardware and software. The small size of many African national markets may mean that this might best be done through cooperation, or the development of complementary industries in a group of countries in a region, rather than through competition. Such a case is persuasively argued by Woherem.[33]

Most of the foregoing ignores perhaps the chief underlying problem of IT for Africa: it is an ongoing financial commitment, not a one-off investment. IT only flourishes in a whole socio-economic culture comprising commercial structures, enforceable contracts and other commitments, and human capital, in the form of trained and appropriately-oriented personnel. But the entry into this culture implicitly involves an ongoing investment which only starts with the initial hardware and software acquisition. All too frequently a budgetary allocation, or a donor commitment to the provision of a system, is considered in total isolation, and the future (if it is considered at all) is left to chance. The obsolescence cycle of computer systems has shortened progressively, so that in an ideal financial environment whole systems should be renewed every 2–4 years. Even where more pragmatic decisions have to be made, renewal is an utterly unavoidable constant, more pressing than any of the well-publicized concerns over physical infrastructure and environment.

There is also an ethical dimension to consider, Olden's trenchant and much-cited polemic has set out the core of this. He suggests that, while the technical problems can be overcome, the concentration of resources necessary to apply information technology is likely, in the first place, to be paid for at the expense of services to the masses.[34] The question is how far IT is of true benefit to the whole African populace and how far it is effectively a reinforcement of the hold of an educated elite on the springs of power. Anecdotes of those provided with computers preferring to use them for lucrative consultancy rather than put them to the benefit of the community they were intended to serve are quite frequently heard.

Olden is quite right to point out that there is little obvious direct benefit from IT for the peasant hoeing his fields, or the herdsman tending his cattle. An obvious reason for this is literacy: even if terminals providing appropriate information were to be made available to all, more than half of the African population would understand little or nothing of what they saw on the screen. Commentators on IT all too frequently draw attention to the availability of sound, graphics and video, icon-driven systems, touch screen and voice response, to argue that literacy is not so relevant to computer use. This painfully underestimates the significance of alphabetic communication and text in computer systems, exaggerates the instinctual component in computer use, and does not really take into account the extent to which so-called computer literacy relies on the types of logical sequences of reasoning nurtured by text-based argumentation. However, even starting with Olden's premise that information delivery to the people should be paramount, there is a case for the computer.

Woherem argues strongly that rejection of IT on ethical grounds would be self-destructive.[35] Tiamiyu, in a carefully argued response to Olden's original article, refers to the value of computers in formal education programmes, in planning and management, and in non-library types of information delivery.[36] He draws attention to the way in which computerized information systems can transfer information to those who will be the ultimate providers of information to the citizen. It is at this intermediate level that IT can, and probably should, be introduced. Those who work with people and seek to inform them on matters of health and hygiene, citizens' rights or the law, need the very best access to the information for which they are intermediaries. Computerized databases, and networks to make their content widely available, could be seen from this perspective as almost a right.

Technology particularly apposite to such needs is now available. Stand-alone or networkable personal computers (and laptops) have advantages in information provision to communities which the older mainframe technology conspicuously lacked. CD-ROM, and optical storage of information generally, has enormous data capacity. This makes database access independent of the tyranny of the expensive and unreliable telecommunications connections which bedevilled on-line services. It can make an expert system (capable, say, of helping a paramedic in an isolated health centre make good preliminary diagnosis of a wide variety of conditions) available almost anywhere, or it can simply provide great volumes of comparatively easy-to-update directory information to community centres. Where bibliographic databases are concerned, it is true that a CD-ROM can actually increase frustration and possibly divert attention away from locally-available sources, by drawing attention to publications that are not held locally, or are prohibitively expensive to obtain via document delivery services.[37]

Ultimately, however, Woherem is right to argue that IT cannot be ignored. Nations have to accept that even if they were to turn their faces against it, international business, aid agencies and others would still use it within their borders and accentuate their deprivation. The problem is in devising national information policies which will enable sensible, affordable, widely-beneficial utilization of technology. Woherem advises that:

> Governments of African countries, according to their perceived needs and national capabilities, should invest in an IT policy/strategy – come out with a master plan for IT acquisition, effective use, diffusion and sustainable development, link IT policy to their overall economic and industrial and other related policies; make centres for R&D in IT

available; make funds available for IT projects in the country, with the assistance of the business community/organisations and ensure that citizen employees are aware of the benefits and needs for IT and change.[38]

All of this is good sense. It should not be allowed to obscure the extent to which IT policy must evolve and change. A policy valid for more than part of the cycle of a national five-year development plan is extremely hard to devise. This does not invalidate policy as a means of dealing with IT: it just emphasizes the need for a nimble-footed and constantly modified response.

Telecommunications

An IT policy cannot sensibly be separated from a telecommunications policy. Their conjunction is what is often referred to as telematics. The concept is based on the recognition that the computer and telecommunications together are the root of modern information generation, handling and transfer. Since at present very few African countries are far down the road to a dense telematics environment, policy decisions made at this stage can be utterly crucial in creating the opportunity for their entry into the new era to meet national goals and aspirations as closely as possible.

The infrastructural prerequisite for effective development of telematics is the telecommunications network of a nation, and the way it interconnects with the international networks. The first thing about this that needs to be pointed out is that telecommunications in most of sub-Saharan Africa are exceedingly sparse and of a very poor quality. There are simply not good numbers of lines, and those that do exist, work unreliably. Extremely small proportions of homes actually have telephone receivers. The comparison with the USA and Western Europe, where something approaching all homes have telephones, and where the streets and public buildings have unlimited numbers of highly effective payphones, is extreme. The frequently repeated saying that there are more phones in Manhattan than in the whole of Africa, shows up the problem whether it is precisely accurate or not. A continent-wide figure of 1.6 phones per 100 people is distorted upwards by the countries of North Africa and by South Africa. In practice, the majority of

African countries have less than one telephone per 100 people. Nigeria with over a quarter of a million phones has only 0.2 per 100, while the Kenyan rate, though better at 0.8, is still very low. Only a few tiny African island countries have more than 1 per 100, except of course for South Africa. In the early 1990s official figures suggested that there were only about 15,000 fax machines in sub-Saharan Africa (excluding South Africa), and virtually no cell phones. This is a situation which has changed fast, but figures are certainly still not high.

In South Africa, there are about 3,500,000 telephones, representing a rate of 8.8 per 100. This rate, however, like many things concerning South Africa, is deceptive. The white population in both urban and rural areas is well provided with phones: the non-white population, wherever they live, are circumstanced much the same as the rest of Africa. This is significant because intensive research on telecommunications by the University of Natal throws light on patterns of telephone use and need among the black population that clearly have some application to the situation in other African countries.[39]

These findings remind us that social factors are a major concern of good telecommunications policy. They emphasize the importance of the urban–rural link in African telecommunications. Migration to the cities, which is not unique to South Africa, and frequently crosses national boundaries, has left family groups split between urban residents, often of very long standing, and those who remained in the rural areas. The rural population is often predominantly female, with older men and boys outnumbering men of working age. Rural incomes tend to be close to subsistence level, but have an extremely significant element of remittances and welfare payments originating in the urban areas. Rural life is dependent on urban life in practical ways, while urban life has strong ties of sentiment to rural life. The telephone connections that matter most of all in both sectors are therefore very likely to be those between city and country. Improvement of urban access to telephones is obviously needed, but without better rural telephone networks it will disappoint a particularly strongly felt need.[40] The way in which this sets a clear priority for telecommunications expansion programmes in African countries is important in the context of overall national development. There are, generally speaking, indications that improved communications have a measurable impact on development performance, so that better telecommunications provision is more than just a matter of social welfare. This is a point which will be returned to in later chapters.

Policies for increased telecommunications capacity and quality need to be a high priority for African governments. However, there is the difficulty that the local telecommunications market may often be too small to attract competing suppliers who might offer competitive rates. Yet although to the world's major telecommunications companies an African market may be insignificant, they do hold dominant positions in these markets. When it is taken into account that much more than half of a nation's telecommunications investment is likely to be on imported equipment, this matters a great deal. In particular, the investment in maintenance may be tiny, with obvious consequences for the quality of repairs to existing systems.

Much of the maintenance problem, in turn, goes back to the nature of African telecommunications systems, of which over 80 per cent use analog switching equipment.[41] This is unreliable, and spare parts are not easily available for what are basically obsolete systems. Costs to the consumer, for an inefficient service, are extremely high – roughly double those to the average subscriber in Europe, when incomes are in inverse ratio to this. Governments also retain high levels of control through telecommunications regulatory systems which, among other things, subsidize such rural telecommunications as exist, and load the expense on to international traffic. They also tend to prevent customers from attaching their own choice of equipment for computing or communications to the national network. There is generally a lack of vision of the role of sophisticated telecommunications in modern life, so that packet switching and leased lines, for instance, are in short supply. Only South Africa has provided ISDN services and the few leased lines that exist in other countries are for major institutions such as banks, airlines and international organizations.

Some of this is undoubtedly because of a fear of the potential of transborder data flows. The swift and accurate movement of financial information, invoices and freight documentation, personnel records, travel bookings, vital economic and geodetic data, as well as huge sums of money, over great distances, has obvious advantages as well as potential drawbacks. The major disadvantages as far as governments are concerned is that such operations are largely beyond national institutions to monitor, let alone control. There is a legitimate fear that such processes are being manipulated to a nation's disadvantage. The international corporations can now obtain and pass on data in such quantities and at such speed that governments can scarcely hope to match the knowledge they command. Indeed, these companies tend to have access to a greater range of up-to-date information on less developed countries than the governments of those countries themselves. It is suggested that 90 per cent of database information about Africa is actually held outside the country, with only limited access to it from Africa. Yet the significance of the information may be greater for the country than for the company. The information on a database can signal catastrophe for a nation, but to a transnational company it may mean only that there is a need to relocate some of its assets.

African countries are arguably placing themselves in this vulnerable position, at least in part, by policies which either trivialize or demonize telecommunications, and restrict their own nationals' ability to make use of telematics. One very important result of this is that by 1996 only a small number of African countries had full Internet connectivity. Before this, Fidonet, which was established in 1984, had been instrumental in getting limited connection at low cost, for email and newsgroup activity, for good numbers of institutions in about twenty African countries. This brought them, in effect, on to the fringes of the Internet, because subscribers had to use a modem and a telephone line to obtain and transmit data. Reports on the countries with full connectivity vary, but South Africa, Zambia, Ghana, Kenya, Uganda and Mozambique appear to have been the first sub-Saharan countries to achieve this. The Zambian example is interesting because it combined two potential directions that offer themselves to obtain full Internet connectivity. These are connection for profit or by cooperative means. In Zambia, a joint venture was set up between the universities and ZamNet, a private company. In Uganda and Ghana the solution was a commercial one, while in Kenya and Mozambique it has been cooperative, with universities providing access for local users.

Other activity in the Internet field has been considerable, with a host of international projects (about 30 extant in 1995) involved in Internet provision for Africa. This has compounded the problem somewhat. Donor agencies have provided limited Internet connectivity via nodes in the agencies' own national bases, thus providing access only as a peripheral function of a distant network. Thus, Afrikanet (for Cameroon) and RIO Africa (for Burkina Faso, Cameroon, Congo, Ivory Coast, Madagascar and Mali) link to

France; RINAF (for 13 sub-Saharan countries) links to Italy; Afrinet (for Kenya, Zimbabwe, Tanzania and Uganda) to the USA; while NGONET Africa, ESANET, ARSONET, WEDNET, HEALTHNET, GHASTINET and WORKNET (between them covering a host of African countries) all link to London. The technology varies; between them single donors and consortia are involved from case to case; and the subject and institutional focus of the projects varies too.[42] This is as confused as it seems.

Odedra-Straub reports that sponsors and their project teams dominated the 1995 Addis Ababa Symposium on 'Telematics for Development'.[43] She felt that they were more concerned with technicalities than development in the global sense; did not share information, to the extent that some were unaware of each other's existence; and often had only pilot projects which had seldom been evaluated. Despite these very valid concerns, all this activity does have the virtue of building up know-how and skills in Africa, which should in turn contribute to the success of broader solutions, once they emerge.

The emergence of such solutions in the mid-1990s is still problematic, however. Fuller connectivity across Africa is inhibited by the exceedingly poor quality of telecommunications links between the various countries. The colonial powers which installed the original systems were mainly interested in providing connections between the metropolitan country and its colonies. Linking one part of Africa to another was not seen as profitable, and maybe even seen as dangerous as the groundswell for independence grew. North–south links are better developed than east–west links, with parallel systems directed towards London and Paris. What this has meant in practical terms is that it has been easier to phone Nairobi from London than from Mombasa, which is in the same country. To get a telephone line from Djibouti to Lesotho, it has been necessary to go via operators in Paris, London and Johannesburg. The problem is being solved by satellite links which permit the countries which have acquired earth stations to communicate more directly. However, this is still a case of sophisticated communication between antiquated systems, prone to hold-ups and misconnections.

The actual links between countries have limited capacity. For instance, to link the totally digital system of Botswana with South Africa's digital fibre optic and ISDN capacity it was necessary to use low capacity analog circuits.[44] There are proposals to provide the links that would open up these partially sealed local telecommunications markets to each other and to a wider world. They include AT & T's idea of a 20,000-mile sea-bed cable around Africa, or Siemens's modular approach, linking the infrastructure country by country with a series of shorter underwater cables. South Africa which, as we have noted, has the preponderant share of the whole continent's telecommunications traffic, through its state corporation Telkom, is also strongly interested in the choices made over modes of linkage. Many commentators see the South African option as best, because it would offer a solution from within the continent. First of all, however, Telkom has to solve the problem of more equitable distribution within South Africa's boundaries. A Telecommunications Bill, tabled in October 1996, seeks to do just that.

The positive potential which follows from modern telecommunications links within Africa is inviting. Paradoxically the low level of telecommunications investment within most African countries means that to renew their whole systems is not an enormous commitment, if the political will is there. The copper wiring that is more or less universal could be replaced by the totally fibre optic networks which have so far presented an unacceptably high financial investment to the intensively wired industrialized countries of the North. Add to this the scope for introducing wireless communication, and an attractive scenario is opened up. African countries would have an infrastructure superior to anything in the world, and could reap the benefits that would grow from untrammelled Internet access today, and almost unimaginable communications advantages likely to be offered by succeeding generations of networks. These benefits would certainly be financial, in the form of an enormous stimulus to business activity, but would also include gains in the social sphere. In education, for instance, South Africa's African Growth Network already offers computer-aided learning facilities to thousands of skills trainees in sectors such as banking, while the Multi Choice business network broadcasts literacy and other adult education materials to thousands of points within the country. Similar developments could transform learning throughout the continent.

Jegede puts the utopianism of all this in perspective when he points out that:

Three quarters of Africa's population is illiterate (so hooking them to the Internet is out of the question); three quarters of Africa is rural without basic facilities of electricity and telephone (so hooking up to the Internet can only be restricted to the urban areas); three quarters of universities in Africa have depleted library resources, have overworked academics and run computer science departments without computers (so hooking them to the Internet is only solving a small proportion of the problem); and there are currently 200 million personal computers worldwide but less than one per cent of them are located in Africa (so hooking non-existent computers to the Internet is still a dream).[45]

Fortunately his analysis does not automatically have to point to the bleakest conclusions. If, and it is admittedly a big if, the highest quality telecommunications infrastructure were put in place, many of the problems he outlines could be addressed with much more ease than at present. The idea that Africa can leapfrog into the Information Age, largely missing out the Print Age which preceded it elsewhere, is not wholly ridiculous. Unfortunately, it does call for a level of commitment which looks beyond Africa's twentieth-century rulers.

Jegede's comments on the Internet return the focus back to the most distinctive feature of the African information environment: the role of the oral. In the next chapter, by turning to the question of information needs of the people and the responses of information providers, that is inevitably the direction in which we turn.

References

1. Crowder, M. The book crisis: Africa's other famine. *African Research and Documentation*, 41, 1986. 1–6.
2. Frommlet, W. Books -- the first victims of the crisis. *Development and Cooperation*, 3, 1992. 24.
3. Ifidon, S.E. Planning without facts: a comparative study of the uses and abuses of information and information technology. *Library Review*, 43, 1994. 27–36. p.32.
4. Unesco. *Statistical Year Book*. Paris, Unesco, 1986.
5. Ryan, M. AIDS: the frightening facts. *New African*, 220, 1986. 7–8.
6. Ive, O. Cameroon: crushing censorship. *New African*, 249, 1988. 39–40.
7. Fopoussi, D. and NDiaya, B. Cameroon: tightening the stranglehold. *Index on Censorship*, 1992. 35.
8. Mukong, A. The tale of a lesson learned too well. *Index on Censorship*, 1991. 24–6.
9. Chiweza, D.S. Information and politics: limits and ambiguity of the concept of freedom of information in the Malawi of 1961–1993. Paper delivered at SCECSAL XI, Blantyre, Malawi, July, 1994.

10. Sturges, P. The political economy of information: Malawi under Kamuzu Banda 1964–1994. In: Feather, J.P. (ed.) *Transforming Libraries and Educating Librarians*. London, Taylor Graham, 1997. 57–73.
11. Buchanan-Smith, M., Davies, S. and Petty, C. Food security: let them eat information. *IDS Bulletin*, 25, 1994. 69–80.
12. Leach, M. and Fairhead, J. Natural resource management: the reproduction and use of environmental misinformation in Guinea's forest-savanna transition zone. *IDS Bulletin*, 25, 1994. 81–7.
13. Mchombu, K.J. Information support for democratization in Africa. In: Feather, J.P. (ed.) *Transforming Libraries and Educating Librarians*. London, Taylor Graham, 1997. 41–56.
14. Duces, B. World Bank activities in library and documentation services provision in developing countries. *Government Information Quarterly*, 8, 1991. 381–6. p.384.
15. Annis, S. Toward a pro-poor information agenda at the World Bank. *Development*, 2, 1990. 73–6. p.74.
16. Hayward, F.M. A reassessment of the conventional wisdom about the informed public: national political information in Ghana. *American Political Science Review*, 70, 1976. 433–51.
17. Cutter, C.H. Political communication in a pre-literate society: the example of rural Mali. *Rural Africana*, 27, 1975. 9–23.
18. Boafo, S.T.K. Utilizing development communication strategies in African societies. *Gazette, International Journal for Mass Communication Studies*, 35, 1985. 83–92.
19. Ansah, P.A.V. News values: an African perspective. *Development*, 1990. 35.
20. Nwuneli, O.E. International news coverage in Nigerian newspapers. *Gazette, International Journal of Mass Communication Studies*, 29, 1982. 31–40.
21. Escarpit, R. *Trends in Worldwide Book Development, 1970–1978*. Paris, Unesco, 1982.
22. Unesco. *An International Survey of Book Production during the Last Decade*. Paris, Unesco, 1982. p.20.
23. Kibirigi, H.M. Libraries and illiteracy in developing countries: a critical assessment. *Libri*, 27, 1977. 54–67. p.55.
24. Ourgay, M. Follow up materials for literacy retention and continuing education: the case of Ethiopia. In: Asamani, J.O. *et al.* (eds) *Libraries and Literacy. Proceedings of the 7th Meeting of the Standing Conference of Eastern, Central and Southern African Librarians, Gaborone, 4–8 August, 1986*. Gaborone, Botswana Library Association, 1987. 95–101.
25. Moyo, G. Forty years on, novelist Sigogo still going strong. *The Chronicle* (Zimbabwe) 15 November 1996. 8.
26. Msiska, A.W.C. Early attempts at creating African literature: its distribution, local authorship, and library service in Northern Rhodesia (Zambia) and Nyasaland (Malawi). *Libri*, 36, 1986. 240–6.
27. Kotei, S.I.A. *The Book Today in Africa*. Paris, Unesco, 1981.
28. Obiechina, E. *An African Popular Literature: A Study of Onitsha Market Pamphlets*. London, Cambridge University Press, 1973.
29. Obasi, J.U. Bibliographical control of Nigerian publications: social

science primary materials. *Journal of Documentation*, 38, 1982. 107–24. p.115.

30. Osa, O. *Nigerian Youth Literature*. Benin, Paramount Publishers, 1987. p.14.

31. Lungu, C.M. Resource sharing and self-reliance in Southern Africa. *Information Development*, 3, 1987. 82–6. p.85.

32. Zulu, S.F.C. Africa's survival plan for meeting the challenges of technology in the 1990s and beyond. *Libri*, 44, 1994. 77–94.

33. Woherem, E.E. *Information Technology in Africa*. Nairobi, ACTS Press, 1993.

34. Olden, A. Sub-Saharan Africa and the paperless society. *Journal of the American Society for Information Science*, 38, 1987. 298–304. p.299.

35. Woherem, E.E. op. cit. p.x.

36. Tiamiyu, M.A. Sub-Saharan Africa and the paperless society: a comment and a counterpoint. *Journal of the American Society for Information Science*, 40, 1989. 325–8.

37. Nkhata, B.W.M. CD ROM in developing countries: is it a technology for the distribution of information? *Electronic Library*, 11, 1993. 295–7.

38. Woherem, E.E. op. cit. p.158.

39. Stavrou, S.E. *A Study of the Socio-economic Needs for Telecommunications in Rural KwaZulu*. Centre for Social and Developing Studies, Report No.1. Durban, University of Natal, 1988.

40. Morris, M.L. and Stavrou, S.E. Telecommunication needs and provision to underdeveloped black areas in South Africa. *Telecommunications Policy*, 1993. 529–39.

41. Adam, L. Electronic communications technology and development in Africa. *FID News Bulletin*, 45, 1995. 298–306.

42. Jegede, O.J. From talking drums to electronic networking: Africa's snailmobile through cyberspace. *FID News Bulletin*, 45, 1995. 218–24. p.220.

43. Odedra-Straub, M. Contemporary issues in electronic communications in Africa: a summary of the Addis Ababa symposium. *FID News Bulletin*, 45, 1995. 225–7.

44. Africa Telematics Symposium Report: downloaded from Community and Civic Networks Discussion List. *FID News Bulletin*, 45, 1995. 215–17. p.216.

45. Jegede, O.J. op. cit. p.221.

Chapter Two

Information Needs and Responses

Needs and Informal Responses

It is, unfortunately, perfectly reasonable to argue, as has sometimes been done, that the rural population and the urban poor of Africa do not have information needs, what they have is resource needs. Rosenberg puts it in the most direct way when she says:

> Surveys of rural communities made by librarians are virtually pre-programmed to discover information needs. Yet when one reads accounts of village life in Africa, made after living one or two years in a particular village, the lack of access to information is never expressed as a problem or its reverse a solution.[1]

What she says is fair. Most surveys of information needs have to be read with a highly critical and questioning attitude. They do tend to start with the solid assumption that everyone, wherever they might be, has information needs. It also seems to be a basic assumption that some fixed and rather formal institution (very much like a library if it is librarians carrying out the survey) will provide effectively for those needs. As an indication of the type of questions that may be involved, the following is part of a transcript of an interview with a Tuareg herdsman conducted by a Ministry of National Education researcher in Burkina Faso.[2]

> Q. You'd said earlier that you would like to learn a certain number of things. Would you accept the advice of someone, a Muslim, who came to live among you in a straw hut to teach you these things?
> A. Yes.
> Q. You are undoubtedly aware that there are grains which, with

49

sufficient rainfall, yield a good harvest, and that there are others which
yield little or nothing. Would it interest you to know the 'why' of all this,
or would you be only interested in the results?
A.   I am interested in everything that would help me.
Q.   That's important: your willingness to accept advice from the person who would come to live here is good. Would you prefer he only state
what is to be done and not why it must be done just so?
A.   No, I prefer that he explain why.

In this exchange the official virtually makes any response other
than the desired one impossible. It might be slightly unfair to use it
out of context to pillory the quality of research findings generally,
but it illustrates Rosenberg's point very well. Most surveys are not to
be treated as hard evidence: they only provide clues.

If a survey is open enough, many respondents will actually tell the
investigators that they have no information needs. They will say that
clean water, adequate medical attention or supplies of agricultural
inputs are all more important to them than information. For
instance Sturges and Chimseu in Malawi, although getting interesting responses to their questions concerning what villagers
needed to know, were told directly on several occasions that it was
not information that was most needed.[3] Francis and Rawlins-
Branan were told by farmers in Zambia that their chief concern was
financial and other inputs (although how the farmers would handle the matter of financial credits without good information is
interesting).[4] Mchombu, again in Malawi, found that as many as 31
per cent of respondents in one of the villages he studied could
express no information needs at all. The starkness of this response
was, however, mitigated by the fact that:

> Whenever respondents were asked to state their information needs in
> the context of an ongoing activity, quite often they were able to
> articulate information needs in very specific terms, contrary to situa-
> tions when these needs were asked for in abstract terms.[5]

People clearly do not see information as being as important as the
satisfaction of basic needs for survival. Any information worker who
ignored this basic principle would be foolish in the extreme, but
that does not mean that information service should be ruled out of
consideration for the poorest members of society. On the contrary,
the surveys do genuinely show information needs, though not
everyone is able, or willing, to express them. These needs are very
seldom library needs, which is what many investigators have been
seeking. They are ordinary everyday needs, which become partic-

ularly urgent when the citizen is faced with problems associated with change and development.

When asked to identify a recent work-related situation that had involved problem-solving or decision making, Zambian farmers gave responses which could be grouped into 27 different categories of problem.[6] These varied from dealing with farm pests, boundary disputes, choice of seed types, to coping with soil drainage problems, all of which would require information if they were to be brought to a satisfactory resolution. Mchombu, in two Tanzanian villages surveyed as part of his INFORD project, found that respondents expressed needs related to agriculture, health and hygiene, and cooperatives and other income generating projects.[7] Earlier, Aboyade in her classic RUDIS project had also identified information needs relating to practical matters, but found a desire for material which would entertain or meet people's religious interests.[8] Another study by Kaniki in South Africa dealt with a rather more varied population, including students, unemployed and self-employed people, with numbers of respondents split almost equally between men and women.[9] His findings there showed a need for information on employment and education related topics.

Women, who in the rural areas carry a disproportionate load of the economic responsibilities in addition to their usual home and family concerns, have acute information problems.[10] Their access to credit packages, both as women and as farmers of small landholdings, is poor.[11] Many of them indeed prefer to avoid indebtedness for obvious reasons. However, information and advice tend to come as part of the credit packages, often leaving women farmers with serious gaps in their knowledge. This kind of evidence from quite a good number of other surveys should not be ignored, even if the surveys tend to rate information more highly than respondents would do themselves.

Before going on from a tentative recognition that needs do exist to suggesting systems to serve them, we need a much clearer idea of how people meet their needs at present. The surveys and other literature offer some indications regarding this. First of all, it would be a mistake to assume that the information needs articulated by survey respondents go unmet. A high proportion of people solve problems from basic knowledge which they attribute to family and other community members, or indeed to their own exploration of solutions and experimentation. Mungunda and Mumbuna's survey of Zambian farmers' livestock knowledge indicated that as many as

84 per cent gained their essential knowledge in this way.[12] McClymont, working with commercial farmers in Zimbabwe, obtained
very similar findings, 78 per cent having either learned from
experience, or from friends and neighbours.[13] Kaniki, in the study
already cited, discovered that 75 per cent of the farmers he inter-
viewed very often relied on personal experience, and that 35 per
cent (closely overlapping?) frequently resorted to family and neighbours.[14] In doing this, they are actually very often tapping the
reservoirs of orally transferred indigenous knowledge that we have
already identified as retaining the utmost significance in the African information scene.

Until very recent times, a totally oral society was the norm in
virtually every part of Africa. Despite the apparent influence of the
printed word the oral mode still predominates, most notably
among the rural population. Two types or levels of oral communication can be distinguished, the general and the specialized, each
in its own way contributing to the strength of African culture and,
what is important for our purposes, the information system and
knowledge base which is an inseparable part of that culture. The
general aspects of oral communication are those affecting people's
everyday exchanges. They concern the ways in which information,
ideas and feelings are conveyed from one person to others. They
involve the presence of subtle layers of added meaning arising from
who is addressed, where, how and by whom, as well as the use of
gesture, tone of voice and particular modes of speech. The richness
of Africa's oral culture in terms of its general characteristics can
easily be witnessed wherever people meet, be it in the village, in the
market place, or on public transport.[15]

The more specialized aspects of oral culture can be defined by
the ways in which society selects certain types of information for
special treatment and public use, embodying them in formal patterns such as poetry, song and story. Accordingly, the oral medium
has specialized practitioners such as the *griots* of West Africa, story-
tellers, singers, praise poets, soothsayers and traditional healers
who have had well-defined roles and forums permitting the exposi-
tion of the communal knowledge and wisdom for which they are
the major repository. Outsiders have long been aware of this
specialized cultural role, and have even sometimes sentimentalized
it thus, for example:

As the sun nears the western horizon, bringing all occupations to an end, and the sounds of the village are augmented by the chorus of crickets and bullfrogs, a fire is lit and quickly becomes the focus of evening activity. Several quiet conversations can be heard; someone drones a tune; another plucks a harp; others lie down and are lost to the world; and even the usually noisy youths and young women are less boisterous. Suddenly village elders are encouraged to tell a story, and at once an eager crowd of men, women and children throng around the fire, ready to hear such tales as *Anansi the blind fisherman,* or *Omanheme who liked riddles.*[16]

It is important to set aside such views of the oral culture as quaint and charming, but irrelevant to modern life. The significant thing is that the oral culture also holds important functional information. The acceptance of this principle leads inevitably to the questions 'How is practical traditional knowledge accumulated?' and 'What exactly do the people know that is useful?'. In answer to the first, it is clear that much traditional knowledge is rooted in generations of experience and observation. The nature of peasant life is well summed up by the following:

> They build and repair their houses; they prepare food and fetch water, fuel and other domestic supplies; they spin, weave, and sew clothing; they keep animals, slaughter them, and tan their hides; they make tools, pots, baskets, furniture and ornaments; they generate remedies for their ills; they run their own systems of conflict resolution and work hard to keep a variety of spiritual agents appeased.[17]

Over the years Africa's peoples have done all these things, and they have gradually found when, where and how best they should do them. This has cumulated into a body of knowledge precisely adapted to the specific conditions of the particular localities and conditions in which they have lived.

The oral tradition is particularly rich in agricultural knowledge. In terms of crops this has been based on the way in which farmers have maintained, combined and selected the indigenous varieties which agricultural scientists refer to as landraces. Over the years this has been done with the matching of a wide diversity of crop varieties, whether self-pollinating, cross-pollinating or vegetatively propagated, to difficult and often marginal farming environments. In all this, security against pests, diseases and adverse climatic conditions has always been very much in the farmer's mind. Yet, it has been done very much in a spiritual framework which, to the outsider's eye, may seem to cast suspicion on its validity. Farmers in Northern Ghana, for instance, employ the mediation of chiefs, soothsayers and earth priests (*tendana*) to obtain messages from their ancestors and gods to assist in agricultural problem-solving and decision making. The messages give guidance on matters of wind, rain, crops and livestock, and have prompted an innovative and effective approach to the immediate farming problems of the community.[18]

The spiritual or intuitive dimension of traditional knowledge exposed by both casual observation and systematic study does present a mental barrier to cooperation for professionals educated in the rational traditions of the North. To counterbalance this, there is ample evidence that in the oral environment information needs of various sorts are satisfied by the use of observation and experimentation of a kind quite familiar to the formally trained scientist.

The case of Nigerian responses to an agricultural pest, the variegated grasshopper, illustrates this very well. Investigators found that in those features of knowledge of the grasshopper which were susceptible to precise quantitative data, sophisticated experimentation and biochemical analysis, formal science transcended local knowledge.[19] They also found that in several features such as the food preferences of the grasshopper, levels of damage it inflic-ted on the cassava crop, and its egg-laying behaviour, farmers' knowledge was broadly equivalent to that of scientific investigators. In yet other areas, they found farmers' knowledge contained significant information which had not been observed by researchers. This included detailed awareness of outbreaks of grasshopper attacks not formally recorded, detail on the range of crops attacked and their local economic significance, and the role of the grasshopper as a food item which was particularly valuable in the diet of women, children and poorer members of the community.

This kind of knowledge had its chief strengths in things which could be observed by a long-term local resident. The grasshopper and its activities are clearly visible to the naked eye of the observer, and information about the extent and variation of outbreaks can be accumulated in conversation with other farmers. This may seem to set quite strict parameters to farmers' ability to achieve substantial comprehension of a particular agricultural issue. Despite this, farmers have also shown the ability to understand the processes of a microscopic pest like cassava bacterial blight, accurately assessing the significance of rain storms and the spread of the pest through the use of indirect inference.

Although farmers' knowledge is essentially qualitative, there is a great deal of measurement involved in their work.[20] For this they employ local units of weight, area and volume, such as the guinea corn stalks woven together which are used in Kwara State, Nigeria, to calculate the layout of a yam vine trellis. Such units are variable, but they contribute to effective estimates of distances, weights, areas, times required for particular tasks, and typical yields per acre. Such measurement is easily adequate for the farmer experimentation which can be found in many locations.

In areas of farmland near the Volta lake in Ghana, for instance, farmers have been forced into experimentation and innovation by the problems of desiccation, deforestation, climatic change and invasion by savanna weeds which they experience.[21] The cultivation of the cowpea has been introduced and farmers have experimented with a number of variations of crop rotation to obtain an optimum effect. Other innovations include introduction of cassava varieties which mature earlier than the ones previously used, improvement of fallow regeneration by developing methods of preserving young tree seedlings and the exploitation of particular species of tree which grow well locally and whose presence is conducive to the cultivation of maize, cowpeas, cassava and plantains.

Farmers in Zambia have been shown to have developed elaborate classifications of soils which would provide a solid basis for experimentation.[22] These classifications are not intended to be universal, but relate to the area in which the farmer lives. The method of classifying soils which farmers use focuses on both the advantages and the limiting factors of a given soil. Soil scientists are uncomfortable with the categories such classifications include, because they do not easily match the technical categories which the scientists themselves employ. In this the scientists miss the point. The locally developed categories are based on a wide range of criteria, including observed crop performance, that place the greatest emphasis on the fertility status of a soil. Classifying a soil according to its position in an array organized by inherent chemical properties, as scientists would prefer, is not adequate for the farmers' purposes. Much more richly descriptive categories are needed to serve their needs. The kind of intimate soil knowledge the farmers reveal through their classifications is a prerequisite for matters such as seed selection, where careful experimentation is essential.

An excellent example of farmers' experimentation in practice is the rice-growing of the Mende of Sierra Leone.[23] Travellers' accounts, from as long ago as the seventeenth century, show the Mende carefully matching rice varieties to soil moisture conditions. The harvesting practices still used are the basis for selection of new seed. Early-ripening types are taken by farmers desperate for food early in the season, and later-ripening types will be left in the fields for gleaners. Seed from the former is eagerly sought because of the high status of early-ripening crops, and its qualities are tested in trial plots. Tested seed which gives good results is then used for the next crop. This process is continuous because of the Mende's perception of rice as a constantly changing resource, which must be worked with to obtain ideal results.

Traditional medicine also contains a corpus of valuable knowledge but within a spiritual framework that led colonial governments and Christian missionaries to condemn and suppress it as witchcraft. This failed to give credit to either the broad religious and social role the traditional healers played in the community and the contributions which they could make to public health. The traditional healers of pre-colonial Zimbabwe, for instance, encouraged the community to select village sites in high places, with clean water sources, above the malaria zone. They sought to treat their patients not merely as sufferers from specific diseases and conditions, but as whole people in whom the spiritual influences the physical. At the same time, they employed considerable empirical medical knowledge, a large part of it herbal. More than 500 different types of plants were used for medical and veterinary purposes in early twentieth-century Zimbabwe and the clinical effectiveness of many of these is now witnessed by modern medical researchers. Some modern African states have recognized the importance of traditional medicine, for instance Zimbabwe in its Traditional Medical Practitioners Act of 1981.[24]

The problem with traditional medical knowledge is that it is flawed knowledge. It can easily be shown that ordinary people, reliant upon it, all too often lack essential information capable of saving lives and enhancing standards of living. When people turn to indigenous knowledge resources, as they can be shown to do in a wide range of circumstances, they may or may not obtain a safe or useful answer. To elaborate on this a little further, two medical examples will give an idea of the way in which people use traditional medicine, and the extent to which there is a need for an alternative source of assistance.

Guinea worm, a parasite which lives under the skin of its human host, protruding through a painful ulcer, has been common in many isolated rural areas of Africa and south Asia. It is painful and debilitating, but not fatal. Its eradication can be quite simply organized if residents in an infested area can be persuaded to subject their drinking water to a very simple filtering process. The cheapness of this process would more or less justify the identification of guinea worm eradication as an information problem, rather than one of medical inputs. Intensive investigation of local knowledge of the guinea worm in Nigeria discovered that less than 3 per cent of identified sufferers from the parasite sought treatment in hospitals or clinics.[25] The traditional view was that the worm was potentially present in everyone and was responsible for a variety of unpleasant rashes, aches and pains and other symptoms that people experienced from time to time. There was no real way of treating this in the traditional view, although various palliative treatments could be adopted to soothe particular symptoms.

Similarly, the inhabitants of rural Africa suffer a range of eye conditions, including cataract, corneal disease and bacterial infections. Many of these eventually result in blindness, which affects about 1 per cent of the population. The evidence from a number of African countries tends to suggest that a proportion of this figure is actually attributable to the use of traditional eye medicines, probably in the form of self-treatment. A survey in the Chikwawa District of Malawi showed that traditional healers were treating considerably more patients for eye conditions than the personnel of the formal clinics.[26] They used a variety of herbal and other treatments, but none attempted surgical correction of conditions such as cataract. The evidence left the investigators happy to believe that traditional treatments, when administered by healers, were effective for self-limiting, non-blinding eye diseases. Even then the inability of traditional healers to deal with various blinding conditions was clear. The survey revealed that more than half of the healers they investigated knew that surgical procedures for cataract were possible, but this information was seldom passed on to patients in the form of advice or referral.

In fact, it is important to recognize that traditional medicine is not such an effective means of disseminating health awareness as it may be in treating sickness. As an instance of this, a study undertaken among rural women in Central Tanzania found that only 34 per cent felt sure that malaria was caused by the bite of the mosquito.[27] Many of these rural dwellers thought it was due to eating unripe maize or wild berries, and some even thought it was brought by the wind. Malaria is not new to East Africa, nor is it uncommon in Central Tanzania. It is examples of ignorance like this that have led many to shun and even despise indigenous knowledge as merely a form of superstition.

The best inference that can be drawn from these and other examples is that if modern medical advice and treatment were offered in a way which harmonized with traditional knowledge, it would be possible to increase greatly their acceptability. In fact this was precisely the suggestion made by the Malawian investigators who suggested ongoing collaboration with traditional healers for blindness prevention, which would involve training programmes intended to lead to referral to clinics when appropriate. What is more, they made it clear that the association of witchcraft or sorcery with the practices of the traditional healers should not be regarded as a barrier to such cooperation.

Significantly, one group of outside interests which are far from shunning traditional knowledge because of its perceived imperfections, are the research-based industrial companies of the North, particularly in the agribusiness and pharmaceutical sectors. What has been described as a 'resource rush' has been taking place in the 1990s, whereby researchers have been seeking to obtain, test and adapt traditional knowledge of bio-resources with commercial potential. One way which is being explored to protect knowledge that has always been seen as a public good, rather than a source of private profit, is by treating it as a kind of community-owned intellectual property.[28] Since the companies concerned patent their products and market them in the developing world under strict protection from infringement, this is perhaps the best way to contest the issue. Whatever the outcome, the interest of big business in indigenous knowledge is a major endorsement of the value of its content, albeit an ironic one.

It would also be a mistake to concentrate on indigenous knowledge as a fixed corpus from the past preserved for today. This is much too restrictive and, among other things, it fails to take into account the way in which oral society accommodates new knowledge. Countless innovations from the bicycle to the radio have been tested, adapted and finally absorbed into even the remotest parts of rural Africa. Even in remote rural areas the extent of 'modern' knowledge is invariably underestimated. Taking the example of political information, it has often been assumed that rural populations are politically ignorant to the extent that many people do not understand what a vote is. Certainly in many parts of Africa difficult terrain, extremes of climate, poor roads and lack of vehicles limit travel and the access to information. Access to the modern information media, that are ubiquitous in more developed countries, is also poor. This gives plausibility to the idea that African people must be poorly informed politically. However, a number of surveys by no means bear this out, indeed, they suggest something quite different.

The ability of people in rural areas, literate or not, to name their political representatives and identify the content of issues of current political concern frequently outshines that shown by people in similar surveys conducted in the United States and Europe.[29] Perhaps this could be explained to some extent by the jaded appetite for political involvement which citizens in the West have developed as a consequence of the sheer volume of political information that confronts them both at election times and in the intervals between. Perhaps also the comparative paucity of political information by Western standards in most African countries sensitizes people to what little is available and encourages them to retain and remember it. Whatever the reasons, the basic findings remain and suggest the importance of oral communication in the political process.

There is also a danger of regarding oral society and indigenous knowledge as basically rural. Indigenous knowledge also encompasses a multitude of urban themes – small-scale business and industry for instance. The resilience of the informal sector in most African countries, despite a hostile business environment and neglect by government, is something often overlooked.[30] The informal sector is mainly the preserve of micro-enterprises usually under individual or family control and conducting transactions with little intervention from banks, accountants or tax inspectors. Credit, when needed, is obtained through family and personal networks, or from the informal banking sector. Prices and terms of payment likewise vary according to the dynamics of human relations. Such businesses tend to stay small even when successful. Excess funds are distributed within the family network, or used in luxury expenditure, but seldom form the capital for expansion. To survive and prosper, small businessmen or industrialists must be capable of reacting to changes in state policy and the shifting nature of the business environment.

In other words, they have pressing information needs. Although not common, to succeed on a larger scale is possible, and the example of Nnewi in Nigeria shows that similar rules apply. Nnewi is a community which has emerged during the 1980s as an important centre for the production and trade in motor vehicle parts. Some of the reasons for the growth and success of its approximately twenty large locally-owned firms is due to a perceptive choice of alliance with the emerging industrial economies of the Far East. Much else is, however, rooted in the same community networks as the micro-enterprises. Infrastructure (roads, water supply, electricity supply) were acquired and improved in this way. The personnel of the industry is drawn from local people, usually without much formal education, but with strong ties of family and friendship. As a local magazine, quoted by Vaughan, put it, 'No degree or diploma is needed; graduates and the faint hearted keep off. Requisite qualification: street acquired training and experience'.[31] These are precisely the qualities that augment the body of business knowledge in African communities. Again, one can ask if they are sufficient for the expansion of business activity to the point where it can fully support the apparatus of a modern state. The answer might seem to be that they are not, and that for more extensive industrial take off, there is a need for altered circumstances, including greater accessibility of business-related information of all kinds. At present, though, most information needs are satisfied from within the informal networks.

Although these networks are to some extent enclosed and private to a family, a clan, a local community, there are also lines of transmission that spread knowledge more extensively. In areas where markets are well developed, they are a prime focus for information exchange, and those who go to market may as well be there for information as for tradeable goods. In rural parts of West Africa, many communities have at least a small market, and there has tended to be a market within at most a day's journey from most of the farming population. The trade is in a variety of goods with foodstuffs and cooked food predominant, but livestock and craftwork items from the locality are common, and consumer items like cloth and stationery brought in by traders from towns are also sold in such centres. The efficacy of markets for information exchange is almost a byword, and investigation of the market communication network confirms this.

In their research towards a disease surveillance system in a part of Oyo State, Nigeria, Brieger and Kendall carried out thorough research of markets and their catchment areas in the Ifeloju District.[32] They consulted the chief of the market and his council, villagers in hamlets served by the market, and the truck drivers who took people and goods back and forth. In their efforts to identify representatives who would bring reports on disease incidence to markets as a central information collecting point, they sought those who were regular attenders and who were socially acceptable for this delicate assignment. The results of the project, when verified by other means, showed that the representatives achieved high levels of completeness and accuracy in their reporting. Although their focus was on the market's ability to support a particular function, they showed very clearly the precise structures through which information from the hamlets could flow to the local market. What is more, the attendance of outside buyers, traders and lorry drivers linked the markets to the towns and cities for flows of information both inwards and outwards.

The market is perhaps the best but not the only focus for informal information exchange. Indeed, since it is less common outside West Africa, it is necessary to look at other points of exchange too. Mchombu's research, which is probably the most extensive yet undertaken with information needs as its explicit focus, showed church or mosque as more or less equally popular (each cited by almost exactly 40 per cent of respondents) in his Malawian survey.[33] Health centres, at about 25 per cent, were also cited frequently, and percentages somewhere in the teens mentioned beer drinking places, communal wells, the chief's place and the homes of friends. Mentioned by less than 10 per cent were bus stops, the village school and official meetings. Mchombu sensed a tension here between traditional and modern, with place of worship and market-place now rivalled by the health centre as the most common location for information exchange. He also found that the site of the traditional power structure (the chief's place), although diminished in status today, still compares favourably with political/public meetings. To illustrate the variety of sites at which people are conscious of this type of exchange, Sturges and Chimseu, again in Malawi, were told that funerals, beer brewing and drinking occasions, group mat-making and grain-pounding sessions, and games such as *bawo*, were good opportunities to pick up news and information.[34]

The same Malawian research also threw light on people's perception of what made information trustworthy. Chiefs and village headmen are important in information transfer, particularly in more isolated and underdeveloped communities. It is part of their official role in the Malawian system, which allocates certain responsibilities to traditional authorities, to pass on information by calling formal meetings. They also, however, mediate a wider range of transfer. The groups of villagers who participated in the research consistently made distinctions between the weights attached to various sources of information. Information which people acquired at informal social occasions was often their first introduction to something new, but it often merely had the status of rumour. If the information cross-checked with something heard on the radio, or mentioned by an official, it could begin to be treated seriously. For it to be wholeheartedly accepted it required the endorsement of chiefs and other local leaders.

This is also quite typical of other African countries. In Nigeria, the discredited federal state is rivalled in many areas by powerful local rulers and chiefs who have seized the initiative by providing leadership on many issues, including particular community development programmes.[35] In a chaotic polity their ties to community, family and clan, enable them to function as providers of social cohesion and community development. It should be pointed out that commentators on this do not regard it as a wholly positive thing. They suggest, for instance, that while the complex and informal network system within which traditional authority operates does serve to project local values and aspirations, it has also enhanced the status and privileges of the traditional leaders' allies in the local bureaucratic and commercial classes. Our purpose here is not the uncritical endorsement of the role of traditional authority in the relationships which govern many things in rural life. Rather, what concerns us most is its role in the distribution and acceptance of information.

When we look at the African information scene, we find information and other related needs satisfied from personal knowledge or by experimentation; we find resort to traditional wisdom, through the mediation of chiefs and other local authority figures; we note the significance of markets and other informal meeting places for information transfer. All of these relate to societies organized on a radically different basis from that which is posited as the starting point for formal information services like those found in Northern industrialized countries. The social microprocesses which we have illustrated to a small extent here are extremely location-specific and reflect the way in which African rural society, and to a significant degree urban society too, is characterized by autonomy of the individual and family from the official system. Both the rural peasant and the urban entrepreneur or streetwise individual have never been fully coopted by the system. The tiny base for income-related taxation and the very low figures for those in formal employment in most African states are illustrations of this. To a great extent it is a reflection of poverty and deprivation, but it is also evidence of parallel economies, parallel systems of social organization and distinct belief systems.

With the influx of rural people into the towns, Hyden argues that:

> The distinction between rural and urban life has grown less apparent, and forms of social interaction and modes of conducting business increasingly reflect indigenous – originally rural – practices.[36]

What we discover answering people's material and mental needs is something which Hyden calls the 'economy of affection'. The term is intended to apply to precisely those networks of support, communication and interaction among groups connected by kinship, community, religion, etc. In this economy, households cooperate to safeguard the community through structures which tend to be invisible to the outsider, while each household tends to retain its essential autonomy. The household may take up some aspect or other of modern economic production, but will do without automatically surrendering its own priorities. Thus in the case of adoption of high-yielding crop varieties, the household will not necessarily use this to produce a surplus which will increase family income. Rather, members will tend to use an innovation to reduce the time spent in food production so as to shift their attention to other activities to which they accord a high priority. The way in which African wage labourers frequently prefer not to take advantage of productivity incentives to increase their cash income, but choose instead to decrease the number of days laboured, is just one instance of the values of this economy of affection in practice. The flow of funds from town to country, as people who have moved away continue to support the families they have left, temporarily or permanently, is an essential feature of rural family budgets. At the same time it is the central symbol of the enduring strength of the economy of affection.

The holistic culture of the village, and its wider influence through the economy of affection are often clearly at odds with the intentions of development planners. For instance, a rural area near Gokwe in Zimbabwe had a row of toilets built for it by a development agency. When the developers returned to review this project, they discovered that the toilets had not been used as such, but had been converted into a set of convenient grain stores. It was the planners' idea that the community needed toilets, while the villagers felt that they needed grain stores. When consulted in advance, the villagers of Upper Guruwe rejected an elaborately-planned irrigation project, because of the conditions attached to it. Each household would have been required to devote two acres to fruit-growing for the market, so as to be able to repay loan finance, and only to use half an acre for maize, their staple crop. They clearly felt that this was an unacceptable balance and were prepared to do without help rather than accept it.[37]

In a devastating analysis of this kind of miscomprehension, Robert Chambers, a persuasive representative of a new approach to development planning, describes it as resulting from dogmatic errors in development theory and practice.[38] In his attempts to account for the prevalence of such error he offers four types of explanation. The most pervasive of these may be quite simply the sheer arrogance of power engendered by the relative positions of professional development planners and rural peasants. A second, related form of error can arise from the transplantation of professional values, beliefs, methods and technology which are perfectly valid in the conditions prevalent in the North, but which are invalidated by their use in the South. Third, he points out that change in development realities may lead to the irrelevance of plans devised on the basis of out-of-date information. Finally, he suggests that the modes of learning adopted by planners are inadequate, and more specifically criticizes two methods – the brief and biased rural visits often used to assess the validity of projects, and the large-scale questionnaire surveys which always impart such an air of scientific veracity to any plan with which they are associated.

In all these categories there is an important element of inadequate information, though the first two may involve planners flying in the face of available information because it conflicts with their priorities. For the final two categories there is the possibility that information properly collected, shared and discussed, could rectify the damage threatened by inappropriate projects. Approaches contained within such terms as Farmer First and Participatory Rural Appraisal offer just that sharing and openness to the ideas of the community. They are in effect a recognition of the economy of affection and its distinctive priorities and linkages. Pretty refers to these approaches in this way:

> Systems of learning and enquiry are needed to seek the multiple perspectives of the various stakeholders, encourage involvement and action, and resolve conflicts for the common good.[39]

Unfortunately, the one bond that has linked together the colonial civil servant and the modern-day development planner has been their lack of a proper appreciation of the strength of the information system and knowledge base which is an inseparable part of African culture. Colonial administrators, traders, missionaries and settlers more often than not dismissed oral society and indigenous knowledge as primitive and contemptible. Subsequently, governments of independent states and their advisers have still tended to view the citizens of African countries, particularly the majority who live in the rural areas, as the ignorant, passive and stubbornly uncooperative potential recipients of 'modern' information that has somehow been legitimized by the printed word.

Information systems based on the participatory principle offer the possibility of more sensitive and therefore more effective planning. They also promise better general access to information for people at present served well, but narrowly, by their natural mode of communication. We shall return to these ideas in the final chapters of this book, but first it is necessary to discuss the existing formal information systems which have been provided to meet the information needs of the citizen. We will treat the most widespread and effective responses first, which means that our introduction of the topic of libraries ends this chapter. Before that we will discuss agricultural extension services and other welfare-related information and assistance services.

Formal Responses

Agricultural Extension

Extension systems, particularly those for agricultural extension, deserve to be discussed first in the list of responses to information needs both because they have been widely available for the longest time and because they represent the biggest investment in information service in many developing countries.[40] Indeed, in some African countries extension workers are the second most numerous group of public employees, exceeded in number only by school teachers. Extension services have their origins in mid-nineteenth-century Britain and were introduced as part of the colonial administration in a number of African countries at the beginning of the twentieth century. Their original purpose in Britain had been to introduce farming innovations to small farmers whose livelihood was in crisis, and this still remains one of their central aims in Europe and North America. The introduction of such systems into the African colonies of European countries, was to expedite the introduction of farming systems producing cash crops for export to Europe. They are found today in both anglophone countries, for example, Zimbabwe's Agritex, and in francophone countries, for example, the Senegalese PNVA (Programme National de Vulgarisation Agricole).

Extension services were generally seen by those who introduced them as a means for the transfer of technology. They were to be a channel by which the results of agricultural research could be disseminated to practising farmers. This idea that the extension services should be a direct link between research and the farmer is still part of the ideology of the services. The systems were, and still are, largely geared to a top–down information flow. The research centres deliver results from the scientist to the extension service. There the results are packaged for the extension agents to deliver to the farmers.

The whole process was posited on the belief that practices based on research results would be superior to existing farmer practices, because they had produced better performances in research station tests. This in turn looked back to a positivist scientific viewpoint which saw the world as something that could be broken down into a series of specific situations susceptible to scientific investigation, from which accurate and universally applicable laws could be derived. These laws could be used for discovery of generally-applicable agricultural innovations. The discoveries made at the research station could then be disseminated among farmers by a series of stages, first to a small group of forward-looking individuals, and then gradually to the wider community which would observe the benefits obtained by the original adopters of the technology.

The so-called Green Revolution of the 1960s which introduced new varieties of high yielding food grains to the commercial sector of agriculture in many developing countries, and consequently succeeded in raising the national output greatly, was the classical example of this process. It was spread through the agency of extension services.

This type of transfer did not, however, occur effectively in more than a certain number of rather specialized cases. These tended to be where a fairly homogeneous group of farmers was targeted with a particular form of cultivation which was conclusively shown to meet their existing requirements. Generally, the type of extension service conceived within the transfer of technology model achieved only fragments of success when it came to deal with changing the practices of smaller farmers. In attempting such changes, extension services were part of a wider development programme for the rural areas, which took a series of different forms over the years, as attitudes changed in the development agencies and national governments. As early as the 1950s the colonial administration in many parts of anglophone Africa had attempted to mobilize local communities through an approach known as 'Community Development'. The main emphasis of this type of programme centred around encouraging rural communities to work together to construct facilities such as bridges, schools and clinics. The approach was not successful for a variety of different reasons, the principal one being that the local organizers did not know how to integrate community development projects into the social, cultural, economic and agricultural structure of the local community.

Although some countries still continued to follow such an approach, the favoured system in the 1970s was known as 'Integrated Rural Development'. This involved a concentration of efforts on some major project or projects, usually administered by a variety of semi-autonomous agencies. Examples were the Action Priority Zones Programme in Cameroon, the Lilongwe Land Development Programme in Malawi and the Special Rural Development Programme in Kenya. The majority of these programmes have subsequently been criticized for the inappropriate matching of proposed technical changes to small farm conditions. According to the detailed studies of Uma Lele, what was lacking was a sufficient knowledge of, and sensitivity to, local institutional patterns.[41] What was required to make many of these projects successful was a systematic acquisition and use of local knowledge. This seldom formed part of Integrated Rural Development programmes, and the spectacle of development experts wringing their hands over failed projects, and bemoaning the fact that Africa was somehow different, was a common occurrence.

The 1980s saw a greater recognition that much of the difficulty in project implementation does not necessarily rest with Africa's farmers. Rather, it arose from development planners who attempted to impose projects on local communities without any serious attempt at gaining an understanding as to how those communities worked and functioned. As a result, the emphasis in agricultural development shifted to 'Farming Systems Research' which was developed from the premises that:

a. previous work failed to take the information needs of small farmers into account;
b. there was a gap between the education, values and interests of researchers and extension workers on the one hand, and farmers on the other;
c. studies had often considered too small a sample;
d. the impact of social and political institutions on household decision making has been neglected;
e. research findings were seldom disseminated in a form usable by the farmers.

Farming Systems Research attempted to reverse these failures by developing

> research programmes which are holistic, inter-disciplinary and cost effective in generating technology which is appropriate to the production and consumption of rural households in specific micro-environments.[42]

During the 1980s more than half the countries of Africa initiated research programmes of this type. They have been able to draw on work from other disciplines such as cultural anthropology, whose practitioners, unlike economists and development planners, have always been more concerned with societies as they were and as they are, rather than as they should be.[43] The shift towards rural development planning which involved the social science researcher naturally led to a need to improve the collection and processing of information about communities. As the other side of the coin, it also strengthened the conviction that it was necessary to improve the quality of service required to disseminate agricultural information to those same communities.

The social scientist was, in effect, introduced into the model as a broker between scientist and farmer. This was a substantial step towards the humanization of the transfer of technology model, within which there was a strong tendency to blame the farmer if scientifically developed technology were not taken up. However, it still maintained the distinction between the scientist as the developer of technology, and the farmer as recipient. It still used a one-way top–down channel. In the 1990s the approach which has become intellectually dominant, if not yet the main way in which agricultural research and extension are oriented, goes by a number of different names in which 'participation' is probably the key term. The terms Participatory Rural Appraisal and Farmer First were introduced in the last section. To these terms could be added many others, such as Farmer Back to Farmer, Farmer First and Last, and Farmer Participatory Research.[44] What they tend to mean in practice is best illustrated by an example.

Farmers in the Machakos District of Kenya, working with an ICRAF project, identified a series of agroforestry problems related to poor soil fertility, inadequate soil moisture, dry season fodder shortage and lack of wood for fuel and construction.[45] Ten farmers tried variations on alley cropping of a tree suitable for mulch and fuelwood and the planting of scattered fodder trees in their grazing lands. The researchers then took part in follow-up activities directed at soil conservation, based on the farmers' reactions to the experimentation. These activities were in turn monitored and community members not previously involved in the experimentation began to request seedlings to try their own versions of the practices that were being tried. These were not simply the taking up of a 'package', but creative exploration of alternatives. One woman, for instance, took material cut away from the *bomas* (hedges) of her cattle pens and allowed it to be trampled by the cattle, soaked with urine and baked into the soil and manure floor of the pens. This very swiftly composted the cuttings. Details of this practice were then fed into group discussions and combined and compared with other experiments and established practices. The whole series of activities, of which this was a part, combined farmers' inventiveness with the knowledge and access to resources of the researchers in a rich and evolving agroforestry development process.

It is still a problem, however, that the introduction of this approach into a wider dissemination activity depends on extension services which, at present, have a very hierarchical structure. At the apex is an administration with at least partial graduate-level recruitment. These technical officers and supervisors plan and administer the service and prepare the information packages which are to be fed into the system. The typical extension service will have access to printing and other technical facilities for this purpose. Writers at the Agricultural Communication Branch of the Ministry of Agriculture and Livestock Development in Malawi, for instance, provide information input for a variety of print and other media.[46] They create material, based on research results received, to take the form of circulars, newsletters, magazines, booklets, radio broadcasts, cine films and puppet shows. The Branch has separate design and writing/editorial sections, the latter employing the staff of writers, all of whom have agricultural expertise. Their task is to rewrite and edit the material they receive into forms which they consider will be the most suitable for the target community, including translating from English into Chichewa.

There is then an intermediate group, with posts designated by titles such as agricultural superintendents and project officers. They work at the centres from which the field activities are directed. To continue with the Malawian example, these are the local offices of the eight Extension Planning Areas into which the country is divided. From these offices the day-to-day work of extension is supervised, and it is here that the Training and Visit system is put into practice.[47] The Training and Visit system has been widely used in extension services since the late 1970s as a means of effective management. It introduces clear objectives, a reporting system and regular schedules into services which had often previously operated in a less business-like fashion. In a typical Training and Visit system the field agents work a two-week cycle including one training day at the district administrative centre. On this occasion the administrators, plus any visiting specialists, train the field agents in the subjects that form the content of the extension messages they are expected to take out on their visits to their farmer clients during the remaining days of the cycle. Training and Visit is thus a means of providing a regular and controllable flow of messages out via the extension system.

The third level of employment is that of the extension agents themselves, designated by titles such as field assistant, or, if they have some specialist role, as farm home assistant or veterinary assistant. It is usual for them to have a two-year agricultural diploma to qualify for this work, but in some countries there is an even more lowly cadre of field overseers or paraprofessionals. Each agent will serve a large number of farm families scattered over what may be an extensive tract of country. Ratios of one agent to about 1000 farm families are normal, and in some places an agent may be responsible for several thousand families. This could be a thankless task in the years before Training and Visit was well established, as Wiggins points out:

> In sub-Saharan Africa extension agents are all too often sad figures, abandoned in the bush with little or no support, infrequently supervised, with no messages worth passing on to farmers, and with few incentives to get on with the work. Farmers do not appreciate the agents' work, and only make use of them when they can gain access to some input – especially if subsidised – such as seed, fertiliser, chemicals, tractor hire, or farm credit. Consequently agents are demoralised, with little enthusiasm for their jobs.[48]

Sadly this still captures the worst features of the extension agent's life very clearly.

Fortunately this has not wholly destroyed faith in extension among rural inhabitants. Sturges and Chimseu in Malawi found that farmers generally endorsed the extension system as a means of obtaining information in principle.[49] There were plenty of criticisms of it in practice and the system was often referred to quite explicitly as being in crisis. The extension agents were widely said to be no longer visiting every part of their areas on a regular basis. One or two, indeed, were said to be more concerned with their own farming activities and with manipulating credit opportunities to their own advantage. Women often felt particularly neglected, with the farm home assistants, who are supposed to advise on domestic skills, hardly reaching the more isolated communities. For health information, women felt compelled to walk long distances to the clinics. Yet despite all this, the villagers did look to extension as a system in which they believed, and which they hoped to see restored.

To back this impression that there is a core of faith in extension, in a number of surveys farmers cite the services as their chief means of obtaining information, once their personal and immediate community resources have proved insufficient. Namponya, for instance, found from his own interviews with over 200 farmers in Malawi that 59 per cent saw extension workers as their main formal source of information, and that other studies in Nigeria and Kenya asking a similar question produced very similar percentages.[50] The

Malawian Ministry of Agriculture's MARE Project even obtained a response that 72.5 per cent of farmers would consult extension workers for agricultural advice, and only 13 per cent neighbours and family, but the scale of this response is probably not surprising in a survey conducted under official auspices.[51]

From the other direction, Sturges and Chimseu asked extensionists to discuss their work in terms of problems and possible solutions.[52] The agents brought up a wide range of topics, often concerning the ability or willingness of the farming community to absorb their messages. Among a variety of reasons suggested for this, was many farmers' financial indebtedness and consequent shunning of contact with officials. Lack of materials (fertilizers, weedkillers, etc.) for practical demonstration purposes was a serious hindrance. Simple transport was a major difficulty for extension agents serving very widespread areas on foot, or on a bicycle, along unreliable dirt roads. Lack of coordination between agencies involved in rural development was cited as a difficulty. The sheer number of clients (800 or more farming families each is normal in Malawi) naturally bulked large in this identification of problems.

Agents also mentioned slow official response to requests for specific information (such as a particular agent's need for facts on bee-keeping), or poor response to initiatives that called for information back-up (such as a veterinary assistant's encouragement of rabbitry). Interestingly, there was a frequent and clearly expressed desire for access to written materials for reference in times when information was needed. The District or EPA offices seldom had more than one or two books for this purpose, and respondents cited their need for books on practical subjects like nutrition, cookery and livestock keeping, as well as on relevant background topics like the activities of funding agencies, such Unicef, USAID or the Save the Children Fund. They relied greatly on the Ministry of Agriculture's *Guide to Agricultural Production in Malawi*, but this could only meet basic information needs.

The unsatisfactory state of agricultural extension is attributed by Wiggins not to the nature of the services themselves, but to the fact that:

> Much agricultural policy can be described as uncoordinated, adhoc, and arbitrary; in part, it is a reflection of political processes, in lesser part, the result of technical inability to formulate better policy. More-

over, policy objectives are frequently expressed with little regard for feasibility.[53]

The effect of this on extension is that:

> Because policy objectives tend to outstrip the resources available to achieve them, this leads to overload on the agents. Moreover, it also leads to them trying to do jobs for which they have neither the training nor the experience. The resultant pressure of being expected to do more than they are able both quantitatively and qualitatively demoralises the extension staff.[54]

Clearly no system can effectively deliver information when the information itself represents the confused state of its source. A participatory approach to extension offers possible ways out of this fundamental difficulty by linking extensionists to farmers in a loop that, in turn, connects to the official sources of information that ought, ideally, to enrich local knowledge. This would effectively replace the unidirectional character of existing communication with a participatory information environment, in which extensionists could spend time

> helping farmers to document results, as well as to encourage the use or revitalisation/adaptation of traditional means of communication, education and training (*griots*, theatre, traditional masks, age-grade group competition, etc.).[55]

This and related themes will be dealt with in the Chapter 6.

Social Welfare Services

As we have indicated, agricultural extension may be the only official presence in isolated communities, compelling people to turn to the agents for information on a range of topics beyond their knowledge. In other cases, however, there might be quite a range of services dedicated to giving assistance, advice and information. For instance, Aboyade describes the activities of the community development workers (CDWs) who, at the time she was writing, were employed by the Nigerian Ministry of Social Development, Youth and Sports.[56] The Nigerian CDWs had a wide field of responsibility, including promoting and facilitating self-help programmes which might, in some cases, involve technical assistance and matching grants. Women's programmes were provided, often in cooperation with organized women's groups and churches, maternity centres, etc., to develop domestic skills like cookery. Local women's group leaders and volunteers were trained at residential courses to go back into their communities and further spread useful knowledge. Village integration work was also promoted by activities including leadership training courses and promotion of the concepts of model village organization. These various programme areas added up to a very wide range of involvement covering almost every aspect of rural life. Ideally the CDWs were using a number of communication techniques, varying from formal courses, to organizing local committees and volunteer groups, to informal interaction with individuals and community groups.

Such a form of service relates quite closely to the use of animation in francophone Africa. The concept of animation as a distinct form of activity deserves some mention at this point. In francophone countries there is a large cadre of people trained in the skills of animation – many more, for instance, than are trained as librarians. The skills they are taught are those of helping community groups to organize themselves for cultural or practical purposes, and providing leadership, at least in the formative stages of these activities. As such, their work involves the passing on of a good deal of information, and responding to the questions and problems of those with whom they are working. With some groups the *animateurs* can pass on information in written forms, but much of their work uses group discussion, dramatic or musical presentation, practical demonstration and other fundamentally oral means of communication. The sorts of groups they work with include youth groups, women's groups, sports clubs, trades unions, community development groups and many more, depending on the purpose for which animation has been employed. Their status is as employees of a number of different types of government ministry (Culture, Youth, Sports, Women's Affairs, etc.) and a whole range of NGOs.

This may not sound very different from what we have been describing in a number of anglophone countries, but the emphasis on the *animateur* as someone whose role is defined by attachment and involvement with community groups is crucial. The base of the *animateur* should not be seen as an office somewhere in a government-owned building, but out in the *bidonvilles* and villages, attached to some group which might not have fixed headquarters or offices. At the CDEPS provided by the Ministère de la Jeunesse et des Sports in Pikine-Goudiewe in the outskirts of Dakar, there is a project for Promotion de la Jeunesse (promotion of youth activities) where an *animateur* sets up partnerships with local youth societies. Training courses are then provided to members of partner societies, in subjects such as work with audiovisual equipment, project management or communication skills. One need that has emerged from the contacts involved in the project, is for a counselling service for young people, providing help with health, psychological and social problems. The project is being given a room for this purpose at the CDEPS with a confidential phone line, and visits from experts in particular relevant topics for clinic sessions. The activities of the Centre are being made more relevant and the capacity of local organizations to serve their members is being strengthened simultaneously by this animation activity.

The *animateurs* may be, at root, an instrument of government policy, but this is not the chief rationale for their existence. They play an important role in the two processes for which the French terms are *vulgarisation* and *sensibilisation*. The former is making specialized knowledge accessible to the public in ways they can understand. Hence the denomination of agricultural extension as a programme of *vulgarisation* in the francophone countries. The latter is making communities aware of and promoting understanding of new knowledge: it is a kind of consciousness-raising. Popularization of ideas and promoting awareness are thus central to the work of the *animateur*.

Certainly the activities of Nigerian CDWs have much of the same character, but the efforts of this kind in anglophone countries are comparatively piecemeal and lack an underlying concept such as animation. 'Social welfare' is one concept, however, which does provide a certain degree of unity for activities across a range of government and NGO agencies.[57] It tends to refer to a community-based activity rather than an involvement with individual casework. After the coming of independence in Zimbabwe in 1980, the government began with a commitment to using economic policy to promote fairer distribution of wealth and the development of social welfare facilities. Government expenditure on social programmes, health and education was increased sharply to try to meet policy requirements based on popular expectations. Even after structural adjustment programmes were adopted in 1990, social welfare priorities were retained as policy aims, so as to ameliorate the effects of economic changes. The training of Zimbabwean social workers, particularly at Harare Polytechnic, was designed to meet the personnel requirements of the original policy direction, through an emphasis on involvement with development projects, particularly in the rural areas. This ethos has pervaded the Department of Social Welfare and contributed to an emphasis on proactive programmes for young people, the elderly, women, etc. Harare-trained social welfare workers have also been recruited by NGOs for programmes such as setting up production cooperatives for unemployed young people, or AIDS awareness campaigns.

The involvement of NGOs in social welfare activities, including those with an information element, is also very important in other countries. When government, or local government, programmes are so frequently seen to be in such disarray and financial difficulties as to be more or less ineffective, the intervention of other organizations can be crucial. A fairly typical NGO might be something like the Akanani Rural Development Project in the Northern Province of South Africa. The project aims to empower rural women with skills, among which literacy features very high on the list. Women's groups are informed, for instance, about their rights to own land, whether or not they are married, and encouraged to develop solutions to community problems through group discussion. Akanani also runs income-generating projects, such as brickmaking, baking and organizing a market, so as to help women develop economic independence. The literacy groups mainly consist of women, although some men who have been inspired by the example of their wives have also joined. The facilitator of these activities is someone with roots in the community served and the whole emphasis is on a mix of activities including some which have an undoubted information content.

NGOs with a wholly information focus are not particularly common, but one type that should be mentioned is the Citizens' Advice Bureau (CAB). Based on British experience, the CAB was introduced into Cape Town, South Africa in 1961.[58] Bureaux were also opened in other South African cities soon after. The essence of the CAB is close involvement with clients, who are assisted with the kind of information they need to solve their problems and survive in a difficult and even hostile world. CABs are staffed by trained volunteers, who are assisted by lawyers, doctors and other professional people (also volunteers) called on by the bureaux when necessary. Although it might be expected that a volunteer organization originating in the white South African community would not be able to offer a whole community service, the heavy case load of the existing bureaux does include problems from all groups in society, including many domestic workers. Although the South African CAB is a rather isolated phenomenon, aspects of its structure, particularly as regards training and record-keeping, provide useful models of information service to the community.

The extent to which NGO activities can dominate social welfare activity is shown by the example of Gambia.[59] The relevant government ministries have been too cash-strapped to provide development-related services, local government has likewise lost any initiative it held in such activities, and even the village development committees set up to enable democratic input to the development process have been a mixed success. Gambia, as a tiny, accessible country has attracted what is probably more than its fair share of NGO involvement. The NGOs have, by default, taken on the totality of roles which might, in an ideal world, be performed by official welfare institutions. Communities have tended to be happy with the heavy commitment of NGOs for a number of reasons. They were seen as politically neutral, more open to the interests of women, young people and the poor, and more participatory in their planning processes. The NGO involvement has been most significant precisely in areas such as preventive health programmes, literacy programmes and institution building, where information is central, or very significant. The point is not that NGOs are marvellous, for plenty of negative stories can be told to counter such a view. What is significant is that when people have the opportunity to make the choice, they prefer organizations with participatory ways of working.

Perhaps the most substantial negative side of NGOs is that their involvement is unevenly spread, largely uncoordinated and could even be regarded as opportunistic. Those experienced in working with NGOs witness to their value:

> NGOs are not simply gap fillers in service provision *vis-a-vis* government and community efforts, but rather, as is the case in Malawi, they are a major instrument for socioeconomic improvement and change. They are also a more credible witness to official government claims about the social and development needs and problems in seeking external assistance. Without NGOs there would be little that a government could achieve in the cause of social welfare and socioeconomic development.[60]

However, attempts to coordinate the social welfare work of NGOs in Malawi illustrate precisely the problems created by their hetero-geneity in terms of aims, objectives, methods of operating and organizational culture. They can be seen, on occasion, as happier in competing with official bodies and fellow NGOs than in cooper-ating for a balanced approach to the needs of a given country. Be that as it may, they can be discovered everywhere in Africa not just alleviating people's material needs, but disseminating information and responding to gaps in the knowledge of individuals.

Health matters are probably the biggest area of life where infor-mation can play a major part in enhancing social welfare. Health education and health information are widely recognized needs in developing countries. Everywhere there is evidence of major pro-grammes to control diseases and conditions through immunization programmes, in the form of the posters and other advertisements by which the programmes are promoted and publicized. Likewise, there is similar evidence of the ubiquitous campaigns to encourage different behavioural patterns, particularly in relation to hygiene. This is particularly so in the case of AIDS, which, in the absence of a vaccine or cure, can only be attacked by information and educa-tion programmes. To take the example of Zimbabwe again, the country has a system of Health Education Officers organized on a provincial basis.[61] The actual health education activities which they supervise have been performed by a variety of people, including nurses, environmental health technicians, village health workers and school teachers. In a way that is unfortunately typical of such services, specific training for education activities has been unevenly available. Also, Zimbabwe has often been short of health educa-tional materials such as posters. Talks, the content of which has been backed by radio announcements, have tended to be the main means of information dissemination. These have achieved some success in getting essential messages across to the community. Unfortunately, the swift spread of HIV and AIDS is evidence of how frail such successes can be.

Surveys show that people know that the best place to get reliable AIDS information is from a clinic, a nurse or other community health worker, a school teacher or priest. People also distrust the information picked up on buses, in bars or discos, from friends and acquaintances, or even from traditional healers. Many have some grasp of the essential means of HIV transmission. However, behav-ioural change is much harder to effect. Young Zimbabwean women in a survey by Munodawafa felt that male sexual attitudes were a major barrier to change.[62] These attitudes are characterized in the survey as the habitual, and socially accepted, promiscuity of men. In fact, the problem goes deeper, because favoured sexual practices such as *mushonga wekupfeka* (or dry sex), which are common both within and outside the marriage relationship, raise the likelihood of transmission by increasing the incidence of genital lesions. Good information by itself is just a beginning in attacking the entrenched behavioural patterns that help disease spread.

The Zimbabwean health education situation has continued to serve as a particularly useful exemplar of the complexity of the African welfare information scene.[63] In 1989, the 6–7000 village health workers employed by the Ministry of Health were transferred to the then Ministry of Community, Cooperative Development and Women's Affairs, along with about 1000 community workers responsible to different ministries, and redesignated as Village Community Workers (VCWs). At one level this recognized the genuine case for a wide-reaching community service function, but at another it diluted the carefully nurtured health education capacity of the country. The role of the new VCWs was to work with elected Village Development Committees, to perform the tasks originally performed, and often duplicated, by community development workers, local government promotion officers, home economics demonstrators, the village health workers, and others such as school teachers.

The VCW concept was of a local community member, who was expected to put in about 100 hours per month getting involved in the whole range of community development and welfare activities, in exchange for a nominal salary. This move towards an all-purpose cadre of community workers is important because of the sense it expresses of the way in which community needs and problems interlock, and cannot simply be separated into packages called health, work, development, etc. The progress of the South African Reconstruction and Development Programme (RDP) suggests that the lesson has not filtered that far, because the programme documents propose a welter of information and advice services provided for health, arts and culture, telecommunications, and the police, not to mention agencies such as the national research facility, the Centre for Scientific and Industrial Research (CSIR), which is exploring the idea of information kiosks. Somewhere between the unifying approach and the tendency to provide many specialist services there are lessons to be learned for information services.

Libraries

Libraries will be a focus of much of the discussion in the following chapters of this book, but it is appropriate to introduce them at this stage. As suggested earlier, they are not the most widespread form of response to information need, nor are they the earliest response to be fully established as a service in Africa. Agricultural extension services were thoroughly well established much earlier. However, it is true that there were libraries on the African continent from early times. It is fairly common to see the great library at Alexandria in the centuries before Christ quoted as Africa's claim to have a library history more significant and more ancient than most of Europe. This is somewhat disingenuous. True, the Alexandrian Library was on the African continent, but it was a product of the hellenized Mediterranean culture, and held works of scholarship in Greek and other non-African languages. In one major sense, however, it was similar to Africa's other early libraries, in that it was on the fringes of the continent and was established by outsiders. Indeed, the history of written records in Africa is that they were the product of Muslim and European traders, slavers, military invaders and missionaries. Indigenous African scripts have existed in some numbers but they have never had the currency across wide regions that has been achieved by the Roman and Arabic scripts.[64] Indeed, African languages were generally given orthographies by outsiders so that the Bible and other religious books could be made available to converts.

The first libraries in sub-Saharan Africa were in the Sahara itself, where cities like Timbuktu and Djenne had mosque libraries in the sixteenth century.[65] Trading communities on the east coast, such as Mombasa, Zanzibar and Kilwa, also had similar libraries centuries ago. In South Africa, Europeans set up a small public library in 1761, and subsequently the gradual appearance of similar libraries can be traced, following the spread of colonial occupation. They were usually to be found where the most numerous groups of European settlers congregated, in countries such as South Africa, Kenya, Senegal and Zimbabwe, and they were almost invariably for the exclusive use of Europeans. Even though in independent African countries libraries are explicitly for the use of all, the exclusiveness of libraries has persisted. Language has been a major agency of this. The colonialists brought their languages with them to Africa, and the widespread use of these languages by the post-colonial elite has continued to symbolize the separation of the written culture, and its libraries, from the oral, indigenous African culture. European languages have also symbolized the division of library traditions.

By the 1960s, when the colonial period ended for most of Africa, the three European languages which were dominant in the continent were English, French and Portuguese. In the three countries from which these languages, and their associated cultures, emanated, libraries differed in their importance, and in the ways that they had developed. A brief word about the Portuguese influence in Angola, Cape Verde, Guinea-Bissau and Mozambique, will serve as an illustration. Metropolitan Portugal itself is still not an especially well-developed country in the library field, and its pre-independence influence on its colonies reflected this. There were a few old-established libraries, such as Angola's Biblioteca Municipal de Luanda, founded in 1856, and some research libraries dating from the early twentieth century spread throughout the Portuguese colonies. None of these was sufficiently strong to emerge in good shape from the wars of independence and subsequent civil wars which have devastated most of these countries. This can be illustrated by the example of one major city. In Luanda the National Library of Angola barely functions; there are two or three libraries with collections of only a few thousand each which offer public access; and only some special libraries in government institutions show signs of vitality.[66] The combination of a weak library tradition and the disastrous effects of recent history have left little that requires special comment about the situation in Portuguese-speaking Africa.

The French library tradition was also not an especially positive one. France had had richly-stocked libraries since the Middle Ages, but these tended to be the preserve of the scholar and bibliophile, rather than the ordinary information user. The idea of the library as more of a symbol of civilization than an instrument for its progress continued to characterize French library provision until the middle of the twentieth century, and this attitude communicated itself to the former French colonies. Indeed the Democratic Republic of the Congo (Zaire), as a former Belgian colony, experienced some of the more positive library initiatives in francophone Africa. That was, of course, until the disintegration of formal institutions, consequent on the anarchy of the Mobutu regime, choked off most of the opportunities for progress. Mary Maack has shown in some detail just how the French influence worked itself out in Senegal.[67] The general consequence was that at the time of their independence most francophone countries had hardly any libraries, virtually no qualified personnel, and extremely slight public access to reserves of published information. Ironically, in terms of archive services they were much better provided for, having the first national services in Africa: those of Senegal and Niger dating from 1913, and that of Benin from 1914. The interesting thing about the frailty of library provision is that it may have left these countries with more scope to invent their own responses to information needs than has been the case in the former British colonies.

archives

Britain passed on an intellectual inheritance to its former colonies which included the idea that the library, particularly the public library, was an essential feature of the complete nation state. What is more, it effectively prescribed the form such libraries should take by the introduction of models in various of its colonial possessions. The nature of this process, full of misapprehensions and hypocrisies, is tellingly anatomized by Olden.[68]Although in many cases the libraries were initially run on a racially exclusive basis, by the mid twentieth century an African elite was being admitted and the library was being promoted as a means by which literacy could be spread. This approach was, in effect, codified by the Unesco Seminar on Public Libraries at Ibadan in 1953, which recommended that the Unesco Public Library Manifesto be adopted as the basis for library service in Africa.[69]

UK model

Embodied in that Manifesto was something which is often described as the Anglo-American library tradition. Since 1953 the effects of this tradition can be observed throughout Africa, though more obviously in the anglophone countries. At the centre of its influence are national library services that are supposedly the leaders in service provision. However, they have often developed only part of the apparatus of national legal deposit collection, national bibliography, cooperative and interloan services, that outsiders might expect of a national library. What most of them do, is to act as a national public library service, with a central headquarters coordinating regional branches and other forms of service, such as postal loans and mobile libraries. Their success has been, to put it kindly, mixed. What they try to do, and why it works imperfectly, provides much of the substance of the next chapter. But there is also much to say about other types of library because, of course, not all Africa's library activity has been aimed at service to the general public.

There is a special library sector which is comparatively strong, *Special libs*
and generally longer established than other types of library. Some
of the first were geological libraries, such as that established at *libs*
Khartoum, in the Sudan, in 1904, and agricultural libraries, such as
the Forestry Department Library and Herbarium at Entebbe,
Uganda, established in the same year. In 1910, administrative
libraries were required by law in the Belgian Congo, and the
progress of such libraries generally dates from these years. Many
current special libraries are part of government ministries, NGOs
and parastatals, which often gives them good access to the decision
makers, and a chance of competing effectively for funding. They
also, fairly commonly, have useful links with overseas institutions,
which enhances their prestige and gives them chances to acquire
materials as gifts or exchanges. Because the clientele they serve
tends to include influential people, and because they can be seen as
contributing to the economic development of the country, many
current generalizations about the desperate problems of libraries
only partially apply to them.

Most academic libraries date back to the period after the Second *Academic*
World War, when African education began an enormous expan- *libs*
sion. With few exceptions, the very high investment which each
African country has poured into education has included one or
more universities. Many of these have magnificently imposing
library buildings as a central focus of their campus. Writers from
these institutions continually assure us that 'the library is the heart
of the university', but the reality behind the doors of the buildings
tends to be much less impressive. The costs of keeping up a high
quality library collection to support teaching and research in a
university are so astronomical that they have defeated the funders
in most African countries. The footnotes of articles written by
scholars from African universities show that researchers improvise
with what materials they have to hand. The content of what is taught
generally harks back to what the teachers have learned during their
own degree studies, and students rely on notes dictated by the
teachers. College and school libraries usually suffer even greater
deprivation, many existing in name only.

The inescapable conclusion drawn by the observer is that libraries as a response to information needs in Africa have proved a real
disappointment, even in the anglophone countries which accorded
them the most respect. The nature of their failure, and the reasons
for it, have to be addressed by anyone with a serious interest in the

future of libraries. The next chapter will show that forming a detailed assessment is not a comfortable experience.

References

1. Rosenberg, D. Rural community resources centres: a sustainable option for Africa? *Information Development*, 9, 1993. 29–35. p.32.
2. Bugnicourt, J. Views on education and health as expressed by herdsmen of the Voltaic Sahel. *African Environment*, 14–16. 1981. 449–56. p.455.
3. Sturges, P. and Chimseu, G. The chain of information provision in the villages of Malawi: a rapid rural appraisal. *International Information and Library Review*, 28, 1996. 135–56.
4. Francis, P. and Rawlins-Branan, M.J. The extension system and small-scale farmers: a case study from Northern Zambia. *Agricultural Administration and Extension*, 26, 1987. 185–96.
5. Mchombu, K.J. Information needs for rural development: the case study of Malawi. *African Journal of Librarianship, Archives and Information Science*, 2, 1992. 17–32.
6. Kaniki, A.M. Information seeking and information providers among Zambian farmers. *Libri*, 41. 1991. 147–64.
7. Mchombu, K.J. *Information Needs and Seeking Patterns for Rural People's Development in Africa.* Gaborone, University of Botswana, 1993.
8. Aboyade, B.O. Communications potentials of the library for non-literates: an experiment in providing information services in a rural setting. *Libri*, 34, 1984. 243–62.
9. Kaniki, A.M. Exploratory study of information needs in the Kwa-Ngwanase (Natal) and Qumbu (Transkei) communities of South Africa. *South African Journal of Library and Information Science*, 63, 1995. 9–18.
10. Kabadiki, K. Rural African women and development. *Social Development Issues*, 16, 1994. 23–35.
11. Chipande, G.H.R. Innovation adoption among female-headed households: the case of Malawi. *Development and Change*, 18, 1987. 315–27.
12. Mungunda, S. and Mumbuna, M.M. *Livestock Knowledge in Western Province: Part 2, Local Knowledge of Cattle Keepers.* Mongu, Zambia, Dept. of Veterinary and Tsetse Control Services, 1992.
13. McClymont, D.S. *An Investigation into the Communication of Innovation among Commercial Farmers in Zimbabwe.* Unpublished report, no bibliographic details, 1982. Copy in library of Overseas Development Institute, Regent's College, London.
14. Kaniki, A.M. Information seeking and information providers among Zambian farmers. *Libri*, 41, 1991. 147–64.
15. Doob, L.W. *Communication in Africa.* New Haven, CT, Yale University Press, 1961.
16. Barker, W.H. and Sinclair, C. *West African Folk Tales.* London, Harrap, 1917. pp.15–16.

17. Hart, K. *The Political Economy of West African Agriculture*. London, Cambridge University Press, 1982. p.78.
18. Millar, D. Farmer experimentation and the cosmovision paradigm. In: de Boef, W. et al. (eds) *Cultivating Knowledge: Genetic Diversity, Farmer Experimentation and Crop Research*. London, Intermediate Technology, 1993. 44–50.
19. Richards, P. Community environmental knowledge in African rural development. In: Brokensha, D., Warren, D.M. and Werner, O. (eds) *Indigenous Knowledge Systems and Development*. Lanham, MD, University Press of America, 1980. 181–94.
20. Ibid. pp.186–7.
21. Amanor, K.S. Farmer experimentation and changing fallow ecology in the Krobo district of Ghana. In: de Boef, W. op. cit. 35–43.
22. Sikana, P. Indigenous soil characterization in Northern Zambia. In: Scoones, I. and Thompson, J. (eds) *Beyond Farmer First: Rural People's Knowledge, Agricultural Research and Extension Practice*. London, Intermediate Technology, 1994. 80–2.
23. Longley, C. and Richards, P. Selection strategies of rice farmers in Sierra Leone. In: de Boef, W. op. cit. 51– 7.
24. Chavunduka, G.L. *Traditional Medicine in Modern Zimbabwe*. Harare, University of Zimbabwe, 1994.
25. Brieger, W.R. and Kendall, C. Learning from local knowledge to improve disease surveillance: perceptions of the guinea worm illness experience. *Health Education Research*, 7, 1992. 471–85.
26. Courtright, P. Eye care knowledge and practices among Malawian traditional healers and the development of collaborative blindness prevention programmes. *Social Science and Medicine*, 41, 1995. 1569–75.
27. Anderson, H. The participation of women in rural development: the case of Singida region. Unpublished monograph, 1985.
28. Greaves, T. *Intellectual Property Rights for Indigenous Peoples*. Oklahoma City, Society for Applied Anthropology, 1994.
29. Hayward, F.M. A reassessment of the conventional wisdom about the informed public: national political information in Ghana. *American Political Science Review*, 70, 1976. 433–51.
30. Forrest, T. The advance of African capital. Workshop paper for Alternative Development Strategies in Africa, Queen Elizabeth House, Oxford University, 1989.
31. Vaughan, O. Assessing grassroots politics and community development in Nigeria. *African Affairs*, 94, 1995. 501–18.
32. Brieger, W.R. and Kendall, C. The Yoruba farm market as a communication channel in guinea worm disease surveillance. *Social Science and Medicine*, 42, 1996. 233–43.
33. Mchombu, K.J. Information needs for rural development: the case study of Malawi. *African Journal of Librarianship, Archives and Information Science*, 2, 1992. 17–32.
34. Sturges, P. and Chimseu, G. op. cit.
35. Vaughan, O. op. cit.
36. Hyden, G. The invisible economy of smallholder agriculture in Africa.

In: Moock, J.L. (ed.) *Understanding Africa's Rural Households and Farming Systems.* Boulder, CO, Westview Press, 1986. 11–35.

37. Reported in *The Star* (South Africa), 14 September 1996.
38. Chambers, R. All power deceives. *IDS Bulletin*, 25, 1994. 14–26.
39. Pretty, J. Alternative systems of inquiry for a sustainable agriculture. *IDS Bulletin*, 25, 1994. 37–48.
40. Rolls, M.J., Jones, G.E. and Garforth, C. The dimensions of rural extension. In: Jones, G.E. (ed.) *Investing in Rural Extension: Strategies and Goals.* Amsterdam, Elsevier, 1986. 5–18.
41. Lele, U. *Design of Rural Development: Lessons from Africa.* Baltimore, MD, Johns Hopkins University Press, 1975.
42. Eicher, C.K. and Baker, D.C. *Research on Agricultural Development in Sub-Saharan Africa: A Critical Survey.* MSU International Development Paper 1. East Lansing, Dept. of Agricultural Economics, Michigan State University, 1982.
43. Seddon, D. (ed.) *Relations of Production: Marxist Approaches to Economic Anthropology.* London, Cass, 1978.
44. Scoones, I. and Thompson, J. Introduction. In: Scoones, I. and Thompson, J. (eds) op. cit. 1–12.
45. Rocheleau, D. et al. Local knowledge for agroforestry and native plants. In: Chambers, R., Pacey, A. and Thrupp, L.A. (eds) *Farmer First: Farmer Innovation and Agricultural Research.* London, Intermediate Technology, 1989. 14–24.
46. Sturges, P. and Chimseu, G. Information repackaging in Malawi. *African Journal of Library Archives and Information Science,* 6, 1996. 85–93.
47. Mpachika, E.D. *et al.* Contact farmers voice opinions: T & V system of extension in Malawi. *Journal of Extension Systems,* 6, 1990. 67–73.
48. Wiggins, S. Agricultural policy and agricultural extension: the African experience. In: Jones, G.E. (ed.) op. cit. 99–105. p.99.
49. Sturges, P. and Chimseu, G. The chain of information provision in the villages of Malawi: a rapid rural appraisal. *International Information and Library Review,* 28, 1996. 135–56.
50. Namponya, C.R. Agricultural development and library services. *International Library Review,* 18, 1986. 267–74.
51. Malawi Ministry of Agriculture, Evaluation and Action Research Unit. *Blantyre ADD Communication Project: Baseline Survey.* Lilongwe, Ministry of Agriculture, 1992. p.19.
52. Sturges, P. and Chimseu, G. op. cit.
53. Wiggins, S. op. cit. p.101.
54. Wiggins, S. op. cit. p.103.
55. Kohnert, D. and Weber, P.G. The new mission of agricultural research and extension in African agriculture. *Sociologia Ruralis,* 31, 1991. 162–8.
56. Aboyade, B.O. Access to information in rural Nigeria. *International Library Review,* 17, 1985. 165–81.
57. Mupedziwa, R. The challenge of economic development in an African developing country: social work in Zimbabwe. *International Social Work,* 39, 1996. 41–54.

58. Louw, A. Survival information services in South African public libraries. *African Journal of Libraries, Archives and Information Science*, 4, 1994. 91–8.

59. Davis, D., Hulme. D. and Woodhouse, P. Decentralisation by default: local governance and the view from the village in The Gambia. *Public Administration and Development*, 14, 1994. 253–69.

60. Simukonda, H.P.M. Creating a national NGO Council for strengthening social welfare services in Africa: some organisational and technical problems experienced in Malawi. *Public Administration and Development*, 12, 1992. 417–31.

61. Dehne, K.L. and Hubley, J. Health education services in developing countries: the case of Zimbabwe. *Health Education Research*, 8, 1993. 525–36.

62. Munodawafa, D., Gwede, C. and Mubayira, C. Using focus groups to develop HIV education among adolescent females in Zimbabwe. *Health Promotion International*, 10, 1995. 85–92.

63. Higgins, K.M. and Mazula, A. Community development: a national strategy in Zimbabwe. *Community Development Journal*, 28, 1993. 19–30.

64. Kotei, S.I.A. Some cultural and social factors of book reading and publishing in Africa. In: Oluwasanmi, E. *et al.* (eds) *Publishing in Africa in the Seventies*. Ife, Nigeria, University of Ife Press, 1975. 174–208.

65. Wilks, I. The transmission of Islamic learning in the Western Sudan. In: Goody, J. (ed.) *Literacy in Traditional Society*. London, Cambridge University Press, 1968. 161–97.

66. Tali, M. Libraries in Luanda, Angola, problems and prospects. *Cadernos BAD*, 2, 1993. 29–53.

67. Maack, M.N. *Libraries in Senegal: Continuity and Change in an Emerging Nation*. Chicago, American Library Association, 1981.

68. Olden, A. *Libraries in Africa: Pioneers, Policies, Problems*. Lanham, MD, Scarecrow Press, 1995.

69. *Development of Public Libraries in Africa: The Ibadan Seminar*. Paris, Unesco, 1954.

Chapter Three

An Alien Implant

Dependence

The fortunes of Africa during the period since independence have generally been an enormous disappointment. While it is no longer fashionable to blame every current misfortune on the colonial past, it is nevertheless true that the entire continent is still firmly tied to that past in ways that do not usually benefit its people. Dependency is the most consistent characteristic of political, economic, social and cultural relationships since independence. Libraries, as was partially suggested in the previous chapter, provide an example of the persistence of the colonial heritage and illustrate how stultifying can be the effects of the dependent relationship between Africa and the Northern industrialized countries.

As we have suggested, libraries and other formal information systems hardly featured in the life of sub-Saharan Africa in the distant past, but events just before the main era of independence for African countries did something to alter that. A period of serious change in the character of information provision was initiated by a small but significant number of new arrivals on the continent. These arrivals were expatriate librarians who were personally to do much to set the course of library development in Africa during the crucial first years of independence. Evidence of their activities can be traced most densely in the anglophone parts of East, West and Southern Africa in the form of the actual library services that are still largely in place today.

To the expatriate librarians' credit, many of them expressed a clear perception of the problems of establishing libraries in developing countries. They clearly had the intention of developing systems and services that would be properly integrated with the social and political circumstances of their host communities.[1] Many of them were not only aware of the need to tailor library systems to the characteristics and aspirations of a newly-independent Africa, but also recognized both the cultural diversity of the continent and the need to develop services that would accommodate the shifting patterns of a transitional era.[2] Their intentions were undoubtedly of the very best. Yet it is not unusual for good intentions to go amiss, and this is what happened in these formative years of modern library services in Africa.

The legacy the pioneers left failed to meet the objectives they had set. What actually emerged from the early days were systems which reflected practice in the metropolitan countries. In most cases, the expatriate librarians probably had little choice. Having recently arrived in their adoptive countries they usually faced the exigencies of planning an entirely new system, or occasionally reviving and strengthening embryonic institutions. No blueprints existed to assist them and their employers had little time for tentative or experimental beginnings.[3] While the library mission to Africa was certainly well intentioned, it was also guided by a cautious pragmatism, rather than the results of any deep philosophical debate. This is perhaps not too surprising, for if one looks at what the British library profession was talking about in the earlier part of the twentieth century one tends to find a preference for discussing the minutiae of routine and rather less concern with examining the broader issues.

American librarianship, which was another important source of ideas and inspiration, was likewise suffering a period of disenchantment, particularly in relation to public libraries. Michael Harris has described this as follows:

> Discouraged on the one hand by their inability to increase library use significantly, and on the other by their seeming failure to elevate those who did use the library, American public libraries began slowly, almost imperceptibly, to abandon their mission as originally defined by the founders. They were less and less able to provide reasons for processes that were being performed in their libraries, and they began to define 'functions' such as 'recreational reading' or 'informational service' as ends in themselves. They had lost their way, most had completely lost sight of the founders' vision, and the few who could still see it had lost their faith in its potential for fulfilment.[4]

Since library development in African countries in the early days was mainly of new public library services, this stagnation of the Anglo-American library tradition was highly significant. Indeed, it is doubtful if the Anglo-American tradition was really in a fit condition for export to Africa.

It was exported, however, and the advent of independence witnessed a remarkable quantitative expansion of library services. Much of this early effort was concerned with the establishment of structures and the creation of patterns of bureaucracy. There does not seem to have been the time available for discussion as to what Africa's own particular information needs were, and whether new solutions could be found to meet them. Isolated cases where noticeably different solutions were tried were few, and their outcomes were not necessarily happy ones. In Uganda, for instance, the period 1964–6 saw an attempt to provide a large number of library service points around the country, as rapidly as possible. These were linked to an unusually informal central organization and there was a minimum of elaboration in the treatment of library materials. This fairly radical preference for immediately maximizing the impact of service to the community, as opposed to steady concentration on the established procedures for collection building, quickly produced problems. These problems led to the early abandonment of the approach and the replacement of the director of the service. The Ugandan library service after 1966 prided itself on having a headquarters with full processing facilities, a proper catalogue and a formal reference service. A 'real' library system had been restored and a hectic experiment with a different approach had been abandoned.[5]

Unfortunately this slavish devotion to doing things 'properly' persists. A consultant tells the recent story of visiting a library in Zambia to check the impact of a sizeable book donation. The books had made no impact at all, because they were still neatly piled around the library workspace. All were perfectly catalogued according to the Anglo American Cataloguing Rules, and the cards, with plentiful added entries, etc. were tidily bundled up with rubber bands around them. When the librarian was asked why nothing further had been done with the books, the consultant was told that the books could not be made available for readers because there were no catalogue trays into which the cards for the books could be filed. When a sufficient number of trays had been located and assembled, the books still could not be shelved. This time it was

Bureaucracy

because materials to label the spines of the books had not been supplied. Not until materials were obtained and the spines labelled (which took a fairly short time with the consultant sitting at the workbench and helping), could the books be allowed to perform their intended function. Cases of such total disablement by convention are perhaps rare, but they illustrate just how dependence on an idea, or a system, can filter right down to the service delivery level.

AID

During this early phase of library development in Africa, international organizations, charitable foundations and national aid or cultural agencies played a significant part. The work of such organizations as Unesco, the British Council, the Ford Foundation, the Carnegie Corporation, the Ranfurly Library Service (now Book Aid International) and the International Federation of Library Associations (IFLA) has been extensively documented, and the contribution they have made to library development in Africa has received its due acknowledgement. In particular, Stephen Parker's review of Unesco's role in developing countries provides an excellent account,[6] while Beverly Brewster has charted the history of America's contribution between the years 1940 and 1970.[7] The contribution of the British Council has been chronicled by Douglas Coombs, who tells how,

> Since its birth in 1934 the British Council has been instrumental in creating a unique international library network, and has laid the foundations, at least in part, of many public library systems in the developing world.

and, more importantly, suggests that,

> The men and women who have worked as Council librarians overseas have, like missionaries, spread the word of their faith in a strong and free public library service as a powerful weapon in the struggle against ignorance, poverty and tyranny.[8]

More recently O'Connor and Roman have brought the story of British Council work up to date through the more difficult times that have followed.[9] Most of this, however, has been written from the perspective of those working for the donor agencies.

Olden has written probably the first full treatment of the same events which attempts an audit from the user perspective.[10] His findings put a much less optimistic gloss on the story. Yet if the library provision offered was so inappropriate, it seems surprising that newly-independent African states accepted the public library idea with remarkable alacrity. For instance, despite competition from other pressing concerns, several former British colonies enacted legislation very soon after independence, committing governments to providing a free public library service. This was extraordinary considering that the same principle had only been won by the British and American library movements after considerable effort had been expended. In all, it represents a remarkable effort at persuasion by a small number of expatriate librarians, and some equally committed African colleagues. This phase of library development is well represented in a substantial text by Kaungamno and Ilomo of Tanzania.[11]

The African public, however, had not been consulted when library services were put into operation. Indeed knowledge of the needs, and even the composition, of Africa's potential library clientele was virtually nonexistent at the time. Subsequently it has become clear that people's response to libraries has, all too frequently, been one of scepticism and apathy. To the majority of adult Africans, libraries have appeared to have very little to offer. Faced with this, librarians have wrung their hands in anguish and lamented the disinclination of the public at large to accept the obvious benefits that libraries offer. A constant theme of librarians' meetings is that more effort is needed to persuade the public that libraries can help them. Anyone involved with marketing could tell them that you do not just persist in pushing an unpopular product at the consumer, you find out what the consumer really wants and offer them that. This was not, however, a message that was heard very often.

In the meantime, Africa's governments have lost any initial enthusiasm they had for libraries. Librarians have therefore added the exhortation to convince the decision makers of the importance of libraries, to their ritual call to convince the public. This touching faith in the power of reason more or less unsupported by evidence has, unsurprisingly, been of little avail. The reality is that after more than three decades of independence libraries are, at best, grudgingly tolerated by governments, and are placed low on any national list of priorities. The problem is well exemplified by the National Library and Documentation Service of Zimbabwe. Although it was established by law in the mid-1980s, the statute failed to make it clear whether or not it should operate as a government agency or a parastatal. If it were to be the former, government would have an unequivocal responsibility to give it appropriate financial support. If it were the latter, it would be free to obtain funding wherever possible. Hovering between the two potential statuses it has withered away in embarrassing fashion.

In a way, this symbolizes the equivocal status of the library in Africa. But more than this, because the library is an idea that has been borrowed from a very different part of the world, its implementation has resulted in a whole series of specific ambiguities. It is important to examine these in turn to assess the full flavour of what exists on the ground. Buildings, collections, practices and personnel, all repay attention of this kind.

Buildings

The library, from the earliest times and throughout the world, has tended to be perceived as something of a monument to personal, institutional, civic or national pride. Many libraries actually bear the names of donors, cities and nations. No doubt none of those commemorated would have wished to be represented by something which was less than impressive. Indeed, it would be foolish to complain about the architectural magnificence and luxurious furnishing of the world's great libraries. It could be thought encouraging that many developing countries have cared enough about their own libraries to seek something of the same style. The problem is, however, that in some cases this amounts to overbuilding. The collections and services of a library can simply fail to match the pretensions of the building. The initial expenditure on a building, and the cost of its subsequent upkeep and maintenance, can also inhibit satisfying more pressing need elsewhere. Such need tends to be for more numerous service points, stocked with more and better information resources, staffed with more and better educated personnel, and used by greater numbers of the public.

A photographic survey, by Sitzman, of African libraries in a large number of countries suggests that overbuilding has occurred in quite a few cases, particularly with university libraries.[12] What the survey did not show was the emptiness, indeed squalor, behind the facades of library buildings. The best view that can be taken of this is that the buildings are for the future. Thus the massive Margaret Thatcher Library at Moi University in Kenya, is first and foremost a monument to a controversial public figure, not otherwise known for her love of libraries, books or dissenting opinions. It does, however, offer scope for the innovative librarianship which takes place within its towering walls. It should also be recorded that a successful university, such as the University of Botswana, can in a mere ten years exhaust the scope offered by a very large new library building and need the extension of similar size that is planned to begin in 1997.

In terms of scarce resources it is arguable that a large number of simple service points, whether they be public libraries, reading rooms, special libraries or school libraries, offer better value for a government's money than a comparatively small number of architectural gems. Plain but serviceable units, scattered throughout the country and built with the best local techniques and materials, would be a more effective symbol of the true importance of libraries than imposing buildings largely confined, of necessity, to the cities. By this criterion quite a proportion of African library building begins to seem over-ambitious in the extreme.

What is more, the architects responsible for designing African library buildings have often been provided with a brief which takes too little account of climatic and other constraints on building in the continent. These architects, whether they were foreign consultants, who might not always have been fully aware of these constraints, or local practitioners with overseas professional training, have been responsible for some attractive buildings which have not responded well to the demands placed on them. A discreet veil is generally drawn over failures in library design and few have been documented, but their existence should, nevertheless, not be doubted. Such failures are particularly sad when the principles for constructing in African conditions are not hard to establish.[13]

For example, hot weather causes much distress to readers and staff, as well as exacerbating conservation difficulties. Air-conditioning is the solution which springs most readily to the architect's mind, and in some cases buildings which are almost wholly dependent on artificial air cooling and circulation have been designed and put up. In the context of electricity supply systems which are both expensive and unreliable and maintenance services hampered by shortage of spare parts and skilled personnel, a building using air-conditioning is highly vulnerable. When there are well-established building traditions in hot countries which make the best use of natural air circulation, it would not be realistic to ignore them, even if one could rely on air-conditioning more than is possible at present.

Despite the suggestion that librarians, in preparing architects' briefs, may sometimes have paid too little attention to climatic constraints on library planning and design in Africa, it is true that at least one writer has elevated this to a central place in his philosophy. This is Wilfred Plumbe, whose early experience in the hot and humid parts of West Africa led him to identify climate as the major factor to be considered.[14] Important though climate is, the emphasis should be much more on the necessity for buildings to be appropriate to a whole range of social, budgetary and geographical conditions. A realistic view of library building is a major element in the breaking of dependence on imported versions of librarianship.

Collections

Utterly empty library shelves are not an uncommon sight in Africa, particularly in school and public libraries. Only sometimes is this due to the demands of an eager book-reading public. More often it arises from the simple fact that the library possesses very few books in the first place. A building and a librarian's salary may remain, even where a book budget has totally disappeared. When such depths have been reached, the effort required to secure the financial provision that would fill the shelves begins to seem impossibly great. It becomes easier for the librarian to carry on with a pointless daily routine, while trying to ignore the fact that no books and no readers are likely, one day, to mean no job.

Where reasonably substantial collections do exist some of them are distressingly little used. This can have much to do with the unsatisfactory nature of their content and the view of the world which it represents. The African viewpoint is too little represented, and views from Europe, North America, and sometimes Russia and other current and former socialist states, are usually much easier to obtain from the books on the shelves. The reasons for this are various. Africa's meagre contribution to the world's body of published knowledge and the poverty of bibliographical information available on the continent's documentary record are major causes, and are addressed elsewhere in this book.

The African librarian's deep respect for the published output of the major international publishing houses should also be taken into account. This has meant that such funds as are available tend to be spent on material which represents either alien or deceptively 'universal' viewpoints. The late Sam Kotei, Professor of Library Studies at the University of Botswana, liked to draw scornful attention to the irrelevance of much of the expensive material that could be found in African libraries, often citing Grove's *Dictionary of Music and Musicians* as an example.[15] This kind of acquisition is very much in the tradition of British or American libraries, which have had funds sufficient for them to try to provide access to the whole of human knowledge, sometimes without reference to immediate need. This principle has taken root in Africa and influenced acquisition policies, even though financial limitations alone make it quite unrealistic. Indeed it is doubtful if this ideal can be realized, in terms of acquisitions, by any but the most richly endowed American or European library services. To find, as one of the present writers did, a recently purchased and obviously unread copy of a book on the Severn bore (a phenomenon by which tidal pressure causes the British river Severn to flow upstream at regular intervals) on the shelves of a remote public library in a country where drought had for years prevented water flowing in any direction at all in the dry river beds, is the sort of rich irony that arises from this attitude.

The problem of inappropriateness in Africa's library collections has been exacerbated by the gifts and donations of charitable organizations and foreign governments and their agencies. The role of aid in perpetuating library dependence is a substantial one and is worth looking at in a little detail. As Maack points out in an excellent treatment of the consequences of aid for libraries, inappropriate donations can make a library grow without actually developing.[16] Library materials donated by governments are more likely to reflect the priorities of the donors than those of the recipients. American agencies have tended to give books that support the philosophy of free enterprise capitalism. This can be frustrating, or even have its slightly ludicrous side, as when the donation includes multiple copies of a popular exploration of an American ethos such as *I'm alright you're alright*. On the other hand, the approach of members of the Soviet Embassy bearing yet more duplicate copies of commentaries on the works of Marx and Lenin used to chill the heart of many an African librarian. Works from North Korea on the *Juche* philosophy of Comrade Kim Il Sung have been allowed to sit on library shelves merely because they have been donated, with the unreadable, rambling incoherence of the text quite disregarded.

Language imperialism can play a part in this process too. While it tends to be unspoken in Anglo-American terms, the French explicitly regard their library aid as a means of spreading their language, whatever the content of the books. They not only follow this policy in their former colonial possessions, but also have impressive libraries in other countries of the continent, particularly in the ex-colonies of Spain and Portugal, where French influence has reached the point where they treat some of the smaller countries almost as part of the *francophonie*. There is nothing at all inherently wrong in giving readers the opportunity to learn another language and understand another culture. It merely seems a little super- fluous when materials of more pressing importance are in short supply. The agencies of countries like Germany, or the Scandi- navian countries, tend to recognize this and give their help with materials in the prevailing language, whatever that may be.

While government donations are often too propagandist, gifts from charitable agencies have often consisted of the discarded miscellanea of libraries, publishers' remainders, or well-thumbed second-hand volumes from well-meaning philanthropists. For any librarian who has been on the receiving end of such unsolicited 'gifts' to a developing country institution, the experience recoun- ted by John Harris when he was involved with the setting up of the library at Ibadan University will no doubt bring back painful memo- ries. Soon after his arrival at Ibadan, the library received a consignment of 70 large wooden crates. These were the gift of a number of philanthropic organizations based in Britain, which had heard that Nigeria needed books. The crates contained a collection of over 7000 volumes. In anticipation, new shelving was erected to accommodate them, and hundreds of staff hours were spent unloading and sorting them. By the time the job was finished, it was found that over 90 per cent of the material was unusable. To add insult to injury, the library was then faced with the problem of how to dispose of this collection of dirty, grimy texts which were descri- bed as follows:

> There were works on sanitary engineering designed for England in the nineteenth century; there were two volumes of a five volume work on the topography of Wales in 1820; there were books of essays on long dead ecclesiastical issues of Victorian England; there were twelve copies

of Morley's *Life of Cobden*, and, possibly the least useful of the whole collection, twenty five copies of a pamphlet on *How to win the War*, addressed to the Polish people, and in the Polish language.[17]

The library wisely dumped most of these books, but such situations were common, and not all of Africa's librarians discarded useless donations. This stems from the attitude that some books are better than no books. It also relates to bureaucratic constraints within particular institutions that make it wellnigh impossible to discard material, no matter how useless. A bold condemnation of useless material in rural libraries by Obadiah Moyo generalizes easily to refer to all types of library in Africa, and is really the only line to follow. As he has put it:

> Most rural communities have become dumping grounds for any rubbish which occupies space in urban centres. It is sad to note that this rubbish also includes some reading materials which are useless to the lives of rural citizens.[18]

Examples of more recent donation initiatives include that of The Brothers Foundation, based in New York. Its activities are, first of all, of considerable assistance to the American publishing industry. They ship publishers' remainders and out-of-date texts to Africa. This is far less expensive for publishers than incurring warehouse charges and attracts tax relief. The Ranfurly Library Service was in the past a major provider of discarded and second-hand books to the less developed countries. Its Textbooks for Africa project (TAP) was intended to be much more effective than its previous efforts, and responses from libraries in Malawi and Tanzania, were positive.[19] Ranfurly was then relaunched as Book Aid International, which bases its donations on selection by the recipient institutions. Librarians from these institutions are actually taken to Book Aid's London headquarters for this purpose, to guarantee that selection is based on full knowledge of what is available.

The arguments for the continuation of well-targeted efforts are strong, when set against a reality where a majority of Africa's children are growing up in a totally bookless environment.[20] The remaining worry is that, even when donations are not detrimental to library collections, they harm the development of the continent's own indigenous knowledge base, book trade and publishing industry. It is arguable that aid to develop the book industries of a country is potentially a great deal more useful in the long term than book donations. Aid to publishing can quite quickly make a very valuable contribution to the development of libraries by providing locally-published material for them to acquire. Existing schemes of this kind provide aid in setting up publishing firms, or short courses for publishing personnel. Such aid can also apply to printing technology and supplies. Old-fashioned printing machinery is heavy, durable, repairable and still a highly effective technology. Donations of old printing machinery are a worthwhile form of aid, and in many cases more useful than the more impressive but infinitely more vulnerable electronic publishing technology. Help with the manufacture of paper and other materials such as inks is also highly appropriate.

The other book trades are also ripe for development. Until a local bookbinding cooperative was set up in Botswana, any binding had to be sent out of the country. This usually meant South Africa and in the days of apartheid it was not unheard of for customs officials to stop consignments at the border on suspicion that they contained 'subversive' materials. More recently Bulawayo Public Library has been advertising its binding services as a means of raising revenue for the Library. This is an excellent example of low tech solutions to a serious problem. In Zimbabwe, institutions had been known to send binding work to Britain, at massive expense. Seen in this context, the Bulawayo initiative is a valuable contribution to national self-sufficiency.

What is necessary then, is aid that will enable Africa's knowledge base, and thus her library collections, to develop. No amount of book donations can achieve this. Africa's library collections are in such a dire state that a great deal of effort is needed to bring them up to a level which will meet the needs of current users, let alone attract a wider clientele. In research libraries the situation is so bad that the suggestion has been heard that help towards improving bibliographical access to Africana libraries outside the continent is the best way to supply Africa with access to its own documentary heritage. Even if, in the short term, this were true, it would represent a terrible admission of defeat and effectively close the door to future improvement. Politicians may have stressed 'Africa for the African' at the time of independence, but as far as Africa's library collections are concerned it still has a rather hollow ring.

Bibliographies and Catalogues

Even where a basically sound library collection does exist, it can rarely be exploited to anywhere near its full potential without great persistence and reliance on serendipity. Bibliographically, Africa is poorly served. National bibliographies exist in a good number of countries, but they are incomplete, biased towards books (particularly books in the metropolitan languages) and too out of date to be useful as acquisition tools. Subject bibliographies, abstracts and indexes are published mainly in the developed countries and are overwhelmingly directed towards formal literature from those parts of the world. Their use in acquisition exaggerates the tendency of libraries to lack the necessary African perspective and confirms their dependence on Northern publishing. In retrieving references for the user, librarians understandably gravitate towards the well-organized and seemingly comprehensive tools from the industrialized countries, in preference to the struggle they know they are likely to have in finding out about publications from their own or other African countries. On-line access to remote databases is also prohibitively expensive.

As long ago as 1979, at an Intergovernmental Bureau for Informatics (IBI) conference held at Abidjan, a number of African states were challenging America's right to the major part of the world's database information, which was then in the effective control of the large American corporations Lockheed and Systems Development Corporation.[21] In particular, it was claimed that African countries had a right to the information held in those databases that was of African origin. Not surprisingly the argument met with little sympathy. What is more, it was really only directed at a peripheral aspect of the problem. The irony of access to a remote database is that what it contains is likely to be citations of documents, the great bulk of which are not obtainable from within African countries. They can certainly be obtained via document delivery systems based in overseas countries (the British Library's Document Supply Centre, for instance) but at considerable cost.

The best known attempt to create databases for Africa, from within Africa, is the Pan African Documentation and Information System (PADIS).[22] The PADIS programme began in 1980 and is administered by the United Nations Economic Commission for Africa (ECA), based in Addis Ababa. It has two broad aims. The first is to help African countries strengthen their own internal information systems by various means, including advice and training. The second is to set up a decentralized information network for the continent. The latter is to take input from national focal points and feed it into a computerized database which will in turn produce not only bibliographical information but also statistics and referral information on African experts, institutions and development projects. The first main product from this system was the publication of *Devindex Africa* which concerned itself strictly with development literature. Despite the fact that *Devindex Africa* set high standards of bibliographical production, and has a considerable polish in terms of its appearance, there are serious problems. The content shows a high level of reliance on published and semi-published materials from developed countries as well as information from the ECA or UN itself. This suggests that, unfortunately, the service is largely failing to meet the original objective of bringing together Africa's information about itself.

A consultancy by Wilson Aiyepeku further suggested that the organization had a disturbing suspicion of, and unwillingness to co-operate with, other international agencies working on information in Africa.[23] The unease this produces is increased when the mechanisms for feeding PADIS with information from the various sub-regions of Africa are examined. The situation has been confused, to say the least, and seems to have changed at frequent intervals. In East and Southern Africa, for example, a sub-regional grouping named ESADIS (East and Southern Africa Development Information System) was supposed to provide input from the sub-region to a coordinating centre in Zambia. Unfortunately, the centre never seems to have functioned properly. ESADIS was not even alone in the region, for there was a similar initiative known as SADIS (Southern African Development Information System) which was supposed to have its headquarters in Zimbabwe, and in addition had links with the African Bibliographic Centre (ABC) based in Washington. For a time a publication known as *SADEX* was produced which, while it lasted, proved to be fairly useful at informing those interested in development in Southern Africa of what was happening in terms of projects, publications and international cooperative efforts. This publication then vanished from the scene and not a word about SADIS has been heard since.

In 1986, at a regional meeting to discuss 'Informatics for Development' at Victoria Falls, Zimbabwe, a Zambian librarian had the temerity to ask just what PADIS was doing, how it fitted into the

regional information systems that were emerging, and, more perti-
nently, who was supporting what?[24] No satisfactory answer was
forthcoming. At a time when there was this level of confusion, the
financial input into PADIS had been enormous. Its ten-year budget
of US$160 million was high by any standards and the question of
what has been achieved for the money spent on it still remains
unanswered.[25] The reasons why there has been so little to show are
not difficult to guess, and PADIS typifies the projects, over-
ambitious to the point of grandiose, which have soaked up
development money in so many sectors. The emphasis on information technology seems to have blinded those involved to the basic
information gathering and disseminating exercise which was the
original aim. Once set on this course, it has then proved virtually
impossible to redirect efforts on to productive paths. The need for
African databases has been answered, to some extent, by humbler
projects which will be discussed later in this book.

Meanwhile, it has been bibliographies from other parts of the
world which have influenced Africa, notably in terms of its cataloguing. McCarthy argues that Africa's worship of the canon of
Anglo-American cataloguing is yet another aspect of dependence.
He paints a picture of librarians puzzling over tortuous and complex cataloguing rules to the extent that the backlog of
unprocessed books waiting to be catalogued is more extensive than
the actual library collection available on the open shelves. He
describes the whole exercise of cataloguing according to the
dictates of AACR/ISBD (Anglo American Cataloguing Rules/
International Standard Book Description) as being a gross waste of
human time and effort. However, as he says:

> cataloguers all over the world follow them, because they purport to be
> the best Western practice, because there are no decent alternatives, and
> because adoption leads to world bibliographical unity.[26]

This is taken to its extreme when African library systems acquire
magnificent but immensely expensive tools such as the *National
Union Catalog* (NUC) from the USA as a source for authoritative
cataloguing practice. This not only contributes to over-elaborate
and costly entries, but also leads to material that can be traced in
the tool being given unjustified priority in the cataloguing process.
Locally published material is frequently extremely difficult bibliographically, lacking essential details of imprint or appearing in
languages the cataloguers cannot read. It is thus not wholly surpris-

ing if local material is neglected in favour of imported material for which there is published cataloguing authority.

Catalogues in general are uneven and unreliable. Kenyan libraries, for instance, vary from a few which do not catalogue material at all, through a majority which catalogue monographs but not pamphlets or other less substantial items, to some research libraries which are able to produce analytical entries for their users.[27] The complexity of cataloguing practice contributes to this disparity at a very basic level. For instance, students on the Kenyan Library Assistants Certificate course have been taught the Anglo American Cataloguing Rules, in all their intricate details. When Certificate holders are faced with the realities of library practice, this must seem very unreal to them. One asks why, for most purposes in Kenya or any other African country, there is a need for a catalogue entry which provides more than author, title, publisher and date? When, for instance, was the last time in most libraries that the height of a book (measured in centimetres) was helpful to a reader, or a librarian? The name under which an item is catalogued is the key to easy retrieval, yet conventional cataloguing codes show an inability to cope with African personal names. With this in mind, the Kenya Library Association produced a helpful set of guidelines on personal names, but ironically this important contribution to better cataloguing did not become universally known or used in the country.

Classification systems, whether Dewey, Library of Congress or Universal Decimal Classification, are also a source of problems in Africa. Used literally, they place African material in unhelpful or downright misleading relationships. Iwuji points out that the confusion in early editions of classification schemes has never been sorted out fully.[28] There is a lack of specificity about Africa in most schemes, and signs of gross ignorance. African religions, for instance, are treated as superstition. For historical purposes, the regions into which schemes divide the continent are a mess based on colonial divisions rather than the long-term distribution and movement of African peoples. This tendency can be blatantly racist at its worst. There was a chorus of distress from African librarians over the proposed changes in the revision of the *Dewey Decimal Classification* (DDC 20). On the advice of the South African Institute for Library and Information Services (SAILIS), white South African history remained as 'history' in the schedules, while black South African history stayed among 'social problems'. The proposed version of the schedules also gave recognition to the then Bantu-stans of the apartheid system. In hundreds of other, less glaring, ways the most widely used classification systems continue to guarantee that Africa's library collections are organized in alien and unhelpful ways.

Research at Moi University Library in Kenya suggests ways in which the problem goes even deeper.[29] Students were observed to have difficulty using Library of Congress subject headings to retrieve information. The significant thing was that the types of difficulty they encountered varied from person to person and bore a definite relationship to the different Kenyan linguistic groups from which they originated. This suggests that an African system of subject headings might be difficult to devise, but it does point to a need for some effort in this direction. The sad thing is that there is little evidence that African librarians are seeking remedies for such problems by going back to the basic principles of information retrieval. Instead they tend to look to information technology to help them leap-frog whole development stages that call for the construction of tools such as classifications and subject headings which work in the African context.

African librarians frequently apologize to visitors because they do not have automated systems, or alternatively show off the systems which they do have with a pride that has little to do with the functions the systems perform. Funding bodies are regularly approached for support to acquire the means to computerize the catalogues of tiny collections, and automate circulation systems for levels of use that could almost be held in the human memory, let alone stored on an enormous hard disk. There is a very strong case that for all but a few African libraries, automation can add little if it works, and detracts sharply from service if it does not. When there is so much important basic work to be done, it is sad that it is still possible for librarians to look to the computer as if it were capable of solving service problems by some kind of magic.

Personnel

Ultimately, it is Africa's information professionals who must solve the problems outlined above. The character of these professionals will determine what solutions will be proposed and which changes will be accepted. It is sad to report that the record of Africa's library professionals in responding to the need for change has been generally disappointing. Once again, the origins of this problem can clearly be seen in the colonial past. As suggested earlier, the main impetus for the development of public libraries in Africa can be traced to Unesco's Ibadan Seminar in 1953. The Seminar also effectively delimited the structure and character of a library profession and laid the foundations for the education and training of library personnel. The legacy of the Ibadan Seminar spread beyond the concerns of public librarianship to shape the entire library profession in anglophone Africa and influence the profession in other parts of the continent.

The Seminar advocated the creation of a leadership cadre that would be able to provide a suitably elevated professional profile. This in turn, it was felt, would result in a more ready acceptance of the continent's emerging library movement. There was, however, another approach, advocated by some participants, that placed much more stress on training workers who would perform the everyday tasks of librarianship. There has been debate on this ever since. In Nigeria during the 1970s it became particularly heated when Ahmadu Bello University launched an undergraduate degree in library studies. This raised a storm of protest from Ibadan University which until then had dictated the character of the profession's leaders through its postgraduate programmes.

The Ibadan Seminar recommendations confirmed the already-emerging stratification of Africa's library workforce into very precisely defined layers of leaders (professionals) and workers (non- or para-professionals). The status of the expatriates who established services throughout most of newly-independent Africa symbolized this division. Categorization of staff was, naturally enough, a normal feature of the library systems from which they came, but it seems to have been felt that even sharper definition of such divisions was essential to the structure of colonial societies. In colonial or immediately post-colonial Africa the categorization of library personnel took the form: 'professional = expatriate' and 'non-professional = African'. Once established, the division gradually assumed the force of a natural law. After the expatriates had gone, qualified Africans took on not only the professional tasks and responsibilities, but the very rigid definitions of the difference between professional and non-professional staff which came with them. The way in which this developed subsequently shows why it was not a happy legacy.

The legacy is unquestionably alive, and is evidenced in the position of that section of the library and information workforce that is categorized as para-professional. The injustice is that these workers are sufficiently trained to perform many professional tasks, but the system will not permit them the means to obtain professional status and salary. They reached this unfortunate position of responsibility without reward because of the shortage of fully professional personnel immediately after independence. More than three decades after independence, para-professionals are a permanent and distinct stratum of employee, generally on much the same uncomfortable terms as they were before.

The position varies slightly from country to country, but they are usually identified by a diploma in library studies, representing two or sometimes three years of study. There is also an even less fortunate category of librarian, holding a certificate in library studies obtained after anything between six and eighteen months of study. Transition from certificate to diploma is usually possible after further study, but diploma holders are, in the majority of cases, barred from advancement to the professional ranks unless they undertake even more studies in librarianship. To advance themselves, holders of the diploma often study for further qualifications in topics like management and public relations. Some have been able to study for one year at Loughborough University in the UK, where many diplomas are recognized as equivalent to the first two years of a degree. Others take degrees in librarianship at African universities, saved only from terminal boredom by the extent to which the discipline has changed since they first studied it.

To make the staffing situation even more complex, an idea which was developed in Asia a few years ago has received some attention in Africa. This is the idea of the 'barefoot librarian', which threatens to add yet another category of non-professional staff to library establishments.[30] Several types of public service in developing countries have responded to the influence of the so-called 'barefoot revolution', and it is no surprise that this should have been taken up by librarians. The idea is basically that workers are recruited from the community and trained at a very elementary level in the techniques needed to perform the required work, whatever it be. They are then employed, often on a part-time basis, for a small salary or honorarium. In the history of library practice a good number of examples of this approach can be found, although not described by this term. In Tanzania, for instance, rural reading room attendants are employed on this basis, and there was talk that the principle would be adopted elsewhere. It is, first of all, a reaction to the expense of services that are based on current practice in industrialized countries. Secondly, interest in it arises from the perception that established services with their associated forms of staffing have failed to adjust to local needs and circumstances.

The danger which comes from the barefoot librarian is not in the essential concept of a category of worker, qualified more by their base in the community than by the level of their academic achievement, and providing an unpretentious and appropriate service to that same community. Rather, it is that library systems will use the idea merely as a way of nominally expanding their services on the cheap. Unless the need to give effective training to these barefoot librarians, and provide them with constant support and encouragement, is fully recognized, then the system will produce yet another disaffected and inefficient level of employee. The information requirements of rural communities will be poorly served if this happens. Some of those barefoot librarians who do manage to make a success of their work will also certainly develop legitimate ambitions for more regular and better paid employment within the library service. Library employers must anticipate this and provide the channels for advancement that will meet these ambitions. Africa's library services to date have not had an encouraging record in developing such opportunities in their staffing structures, and while one would like to be optimistic about the barefoot concept, the probability is that it will only succeed in creating another even less well-qualified non-professional category of employee.

Although the structure of library employment had from the first been defined in terms of 'them and us', the implications of local professional control of systems (that the 'us' part of the system would one day be African too) was recognized. This had to be achieved through the education and training of an African professional workforce. The form that professional training took was usually dependent on what types of training were available in the colonial or former colonial country. Correspondence courses for the Associateship of the (British) Library Association, then full-time courses in Britain for the same qualification, were an early response. Since the Associateship and the Fellowship (which could be obtained by the same methods) were qualifications which the expatriates themselves possessed, it was perhaps predictable that their African replacements should also wish to obtain them too. The move towards degree level entry to the library profession in the United Kingdom during the 1960s and 1970s had a disastrous effect. Associates and Fellows of the Library Association, who had been among the first librarians in anglophone Africa to achieve professional status, suddenly seemed to be transformed from professionals and demoted, in the eyes of many, to the ranks of the para-professionals. Many of them returned overseas, having little choice but to enrol in various British and American library education programmes, in order for their professionalism to be confirmed anew. They studied alongside a new generation of graduate African librarians who were receiving their first professional training overseas, providing ample opportunity for schisms to occur in the professional ranks. The outcome was that some professional librarians now seemed more professional than others.

The overseas programmes, which over the years have served the needs of the majority of African professional librarians, have been repeatedly criticized as being too remote from the geographical, cultural, social, economic and political realities of library work in Africa.[31] It is the standard currency of debate on library education in Africa to cite instances of members of staff who have been sent to prestigious library schools in Europe and America and returned with a great deal of irrelevant knowledge and a grossly inflated idea of their ability to perform the duties of senior posts in their institutions. Apart from the fact that many of those who proffer these arguments themselves went through this same educational process, much of what they say is perfectly valid. Specifically, overseas postgraduate programmes have been criticized for being too short and intensive, concentrating on theory and broad issues to the virtual exclusion of practice. Further criticism centres around programmes concerning themselves exclusively with issues of concern to the industrial countries, with only minor compensation being offered through the availability of options on comparative and international librarianship.[32] Although these are often taught by lecturers who have a good deal of experience in developing countries, they are not always supported by sufficient information resources on libraries in development.

Despite such criticism, common to many professional fields, the popularity of overseas programmes has never slackened, even when appropriate local alternatives are available. It is not surprising, therefore, that the present generation of leaders in African librarianship contains many who pay generous tribute to the opportunity that was provided for them to study overseas. The worthwhile experiences gained by the individual can be appreciated by reading that excellent, and rare, autobiography of a librarian, Stanley Made's *Made in Zimbabwe*. He had the exhilarating sense that he was 'breaking new ground for sowing the seeds of a new or a hitherto not very well known profession by my fellow Africans'.[33] The fact is that these programmes were originally designed for their home countries, and make very good sense in terms of their own needs. In many ways they are not directly relevant to Africa's needs and require that African students apply a great deal of critical faculty to their content. Despite the ability of many students to do this, the programmes have not always helped African librarians to sort out their views on priorities for the library systems of their own countries.

Partly in response to these criticisms, Africa started to develop library education programmes of its own. This led to the establishment of the Institute of Librarianship at Ibadan University, followed by the Library School in Accra, which subsequently became part of the University of Ghana, Legon. The next stage was the foundation of regional library schools; the first in Dakar, Senegal, for librarians, archivists, and documentalists from francophone Africa, is still flourishing today. This was followed by the East African School of Librarianship at Makerere University, Uganda, originally designed to cater for all the Eastern African countries, which is now reviving from the traumas of recent Ugandan history. More than 30 years after the Ibadan Seminar, most of the countries of the continent have a library school or some type of training programme, and plans exist for quite a few more.

Most African library schools began with certificate and diploma programmes for para-professionals, and in some cases this is still all that is offered. There is no precise international standard for the distinction between certificates and diplomas, nor for that matter any real precedent to guide the curriculum planner who is required to draw up two separate curricula, preserving a clear distinction between two categories of para-professional librarianship. Generally speaking, the certificate is reserved for entrants at a lower level of educational qualification, and may, in some cases, lead on to admission to the diploma. Only the fact that the entrant's educational qualifications are usually below university entrance requirements, and that the programmes offer very little general educational content beyond librarianship, seriously distinguishes them from degree and even postgraduate programmes in librarianship.

To the outsider, the system looks over-elaborate. The existence of two levels of para-professional qualification certainly overstates the quantity of knowledge needed for someone to work in a library. Those who do manage to break out of the straitjacket of non-professionalism and progress onwards through diploma and degree to postgraduate level, certainly find that there is a great deal of overlap and repetition between the various levels. The certificate has little to offer as the path to a career, and the diploma in turn takes holders only as far as the barrier which separates them from the professional posts. Since the diploma undoubtedly prepares them for much of the content of professional work, the para-professional staff working in an African library feel an understandable distress and frustration at the difficulty of progressing further.[34]

Despite years of talk there has been little progress in devising means by which para-professionals can cross the divide to achieve professional status. Indeed, in Botswana, the ladder of education and promotion that enabled one former Director of the Botswana National Library Service to rise to the top from one of the lowest grades has only recently been reopened by the University of Botswana. Even where programmes do exist that in theory make it possible for diploma holders to apply for an undergraduate degree, those diploma holders often find themselves competing for admission against school leavers with better academic credentials, who are often admitted first. Until there is a recognition of the amount and quality of study involved in obtaining these diplomas, librarianship in Africa is condemned to have many of its practitioners in a state of disaffection so serious as to inhibit their will to contribute.

This disaffection is only made worse by the staffing situation at professional level. Despite the rigid hierarchy between professional and non-professional personnel, there is no similar stratification in the tasks each category performs. This has been noted, not only by casual observation, but also through survey[35] and has been graphically highlighted by Aguolu's work on job satisfaction in Nigeria's university libraries:

In one university, one librarian with an honours degree in physics was doing no book selection, no reference work, and no subject cataloguing of scientific and technical publications. He was primarily filing cards, keeping records of gifts and exchanges and occasionally participating in order work. This librarian put his disappointment in this way: 'I think I am wasting my time here.' There were similar cases in other library departments.[36]

In fact one way in which Nigerian librarians have coped with this depressing situation is by researching and writing the articles that flood the professional literature. There has, in fact, been something of a flight from harsh professional realities into the detachment of academic study.

It is not surprising, therefore, to find that library education at professional level is not free from the type of problem previously associated with the training of para-professionals. While in Britain a bachelor's degree in librarianship is considered a fully adequate qualification for professional status, this is not the case in North America, where a master's degree is the bare minimum for most types of post. African library systems have tended towards the American version, which means that even if the para-professionals could be helped to achieve bachelor's degrees in library studies, the system would still often limit their professional contribution. What is more, a postgraduate qualification is often taken to mean not just the postgraduate diploma, which until recently was the most usual qualification at this level in Britain, but a full master's degree. This is certainly the case for many posts in Africa with academic status, and to pile on the weight even further, a doctoral degree is often required for elevation to the most senior positions. As most institutions of library education in Africa feel themselves unready to offer programmes for such qualifications, this paper chase takes many of Africa's most able library personnel overseas for long periods, at a time when their energy and motivation are at their highest and when their services are urgently needed back home.

The rigidity of attitudes towards staffing structures has turned the attention of Africa's library educators too much towards levels of library qualifications, while diverting them away from pressing questions of curriculum content. The content of Africa's library education programmes reflects the fundamental difficulties arising from the conjunction of a library ethos drawn from a Western print-based culture and the needs of developing but information-poor societies. The fact is that Africa's library education programmes are little better in terms of relevance to Africa's needs than those of the metropolitan countries. This is not to say that African library educators have been impervious to the need for curricula to be more responsive to African circumstances, just that the results of their concern are not entirely convincing. As Mchombu has put it:

> The call for relevance over the last twenty years or so had simply led us to dress up conventional subjects in an 'African shirt'. What we often end up talking about is librarianship in Africa, not African librarianship. Library schools have only succeeded in producing librarians who are capable of serving an elite – we have failed to produce people appropriate to our real needs.[37]

The familiarity of the content of curricula in African library schools to anyone who knows library education in other parts of the world can be substantiated from the briefest of glances through their calendars, brochures and prospectuses. Even at diploma level, library management seems to be taught in the usual terms of organizational structures and may include elements on a rich variety of budgeting techniques. This despite the fact that most library systems are comparatively small, have few staff, and often very limited funds to budget for. There is a predictably thorough treatment of cataloguing, classification and indexing, while bibliography, including historical bibliography, still looms large. Options on such topics as bibliometrics, advanced information retrieval and music librarianship, are often offered as if they were relevant to the work of both professional and non-professional. Examination questions that require students to expound the significance of the ancient Etruscan script, or the essential characteristics of analog computers, still pop up among more relevant material.

The plan by Unesco and the International Development Research Centre (IDRC) to create a regional postgraduate information science programme for Africa was a worthwhile attempt to set out a standard for an information curriculum. These organizations published a report in 1985 which described the process by which an appropriate location for a programme had been selected.[38] The choice was Addis Ababa and the school is now known as the School of Information Science for Africa (SISA). The curriculum was apparently designed by a task force on the basis of a world trip visiting institutions of information science education, with a lengthy itinerary including South and North America and Europe.

The objectives of these trips were clearly identified by Unesco and IDRC as being to acquaint members of the task force with the main aspects of the functioning of these institutions and to identify the issues and problems that the University of Addis Ababa might have to face in establishing its own information science programme. The process of making the curriculum relevant to African needs was less apparent. Not until the 1990s did any graduates emerge from this expensively planned programme, and solid though the work done by SISA may be, the question of how far it can justify the investment remains.

The idea of training a new class of information professionals with an information science background incorporating systems analysis, research methods, database management and policy design is certainly attractive. The development of programmes which will largely cater for a narrow band of the population who are already information-rich, is not necessarily incompatible with a more egalitarian approach to curriculum design which attempts to develop an information workforce for service to the majority who are information-poor. The two approaches are, however, distinct from each other and it is essential to ensure that the one approach, equipped as it is with the attractions of technology, and a fashionable image, does not overpower the other. Just as with library education, the roots of information science education must be firmly set in Africa and there are, as yet, few signs that this is fully appreciated. The danger that information science education will be an immensely costly irrelevance, worse than the failures of library education, is a very immediate one.

Conclusion

Africa's libraries and other information institutions urgently need to break the dependence on Northern values which continues to retard their development. Dependence is as much a psychological phenomenon as an economic one. Indeed, economic chains do not always bind as strongly as those of the mind. To break away from an unwanted dependence is, therefore, not at all easy. What is more, in this case it may, in the short term, increase the poverty that afflicts African information institutions. To be poor is bad, but to be locked into relationships that limit the options for breaking out of that poverty is worse. These relationships can be changed.

It is essential for Africa's library and information community to struggle to avoid dependence on international publishing and bookselling companies, to ensure that donor agencies do not set the parameters of what can be done by the nature of the assistance they give, or that telecommunication and computer technology do not create patterns of information flow incompatible with developing country aims. Even more important than this, however, is the need to combat the psychological dependence which is nurtured by modes of thought and philosophies developed in other parts of the world, where both information needs and the resources to meet them are quite different. The imported attitudes and preconceptions of librarianship which dominate in Africa at present both permit and encourage the ways in which this dependency manifests itself. Inappropriate decisions over such matters as the planning of library buildings, the acquisition of materials, or the grading and training of staff, are made not just because advice or commercial pressures from outside suggest them, but because in the minds of those making the decisions there is already the propensity to make them. It is in the minds of the information professionals that we will find the roots of dependence and this is where the changes need to occur that will permit the development of a genuinely African information professionalism.

The institution in which this must take place first of all is the one where ideas on information work are formed, namely, the information and library school. Change in information education is therefore central to eliminating the dependence syndrome and providing the impetus to direct future generations of information workers towards new service priorities more in tune with Africa's real needs.

References

1. Aguolu, C.C. Father of Nigerian librarianship. *New Library World*, 79, 1978. 251–3.
2. Benge, R.C. *Cultural Crisis and Libraries in the Third World*. London, Bingley, 1979.
3. Broome, M. First steps in Tanganyika. *East Africa Library Association Bulletin*, 7, 1966. 18–25.
4. Harris, M. The purpose of the American public library: a revisionist interpretation of history. In: Totterdell, B. (ed.) *Public Library Purpose: A Reader*. London, Bingley, 1978. p.49.
5. Kigongo-Bukenya, C. The Public Libraries Board in Uganda. In:

Wallenius, A.B. (ed.) *Libraries in East Africa.* Uppsala, Scandinavian Institute of African Studies, 1971. 145–62.

6. Parker, J.S. *Unesco and Library Development Planning.* London, Library Association, 1985.
7. Brewster, B. *American Overseas Library Technical Assistance, 1940–1970.* Metuchen, NJ, Scarecrow Press, 1976.
8. Coombs, D. *Spreading the Word: The Library Work of the British Council.* London, Mansell, 1988.
9. O'Connor, B. and Roman, S. Building bridges with books: the British Council's sixty-year record. *Logos,* 5, 1994. 133–8.
10. Olden, A. *Libraries in Africa: Pioneers, Policies, Problems.* Lanham, MD, Scarecrow, 1995.
11. Kaungamno, E.E. and Ilomo, C.S. *Books Build Nations.* 2 vols. London, Transafrica, 1979.
12. Sitzman, G.L. *African Libraries.* Metuchen, NJ, Scarecrow, 1988.
13. Havard Williams, P. and Jengo, J.E. Library design and planning in developing countries. *Libri,* 20, 1988. 160–76.
14. Plumbe, W.J. Climate as a factor in the planning of University Library buildings. *Unesco Bulletin for Libraries,* 17, 1963. 316–25.
15. Kotei, S.I.A. Some variables and comparison between developed and developing library systems. *International Library Review,* 9, 1977. 249–67.
16. Maack, M. The role of external aid in West African library development. *Library Quarterly,* 56, 1986. 1–16.
17. Harris, J. Ibadan University Library: some notes on its birth and growth. *Library Association Record,* 67, 1965. 256–7.
18. Moyo, O. Empowerment of rural people. *RLRDP News Bulletin,* 1, 1995. p.4.
19. Membury, D. The Ranfurly Library Service and the Textbooks for Africa Project. *African Research and Documentation,* 46, 1988. 40–6.
20. Priestley, C. The difficult art of book aid: an African survey. *Logos,* 4, 1993. 215–21.
21. Kuitenbrouwer, F. The world data war. *New Scientist,* 91, 1981. 604–7.
22. Abate, D. Libraries and information services in a changing world: the challenges African information services face at the end of the 1980s. Paper presented at IFLA General Conference, Brighton, UK. August 1987.
23. Aiyepeku, W.O. *International Socio-economic Information Systems: An Evaluation of DEVSIS-type Programs.* Ottawa, International Development Research Centre, 1983.
24. Lungu, C.M, Resource sharing and self-reliance in Southern Africa. *Information Development,* 3, 1987. 82–6. p.85.
25. Gehrke, U. Information for development. Some problems of national co-ordination, regional co-operation and international assistance. *INSPEL,* 9, 1985. 166–98.
26. McCarthy, C. Colonial cataloguing. *New Library World,* 76, 1975. p.55.
27. Thairu, R.W. Cataloguing policies and problems in Kenyan Libraries. *African Research and Documentation,* 40, 1986. 8–15.

28. Iwuji, H.O.M. Africana in LC and DD classification schemes: a need for an Africana scheme? *Journal of Librarianship*, 21, 1989. 1–18.
29. Arap Tanui, T. Psychology and culture in information retrieval: with special reference to Moi University Library, Kenya. *Libri*, 39, 1989. 185–91.
30. Wijasuriya, D., Lim H-T. and Nadarajah, R. *The Barefoot Librarian: Library Development in South East Asia with Special Reference to Malaysia.* London, Bingley, 1975.
31. Lundu, M.C. Library education and training: at home or abroad? *International Library Review*, 14, 1982. 363–78.
32. Tallman, J.I. and Ojiambo, J.B. *Translating an International Education to a National Environment.* Metuchen, NJ, Scarecrow Press, 1990.
33. Made, S. *Made in Zimbabwe.* Gweru, Mambo Press, 1980.
34. Sturges, P. What librarians feel about their careers: a survey of diploma and certificate holders. *Botswana Library Association Journal*, 7, 1985. 9–21.
35. Neill, J.R. Library manpower planning in Southern, Central and Eastern Africa. In: Huttemann, L. (ed.) *Manpower Training Needs. Proceedings and Papers of the Information Experts Meeting, Harare, Zimbabwe, 1985.* Bonn, DSE, 1985. 19–28.
36. Aguolu, C.C. Staffing in Nigerian university libraries. *Library Review*, 31, 1982. p.21.
37. Mchombu, K.J. [Statement in discussion]. In: Asamani, J.O. *et al.* (eds) *Libraries and Literacy. Proceedings of the Seventh Meeting of the Standing Conference of Eastern, Central and Southern African Librarians, Gaborone, 4–8 August, 1986.* Gaborone, Botswana Library Association, 1987. p.198.
38. Roberts, K.H. (ed.) *Regional Postgraduate Program in Information Science in Anglophone Africa: Identification of an Appropriate Location. Report of a Joint Unesco/IDRC Mission.* Ottawa, IDRC, 1986.

Chapter Four

The Search for Relevance

The NATIS Solution

During the late 1960s and early 1970s, after the excitement of the early years of independence when new systems had been begun and the possibilities had seemed infinite, a mood of perplexity overcame Africa's library profession. As governments became disenchanted with libraries' lack of tangible achievement, librarians found the case they argued for the support that might enable them to produce better results was failing to convince. At the same time, however, African librarians were both being heard more frequently at international conferences, and were picking up messages there that seemed potentially helpful. What African librarians were saying at conferences and writing in professional journals and academic theses provided only limited insight into the actual condition of their libraries. Plans, experiments and resolutions were described as if they were functioning reality, and the day-to-day consequences of the problems influencing library development were hinted at rather than faced full on. Many of the documents in the growing archive of consultancy reports and expert missions on library development also tended to skirt round the harsher realities and discuss services as if they existed in a vacuum. There was a tendency to understate the extent of structural problems and the influence of external circumstances.

The message picked up by representatives of the African library profession in those forums where they gave their somewhat clouded versions of the reality in their libraries, was that the issue of libraries and national development was of the first importance.

This followed very naturally from an awareness of a group of Unesco initiatives, centred around NATIS (National Information Systems). A focus on national development, and the offer of solutions through NATIS, came to dominate the agenda for discussion from the mid-1970s through to well into the 1980s. The two elements seemed to fit together beautifully. In the first place, all that librarians seemed to need to do, was make the superficially appealing assertion that libraries could perform a vital role in development. Indeed they said this often. As just one typical instance chosen from hundreds, Alemna claimed in 1989 that,

> Where the government realises that information constitutes the key ingredient in the national economic, scientific and technological development, libraries are bound to flourish.[1]

One does not have to look far in the literature even today to find this mantra chanted as if the mere repetition of it will achieve something. Proving that it is true is quite a different matter, and it is hardly surprising that, in the absence of evidence, those who hold the reins of power ignore it.

Discussing the role of libraries in development in a way that might convince the decision makers seemed even easier if the authority of Unesco, the International Federation of Library Associations (IFLA) and other prestigious organizations could be invoked. Indeed, it was even better than that because the whole thing could be discussed in the context of ready-made plans and documentation originating from these impressive sources. NATIS itself had an impressive appearance. It was a concept which aimed to bring a broad, integrated perspective to the planning of a country's library and information sector. The concept was supported by programmes of promotion through publications, conferences, workshops, consultancies and projects. The story of all this has been well told by Parker, who not only chronicles the history of each individual programme, but also outlines Africa's contribution to their creation and development.[2] A verdict from the 1990s would be that Africa's library professionals spent well over a decade in debating, discussing and writing about these programmes, when their energy and efforts would have been better expended in continuing to grapple with the multitude of everyday problems that beset their services.

Africa's first real involvement with the NATIS concept actually took place in 1970, four years before the NATIS programme was formally called into existence by the 1974 Intergovernmental Conference. A meeting was convened by Unesco in Kampala, Uganda, which was to consider a document to be prepared by Charles Deane Kent, who was at the time Director of the Public Library and Art Museum in London, Ontario. Apart from the final report published by Unesco,[3] the documentation about this meeting is extremely slender. The plan for the meeting was that Kent would prepare a draft library development plan for Uganda which would be not merely the working document for the meeting, but eventually a model for the rest of the continent. The timing was not really propitious. Kent arrived to prepare his model plan just as a formal Inquiry into Uganda's Public Libraries Board was concluding. The report of the inquiry accused the Board, and a number of senior staff members, of inefficiency, incompetence, nepotism, mismanagement and malfeasance, which had brought the library service to virtual ruin. It was in this climate that Kent proceeded with his task.

It is little wonder that the result was not the planning model for Uganda, or the rest of the continent, that Unesco had originally envisaged. Nevertheless, the Kampala Meeting, which included a number of Africa's leading librarians, proceeded to prepare a set of guidelines for library development planning in Africa. The main focus of the recommendations centred around each country forming a single body that would be charged with the responsibility of developing an integrated library and information system that would be fully representative of all the nation's interests. This would be established under the aegis of a government ministry, and would play a decisive role in national development. The essentials of the NATIS approach are contained in this, with all their emphasis on structures within which library and information systems are supposed to grow and flourish. In hindsight, the emphasis seems like the reverse of what was really needed. Flexible response to specific needs in order to build strong specific services was where effort was needed. Structures to ensure balanced and well-planned growth were much less important than the vitality of the separate initiatives that one day, if they were successful, might create the need for structures. Africa's contemporary view of the proceedings is barely documented except for a brief and wholly uncritical account by Kaungamno and Ilomo. This account suggests that the meeting was of extreme importance and great relevance but fails to tell us just why that might be the case.[4]

As Parker points out, for Uganda the postscript to the Kampala Meeting occurred barely two months after the delegates had departed, when:

> The Uganda Army seized control of the country in the absence of the President, Milton Obote, and on the following day Major General Idi Amin, Commander of the Army, proclaimed himself Head of State. There is little evidence to suggest that library development received much official attention during the Amin regime, and with the benefit of hindsight we can see now that in the light of events in Uganda both before and after the Kampala Meeting, the selection of that country as a venue, at that moment in its history, was particularly unfortunate.[5]

The Kampala story is symbolic of the reasons why NATIS and similar programmes have had much less effect on African library and information circumstances than was hoped. In these very beginnings the creators of the programme took insufficient cognizance of Africa's information environment, and proceeded as if political and social conditions were an irrelevance. The idea of a single, national, integrated library and information system as the answer for Africa's library problems emerged from precisely this neglect of messy reality. Although its appropriateness was doubtful from the outset, and indeed, perhaps in a perverse way just because it was concerned with issues one step removed from the struggle to provide services which met specific needs, the NATIS idea continued to strengthen its grip in the following years.

The process by which this happened centred on a series of international meetings. The International Conference on the Development of Documentation and Information Networks in East Africa, held at Nairobi in 1973, was the next major contribution after the Kampala meeting. This conference was held under the auspices of the East African Academy, with the sponsorship of the German Foundation for International Development (DSE). It attracted over 25 participants including delegates from Kenya, Sudan, Tanzania, Uganda and Zambia. The conference endorsed both the NATIS and the associated UNISIST programme that Unesco was also promoting and proceeded to recommend that:

> governments of developing countries should urgently formulate national documentation policies and integrate these policies in the national development plans; that each national government should create or cause the creation of an information unit in each ministry, statutory body and other specialized institution, to collect, evaluate, process, and disseminate information in collaboration with a central

agency in the same country ... that a governmental or government chartered body be created to guide, stimulate, and co-ordinate all information services and to establish national information priorities.[6]

After Kampala and Nairobi, the DSE supported the programme by setting up and financing a series of User Seminars, which took place in various African countries between 1974 and 1981. These were to create a dialogue between librarians and decision makers. The next step in Unesco's own programme was a NATIS meeting in Brazzaville, People's Republic of Congo in 1976. This meeting was to discuss the planning of documentation and library networks in Africa. In addition to participants from the Congo, delegates arrived from Nigeria, Benin, Togo, Uganda, Senegal, Ivory Coast, Cameroon, Gabon, Tanzania, Ghana, Kenya and Sierra Leone. The meeting focused on two main issues: the current situation in planning information systems in Africa; and how the recently published NATIS guidelines could be applied within an African context.[7] The first part of the meeting reviewed the progress that had been made since 1970 in implementing the Kampala recommendations. There was very little to report, certainly nothing of a positive nature, and the general opinion appeared to be that if African governments were indeed taking heed of the Kampala recommendations, there was little evidence to confirm this.

Undeterred by this lack of progress, the participants proceeded to review how NATIS guidelines could be used in Africa. Four main areas were dealt with: legislation, creation of coordinating bodies, Universal Bibliographic Control and personnel. The resulting discussion produced 22 major recommendations, nine of which were addressed to the Director General of Unesco, and the remainder to member states. Among these, Unesco was requested to promote postgraduate library education in Africa, to provide a 'massive' number of training scholarships and to assist in the development of harmonized training programmes in the continent so as to encourage the development of a single unified information profession. Africa's librarians meanwhile were provided with a lengthy list of things to do including:

1. Designing national information policies and incorporating plans for integrated national information systems into national development plans.
2. Profiling user needs and organizing national seminars that would assist in the rapid implementation of NATIS.
3. Strengthening Africa's contribution to Universal Bibliographical

Control through legal deposit and the preparation of national bibliographies.

4. Creating additional capacity for the education and training of the continent's librarians, and incorporating into the library education curriculum courses specifically on NATIS.

Fine as these recommendations no doubt sounded at the time, little discussion seems to have taken place as to why nothing had been achieved in the six-year period since Kampala. Moreover, virtually no insight is provided in the final report as to how NATIS could be appropriately fashioned to fit in with Africa's development priorities and circumstances. Even more interesting is the fact that NATIS as a separate Unesco programme had less than six months to live. Just over two weeks after the final report of the Brazzaville meeting was published, NATIS was swallowed up by the newly-created General Information Programme (PGI), having lost out in its 'battle' with the rival UNISIST programme. Yet the legacy of NATIS lingered on and dominated published comment on libraries and information in Africa for a number of years. Indeed, it still emerges occasionally to haunt anyone in the unfortunate position of trying to write on African librarianship without the support of up-to-date literature or regular professional contact.

The main reason why this story is so sad is that there are virtually no practical results to be shown from Africa's involvement with these programmes. After its years of separate existence, followed by a half-life within PGI, NATIS contributed almost nothing to the development of Africa's information environment. There was hardly a single country in Africa, however small and however lacking in libraries it might be, that did not have a NATIS-inspired model applied to it. The Seychelles is a good example. In 1977, a consultant prepared a plan for a national information system, despite the fact that the Seychelles at that time did not have a single qualified librarian. What is more, the findings of this consultancy could be added to what had been said by four other consultants who had previously visited the islands with a similar brief.[8]

This example is not an isolated one: for instance, discussion of the NATIS principles proceeded in Malawi in much the same way as in the rest of Africa. The Malawi National Research Council discussed NATIS in April 1977 and an interim National Information committee was formed. One of the 'User Seminars' organized by the DSE to create a dialogue between librarians and government decision makers so as to increase official awareness of the significance of information in the planning process, was held in Malawi in 1978, and by 1979 a survey of information resources and library collections had been carried out. Malawi's librarians had high hopes of this process, and Mphundi wrote of the:

> general and universal acceptability of the NATIS concept and objectives as the most appropriate manner of coping with the problem of the provision of information to those who require it in Malawi.[9]

By August 1983 a draft National Information Policy had been formulated. In light of this, Ngaunje, writing in 1986, felt able to suggest that:

> Prospects for the future look bright because Malawi is already looking at the NATIS concept and its implications in Malawi.[10]

However, he was well aware of the chief difficulty, as he pointed out in the same article that:

> In order to ensure the implementation of the information policy, a need exists for a high powered delegation from the government. In doing so, the importance of libraries can be impressed upon the officials.

The crowning irony of the suggestion is that Kamuzu Banda's government had, since independence, systematically and formally intervened to prevent the free flow of information in Malawi.

The story of NATIS and related programmes shows how the attention of Africa's librarians was diverted from the most crucial issues towards attractive but ultimately futile recipes for success. An appropriate point when efforts to promote this approach could have been drawn to a close was provided in 1981. The DSE employed Martin Shio, with the assistance of Augustus Musana, to carry out an evaluation of the user seminars that had been conducted throughout the Southern and Central African region.[11] The purpose of the evaluation was to determine the utility of the seminars in terms of their contribution to increasing the awareness of information as an aspect of planning and decision making. Shio's investigation, which was an opportunity either to show that there was some strength in the equation, libraries = information = development, or help lay the matter to rest, was a disappointment.

The report is vague, inconclusive and lacks the necessary detail which could have settled the issue. He identifies a few good initiatives such as the development of the Institute of Southern African Studies in Lesotho, the establishment of the Swaziland National Archives and the setting up of the Zambian National Documentation and Scientific Information Centre, and implies that they were a direct result of the seminars. However, he offers no real evidence that this is actually the case. More telling, perhaps, is the confirmation he provides of the total lack of progress in preparing national information policies, coordinating library and information services and developing planning models for integrated library and information services that could be incorporated into national development plans. As these were the priorities identified in Nairobi way back in 1973 when the idea of the user seminars was first mooted, the only conclusion is that up until 1981 there had been no real success.

The DSE, which had sponsored the original series of seminars, showed no public sign of dissatisfaction. Furthermore, it was lobbied by librarians from Southern and Central Africa not to discontinue the effort, despite the misgivings implicit in Shio's evaluation report. So there began yet another round of seminars and workshops which commenced with Malawi in 1984 and included Swaziland, Lesotho, Zimbabwe and Botswana, before concluding in Zambia in 1988, when once more an evaluation took place. The objectives of these workshops will no doubt sound familiar, echoing as they do the issues first raised in 1970 in Kampala and resurrected over and over again during the intervening decade or so.[12] Improving planning and decision-making capabilities, assisting socio-economic and cultural development, contributing to national development efforts through the provision of library and information services, sensitizing government officials to the efficacy of information, are all there, and provide a familiar theme that can be traced back to the early 1970s.

Some of the individual papers prepared for this new round of seminars were extremely good, and the reported discussion was very often more candid than before.[13] Difficulties, problems and failures were by now all being highlighted. For this reason alone, this series of seminars was extremely valuable and it is unfortunate that the published volumes of proceedings are not very easily obtainable. Despite these positive aspects, the reader obtains the firm impression from the proceedings that little changed in the years after the original meeting in Kampala. The most frequently recurring themes of the final resolutions cover the following areas:

a. information is a prerequisite to national development, development planning and decision making;
b. developed countries are developed because they are information-rich;
c. Africa is less developed because it is information-poor;
d. as information is the librarians' essential concern, it therefore follows that improved national development will result from more and better libraries and more and better librarians;
e. governments are strongly recommended to legislate for the setting up of national information coordinating bodies that will provide the mechanism for the enactment of a national information policy;
f. all types of information service (although usually only libraries are specifically mentioned) should be banded together to form a coordinated national information network, that will in turn establish regional and international linkages with other information systems and services.

Appealing as these ideas sound, there is little evidence that the assumptions so frequently stated have ever been acted upon or the recommendations implemented. Even when claims to progress have been made, they more often than not represent vague hopes rather than operational realities. Concerns over the validity of the whole line of argument have never been strong enough to dislodge it from the prominent place it holds in the information world generally.

The arguments and evidence to do so exist, nevertheless, clearly-expressed and in an easily retrievable place in the literature. A hard-headed assault was made in 1979 by Tefko Saracevic, when he was commissioned to undertake a study in preparation for the United Nations Conference on Science and Technology and Development.[14] The substance of his case deserves recapitulation here. The study attempted to synthesize the perceptions held by information workers, information users and decision makers in less developed countries, by finding out what they had written about scientific and technical information. Almost from the beginning of his report, Saracevic casts doubt on the authenticity and legitimacy of this written record, describing it as being extremely uneven and pointing out that:

> There is a particularly serious problem with factual evidence on the basis of which statements found in the literature were made, in that the lack of valid and reliable facts, data, statistics, and similar hard evidence

in connection with most of the discussions found in the literature on STI [scientific and technical information] in LDCs [less developed countries] is appalling. ... Hundreds of surveys, trip reports and descriptive articles exist on some or other aspect of STI in LDCs; unfortunately many are shallow. This is particularly true of numerous reports done by and for UN agencies where trip reports are substituted for studies.[15]

Saracevic's critique was subsequently endorsed by Unesco consultant Ulrich Gehrke, who during 1974 had advised the Kenyan government on the establishment of a national information and documentation system.[16]

What Saracevic and Gehrke had to say is extremely important, for their contributions provide the most convincing clues as to why Africa's library and information services have not yet managed to feature in the development process at a national level. A synthesis of both their arguments proceeds as follows:

• Government officials, planners and decision makers exhibit an extremely low level of awareness with regard to the utility of information, and remain stubbornly unconvinced of its efficacy as a factor in the development process. The necessary conviction that would make NATIS work is not evidenced in the top echelons of government service by the people who hold the purse strings. Neither is information taken seriously at the second tier level of administrators and professionals. It is this category of government employee which one would expect to benefit directly from NATIS-inspired services. In general, however, they rarely utilize information in their day-to-day operations and, more importantly, rarely urge their employers to provide new and improved information services. Even on the rare occasions when a reference to information needs does appear in a planning or policy document, it is no more than a declaration of good intent that is not followed through or supported with the allocation of resources.

• Very few comprehensive national information plans and policies have ever been prepared, and even fewer have been elevated to the extent that they have become an integral part of a national development plan or an essential factor in the planning process. Furthermore, no rationale exists as to why information, rather than housing for example, warrants a separate treatment in national development plans with its own agenda and its own policy formulation. Finally, in the few instances where national information policies and plans have been conceived, no evidence exists that any action has been taken to implement them.

• One of the major impediments to governments' acceptance of NATIS and its associated offerings rests with librarians themselves. The library profession is generally poorly perceived, and the inability of librarians to prepare the necessary project plans that could give effect to NATIS only reinforces this negative perception. While the involvement of librarians in planning national information systems is, on the face of it, not unreasonable, the low esteem in which the profession is held has ensured the non-acceptance of NATIS. Just as librarians bemoan the fact that planners and decision makers show a persistent ignorance of the importance of information as it relates to development, so planners and decision makers complain that librarians know even less about development issues. Finally, little solace can be found after examining Africa's education and training programmes in library and information studies. They can best be summed up as being deficient, not only in terms of their content, but also in their ability to recruit suitable faculty and students. They are also clearly failing to provide the appropriate preparation to enable the library profession to communicate with planners, decision makers and high level government officials.

• Existing national information services and systems are usually based on a single, under-resourced, under-staffed and under-developed 'focal point'. The collection of information resources tends to be confined to a single subject or perhaps a small cluster of subjects, which have little direct relationship to national development priorities. The services offered are rarely matched to actual user needs, and the focal points have never succeeded in gaining a significant niche in the development process at a national level. Librarians talk constantly about cooperative services and networks, but most of what they say is idle rhetoric, for in reality they are defensive, cautious, conservative and unwilling to risk ceding their tiny under-resourced empires to a larger national system.

• The information collections upon which these national services and systems are based are marginal, inadequate and over-emphasize bibliographical and referral information at the expense of resources that could provide quick, accurate and direct answers. Major problems exist with these collections in terms of availability, awareness of their existence, accessibility, selection, the facility to screen, synthesize and discriminate between various resources, acquisition, accommodation, dissemination, utilization, as well as the application of information technology. All told the majority of these so-called national collections have so many problems that they are unable to provide the solutions that Africa's planners and decision makers require.

• International and multinational organizations represent the last major piece in the jigsaw which characterizes the failure of integrated library and information systems in Africa. Much of the literature they produce, as well as the studies and consultancies they conduct, are of dubious value. The principal reason for this is that, despite the fact that they are attempting to promote the idea that information is an essential ingredient of planning and decision making, their own reports are virtually devoid of facts and figures upon which informed decisions could be made. Many of these agencies pursue conflicting, contradictory and uncoordinated programme goals, and often engage in internal or inter-agency feuding at the expense of the development programmes they are supposed to be providing.

This synthesis provides a suitable epitaph for this approach to the information needs of Africa. It has been added to and refined by African librarians, and it could be suggested that more or less the last word on the topic, from the point of view of the librarian, was provided by Mchombu and Miti in 1992.[17] If further evidence is needed to show the futility of some of the arguments that have been adduced in support of the case for national information systems, Susannah Davies's powerful introduction to a 1994 special issue of the *IDS Bulletin* on information and development gives them the death blow.[18] Very little that was positive was obtained from the preoccupation with integrated plans for library and information services in relation to national development. Indeed, it failed to relieve the disenchantment that can be found on all sides with the performance of libraries. The only positive effect is that through this disillusionment has emerged a new generation of African librarians who have started to seek their own solutions and to set their own agenda for the future.

African Librarianship

The first whisperings of a different approach can actually be traced back to some of the expatriate librarians who first established

Africa's library services, but the new voice is essentially a voice out of Africa itself. A public debate between those who saw librarianship in Africa as just a matter of applying an established set of practices in different conditions and those who believed that there was a need for something radically different, first began in the early 1960s. Two of the most distinguished British expatriate librarians, Wilfred Plumbe and Ronald Benge, exchanged letters through the pages of the *Library Association Record*. Plumbe had argued that the Library Association (UK) should amend its professional education syllabus and make it more sensitive to the needs of overseas librarians by including an optional paper under the title Tropical Librarianship. The amendments he suggested were not intended to alter in any way the well-established ethos of library service from the United Kingdom. This, he claimed,

> transcends national boundaries and is undeterred by monsoon rains, desert suns, inefficient postal services, nationalist fervour, or the hundred and one other obstacles to study that exist in dozens of countries formerly 'backward' but now developing with alacrity.[19]

The content of his envisaged Tropical Librarianship course was not explicitly stated, but what Plumbe obviously had in mind was a focus on these one hundred and one other obstacles and how they could be overcome.

Benge, while welcoming the attention that was being paid to libraries overseas, expressed his misgivings in the following way:

> Wilfred Plumbe makes many sound proposals but I detect in several of his articles a suggestion that there is something abnormal about the tropics because it is hot and there are insects and hurricanes.[20]

Benge believed that it was more than just the obvious physical, environmental and geographical factors that should give a distinct and separate character to library development in Africa. He recognized that the continent has its own social and cultural values, and took the view that librarianship in Africa should draw inspiration from those values. The book *Cultural Crisis and Libraries in the Third World*, in which he presented a fully worked-out version of his ideas, provoked considerable interest on publication in 1979. It also achieved, for a librarianship text, a large circulation and has continued to be read and commented on subsequently.[21] At about the same time Adolphe Amadi published his relentlessly polemical *African Libraries: Western Tradition and Colonial Brainwashing*.[22] By focusing very hard on the negative effects of colonial influence on the mind-set of the African librarian this book cleared the way for a fresh approach. Indeed, suggestions as to the direction which that approach should take are not lacking in Amadi's work.

Benge and Amadi's clear perceptions and anti-establishment attitudes provided the impetus for what it is convenient, if not wholly helpful, to refer to as 'African librarianship'. Librarians who have sought more worthwhile approaches of this kind have consistently referred back to Benge or Amadi for support, and throughout the 1980s the approach they pioneered has been reflected in conference papers and journal articles. However, for the younger African librarians who have started to adopt this type of approach, life has not always been easy. When an old paradigm breaks down and fails to provide answers that convince, those who discuss this breakdown with openness and candour are often, in effect, challenging not just an orthodox set of beliefs, but the people in positions of influence, whose reputations were built on the acceptance of those beliefs. This has often called for some courage. As Shiraz Durrani put it:

> Over the years, the younger generation of librarians have questioned the basis of library services but their views and creativity have been suppressed as being 'non-professional'.[23]

Despite the resistance of those whose position in the hierarchy leads them to cling to the status quo, new views are emerging and becoming sufficiently accepted to constitute the nucleus of an African librarianship movement. One of the key contributions, as suggested earlier, was 'On the librarianship of poverty' published in 1982 by Mchombu, then a training officer with the Tanzania National Library Service.[24] He made the brilliant, but in hindsight blindingly obvious, observation that the foundations of library work in Africa should be determined by the prevailing social and economic characteristics, and that poverty was an overwhelmingly dominant characteristic of the African environment. He developed this simple principle to argue that poverty required the most positive response from those involved with information work. This to Mchombu meant providing service to the neglected majority of the population who lived, and still live, in the rural areas. Over the years since this article was published, the library profession has begun to absorb the message and accept the challenge to produce a new library and information model.

Mchombu effectively directed the focus of attention to the role of libraries in the rural areas, and the response of librarians to illiteracy. This was not, however, a wholly new emphasis. Two important milestones in the development of the argument had been published during the 1970s in the journal *Rural Africana*. The 1975 issue of this journal looked generally at the problems of communication and information provision in rural Africa, particularly as they relate to rural development strategies.[25] At this stage, the library profession seems to have been seen as having little to offer, because virtually nothing is said about libraries among a great deal of discussion that is actually directly relevant to the question of their potential in rural life. By 1978 an entire special issue was devoted to the topic of rural library provision.[26] This included a surprisingly lengthy bibliography showing that there had been quite a number of voices crying in the rural librarianship wilderness.

The need by the early 1980s was for better and more detailed knowledge on which to build ideas for new developments. Two articles by Adimorah turned the focus directly on to research on community needs. More or less 30 years on from when the Ibadan Seminar had launched the case for public libraries in such a positive way, he characterized the way public libraries had turned out as follows:

> Instead of playing an active role as change agents, most of these libraries play an information suppressing role to their community in failing to disseminate information geared towards bettering the lot of the rural poor. The public libraries still lack the interest or capacity for carrying out an analysis of the community, isolating its needs and satisfying them. They are yet to make a real commitment to the free flow of information, harnessing and providing ready access to information on rural development that would change the social circumstances of the rural poor.[27]

The key thing in this complaint is the statement in the middle that there had been no analysis of community need. In a 1983 analysis of the failures of public libraries in Nigeria, he had made the same point, just as clearly, suggesting that:

> Further research is needed on the information needs of Nigerians and their information gathering habits to enable public library directors to plan society-based services and create a true library tradition.[28]

In fact in Nigeria itself important research of just this type had

already been done in Olabimpe Aboyade's RUDIS project at Ibadan University, mentioned earlier as one of the key documents in
recent commentary on information in Africa.[29] Subsequently there
has been a steady flow of worthwhile research on information needs
by members of the information professions, but it is necessary to
point out that anyone who wants as full a picture of information in
the African setting as possible, must search much more widely to
find it. For instance, one of the very best insights into information
in the African village is still Amaratunga and Shute's marvellously
informative, but virtually never cited, 1982 study of adult learning
in Dome, Ghana.[30] Information researchers should never forget
that it is entirely obligatory to search the literatures of development, communication, education and other social sciences for
adequate data on their topic. In fact, they cite very little from these
rich resources. This has arguably limited the scope not just of their
knowledge, but also of their ability to devise responses to information need.

The research by information professionals has tended to be
better in some particular subject areas than others. Although
agriculture, and rural life generally, may be the most problematic
area, it is very much the best served. The pages of the *Quarterly
Bulletin of the International Association of Agricultural Librarians and
Documentalists* have some claim to have been more fruitful of
interesting studies than any other journal. Work on the expressed
information needs of farmers by Oladele,[31] Adimorah's survey of
farmers' information needs in Imo State, Nigeria,[32] and Aina's
research from the same period[33] are examples of research on
agricultural information. Although all of these came from Nigeria,
related work has been done in other parts of Africa, and a number
of such studies were quoted in Chapter 2.

In contrast, there has been precious little study of the special
information needs and information getting practices of women,
despite the distinct disadvantages they face and the pivotal contribution their work makes to family incomes. One study that makes
more than just a passing reference to women and information, is
that of Nwagha.[34] There has also been less research with a whole
community scope, with Mchombu's INFORD survey in Botswana,
Malawi and Tanzania a major exception to this generalization.
The published Malawian results[35] move away from merely investigating information needs, and show something of the places and
personnel that communities associate with effective information

exchange. Despite the growing popularity of user-related research, there is still a great deal of scope for such work. Techniques can be taken from the social sciences, a qualitative emphasis can be introduced more frequently, attention can be turned to a wider set of information related questions, and various special groups (women have already been mentioned, but linguistic and cultural minorities, such as the San of Southern Africa, should not be forgotten) deserve attention.[36]

Largely on the basis of personal insight, but then using research findings as they began to be published, a set of ideas and indeed a programme for an African librarianship began to emerge. First of all, meetings of information workers were important. As perhaps the earliest relevant example, Aboyade had organized a Federation Internationale de Documentation (FID) Technical Meeting at Ibadan at the same time as she was doing her RUDIS research. This focused on the needs of non-literate societies, and from an impressive programme Ogunsheye's closing contribution drew attention to the crucial question of who would operate new types of service in these conditions.[37] When IFLA held its annual meeting in Nairobi in 1984, there was a pre-session Seminar on Education for Librarianship at the Grassroots Level, at which, amongst other contributions, Kukobo suggested a role as community archivist for the local information worker.[38] The seventh meeting of the Standing Conference of Eastern, Central and Southern African Librarians (SCECSAL VII), in Gaborone in 1986, focused on Libraries and Literacy, and the content of its proceedings confirmed that librarians from the Eastern side of the continent were moving in the same direction as their West African colleagues.[39]

As all this filtered into the general consciousness of librarians, proposals for changed and improved library services began to be formulated. The first fully realized version of such ideas was published in book form in 1987 by Aboyade.[40] One of her key recommendations was that information services should repackage information into forms acceptable to the local population. Sadly, this book has not been widely available outside Nigeria, but the essence of the programme she outlined has continued to be advocated and expanded since. To give only a few fairly recent instances, Chijioke envisaged public libraries as essential contributors to networks for the delivery of community information.[41] Kedem looked at public library services in relation to literacy campaigns and concluded that a variety of new types of service should be introduced.[42] Kantumoya made a number of suggestions for more effective community information services.[43] Dawha and Makinta set out an agenda for rural information services, concluding firmly that 'Rural information services should be based in the public libraries'.[44] The list could very easily be much extended, but these give the flavour of writings that have tended to be reformist rather than revolutionary.

The hardest place for this adaptation of ideas to take place was in South Africa under apartheid, but even there it took place. As long ago as 1988, SAILIS commissioned an investigation of South African libraries and national development. This was particularly interesting because South Africa has a widespread network of public library service points, which were chiefly serving the white population. The report that was written was essentially an attempt to find ways to put this resource to better and wider use.[45] However, it found that:

> All opinion leaders outside the library field considered public libraries to be either an unknown or an inert, albeit a potentially valuable factor in promoting development. (p.5)

More particularly, the black communities, when they were served at all, were not served well.

> Selection committees comprised of whites are inclined to select books that are not used by blacks. In one large library system as many as 70 per cent of the books received by black libraries were considered unsuitable for their communities, despite appeals by black librarians for different kinds of books. (p.3)

The position was particularly exacerbated in South Africa by the fact that:

> Over the past few years a widespread distrust of the written word, especially in the form of pamphlets or news sheets, has developed in some black townships. This is a result of the numerous counter-revolutionary government pamphlets distributed in the townships. (p.44)

As a consequence,

> Public libraries, with few exceptions, play no role in providing information to the urban black community at large. Libraries are almost totally disregarded by this community and are hardly used, except by students

and schoolchildren. Very few educated black people belong to a library or would voluntarily go to a library as opposed to some other community facility. (p.46)

Despite the specifically South African content of this, with its black/white apartheid polarization, much of what was said in the report could be transferred to other African countries with little need for more than altering a word or two. The search for relevance is seen in rather sad form even in the best provided African country. Wallace Mgoqi, Administrator of the Ikapa Town Council, speaking to librarians in the Cape in 1995, criticized libraries as aloof, inaccessible, expensive, alienating, and called for their use to empower people through information, as part of the South African Reconstruction and Development Programme (RDP).[46] That there exists a certain will to do this is clear: just how to go about it, how to create a true African librarianship in South Africa, is still an open issue.

It is in South Africa, however, that some of the best conceptual thinking on new approaches has been published. Peter Lor, for instance, in discussing a new paradigm for South African librarianship has set out very clearly some principles on which it might be based.[47] Several of the propositions he makes as the suggested basis for a new paradigm, can be perfectly well applied anywhere else in Africa, or other parts of the developing world. Following Mchombu in taking poverty (although complicated by the pockets of First World privilege in South Africa) as his starting point, he develops ten propositions. The five most pertinent are as follows:

1. Libraries try to operate at too high a level, and this level should be lowered, without ceasing to strive after excellence.
2. Librarians should commit themselves to the aspirations and values of the communities they serve.
3. There should not be discrimination against users on the basis of literacy.
4. Libraries should give a much higher priority to communication than to organization.
5. Librarians should accept that community information resources have a higher claim on funding than have sophisticated information services.

As a basis of a reformed librarianship for African purposes this is hard to better, but the question still remains whether a reformed librarianship is all that is required. It is our contention that it is not enough: that a reformed librarianship is only part of an answer.

Libraries which are better directed towards the whole community, and which build their services on a realistic assessment of needs and the resources available to meet them, would certainly be a major step forward. Even then it is doubtful whether this would fully address the needs of the poorest, the least privileged and, most crucially, the least print-literate members of society. A new African librarianship has to be set in the context of a new all-embracing information paradigm before it can fully answer their needs.

There is still arguably a failure to consider the continent's information environment as an organic whole, recognizing legitimate needs at all economic and educational levels. These require decisions as to which forms of service provision are appropriate, and as to which needs will be served immediately and which at some subsequent planning stage. This over-arching analysis seems never really to have been attempted. In fact, the level of debate is still that which one would associate with the breakup of an old paradigm rather than the creation of a new one. In such situations the tendency is to put sticking plaster on wounds that require surgery. The contemplation of surgical solutions is frightening, but should not be avoided if a patient is to become fully healthy. For proposals that involve a patient submitting to surgery to be acceptable, however, it must be clear that those proposals are based on clear and sound medical principles. The same is true of proposals that would require such radical changes in the prevailing modes of information provision that they might constitute a new paradigm.

Principles for a New Paradigm

The principles on which proposals for a shift from an emphasis on libraries to an emphasis on total information provision might be attempted are implicit in everything that has been said in the previous chapters. They can be set out in the form of a simple statement with six distinct, but inter-related, elements. We do not claim to have invented any of these elements, but we believe that brought together, each is made stronger and more applicable than any of them is, if taken in isolation. Our contention is that the manifest failure of existing information systems in Africa reveals the need for a new paradigm of information service based on:

1. Financial realism

2. Self-reliance
3. Sustainability
4. Democracy
5. Responsiveness
6. Communication.

does this REALLY help?

Because all of these are themes that have already occurred in various contexts and have been discussed at one level of detail or another, they only require slight further expansion at this point. Then it will be possible to go on to show what might be the implications of their application as the constituent elements of a single approach.

Financial realism is a principle based on Mchombu's precept that information work for Africa must, for any sensible planning period, take the inescapable reality of poverty as a central preoccupation.[48] A number of African states are potentially rich, if their natural resources can be exploited effectively. Others occupy such a marginal natural environment that existence as a nation will always involve struggle. All, even South Africa, if we look at the life of the majority of its people, are poor at present. This does not mean just the financial poverty experienced by institutions, which limits the number and scope of information and library projects, but also poverty as the main fact in the lives of the great majority of potential and actual beneficiaries of services. It can also mean poverty in the information skills that have to be assumed to exist before it is realistic to pursue the practice of traditional librarianship. Information service needs to be designed to help alleviate poverty while functioning within the financial constraints that are the consequences of that poverty. There is absolutely no point in designing services that do not reflect the circumstances of the people and of the national budget.

Ali Mazrui has contended that, if only the will were there, the necessary resources could be found. For instance, he suggests that,

> Even a single major corruption scandal in Kenya is worth the subscriptions of all the journals, in all the disciplines, in all the libraries, in all the public universities of Kenya for the next century.[49]

Yet even if corruption could be eliminated overnight the problems with Africa's libraries would not instantly be solved. The difficulties are more fundamental and more deeply rooted than mere lack of financial resources. The experience of Nigeria in the oil-rich 1970s suggests that sudden flows of money would create the problem for Africa's librarians of just how to use their good fortune to the best effect. The desperate and often thoroughly wasteful attempts of Nigerian librarians in those days to spend their plentiful budgets within the financial year are a salutary lesson for those who think that money is the answer.

Self-reliance posits that if services that are to be completely appropriate to Africa's needs are to be created, ultimately they must emerge from Africa's own intellectual and physical resources. Self-reliance in information is all of a piece with economic, cultural and political self-reliance: a nation which does not achieve it can expect to be the victim of other more powerful nations, in one way or another.[50] At present, ideas on the forms of service (the ubiquitous desire to automate, for instance) are imported from the Northern industrialized countries as if they were the only options available. Information professionals do not ask enough questions about why certain things are done. If they did, they would see that some of these things do not serve the best interests of their clients, or their country. At the same time, donors of various kinds are expected to pay for the implementation of these ideas. It might be good for the donors to pay, in token of the history of exploitation of Africa over the years by their countries of origin. It is not, however, good for Africa that they should pay. It distorts the decision-making process, and effectively hands the control of the whole exercise back to the donors. Olden asks the question as to when, if they genuinely believe that a particular information service is important, African governments will begin to fund it as an essential service, rather than turning to some potential outside source of assistance.[51] Until there is a satisfactory answer to that question, any services that are provided will have a questionable future.

Sustainability follows on naturally from this. The importance of the principle has been set out by Rosenberg in the most challenging fashion, and it provides a real test of the validity of an information service.[52] It means more, however, than that there is merely a reasonable guarantee that some source of funds will continue to be available, at adequate levels, for the foreseeable future. It would not be hard to identify one or two libraries in the North which are so well endowed with funds that they can continue to occupy luxurious premises, and acquire and care for materials on a generous scale, while virtually no one uses them. An institution in this rare position is sustainable, but sustainable more as a museum than a real information service provider. True sustainability means creating something that emerges from the needs, opinions and actions of a community of users themselves. This ensures that they will seek to keep it in existence, despite the difficulties that may face it, because they feel that it is theirs, and that they must safeguard it in their own interests. As Obadiah Moyo points out,

> Rural people unlike their urban counterparts, have to practically participate in matters affecting them, say community health. They would mould the bricks, provide the labour, fetch the water and thatch to see their project through.[53]

This type of initiative, which is the starting point of the projects he supports, is the first test of sustainability. An institution which starts as a response to demand may not, in the end, survive, but it does have the essential dynamic which will enable it to struggle forcefully, and which gives it the chance of true survival.

Democracy demands that citizens should have the information that will enable them to accept the full responsibility of political participation. This principle has driven much recent positive change in information provision,[54] and creates a far reaching requirement for service to the whole of the people, rather than just to minorities who might be literate, articulate, influential, geographically accessible or, even, able to pay. Some of the implications of the principle are set out very clearly by Olden, when he questions the assumptions behind the drive to make Africa part of the paperless society (paperless in this context referring to the application of information technology to information provision).[55] In fact, his contention that technology will leave the majority behind and entrench the privilege of minorities needs to be answered not merely in relation to a future 'information society', but also in relation to contemporary print technology. A truly democratic information service needs to build on the basic assumption that while not every citizen is either literate or computer literate, all have some equivalent set of skills which enables them to function in society and the economy. The precise form that the provision of information services to specific communities must take, would then follow from the balance of skills available in those communities. Thus a university library or an information service to senior government employees could proceed on the assumption of the highest levels of literacy and good computer skills, while at the other extreme, service in a very isolated rural community might reasonably be provided on the assumption of an almost complete reliance on oral communication. Naturally, service at these two extremes would take forms which differed radically.

Responsiveness means providing the information that the people want, when and where they want it. Surveys of users and the development of community profiles are useful in ensuring this, but careful listening to what people say about their needs and the services they obtain is vital, so as to build a feedback loop into the system. In this way a service can be provided which is rooted in clear ideas about users and potential users of information. Official information service has consistently been one-way, and the direction has been top–down. This has failed to shake deep-seated communication preferences and has shown very little capacity to persuade people to accept what officialdom has wanted them to accept. The failure of unresponsive official information systems in the development field has been amply illustrated and explained, most notably by Chambers.[56] To a large extent, what is required instead is a form of just-in-time information service, which answers the needs people reveal to it, when they reveal them. This does not mean passively waiting for specific expressions of need, which was the interpretation of this principle that old-style librarianship tended to offer. A true response to the totality of information need involves taking service out to the public, wherever they are, and positively offering a full range of opportunities that can conveniently be taken up by those who may experience some specific need.

Communication is an emphasis which shifts the balance of service away from providing a response, but not fully accepting the obligation to ensure that it is delivered in a way that recipients can interpret and understand. A service could be democratic and responsive, but still be failing its users if there were not the opportunity for a dialogue which would ensure that understanding and acceptance of information takes place. Ndiaye discusses the relationship between the documentary mode and the communication mode in his synthesis of the form that future information services for Africa might take.[57] In this way he effectively focuses attention on the matter of how information is delivered, but it should not be thought that documentary and communication modes are in any way in opposition to each other. It is the mix and balance of modes which is important. Information workers can use their knowledge of the users to anticipate what will communicate effectively, so as to repackage information from difficult or inaccessible forms into more acceptable forms.[58] These forms might be anything from print or hypermedia, to simple oral delivery, according to circumstances. What is crucial is that there should be a dialogue, or the opportunity for a dialogue, either to deliver the whole response in an oral environment, or to present, contextualize, interpret and, if necessary, modify or substitute some form of information package in a print or computer environment.

References

1. Alemna, A.A. Libraries and the economic development of Ghana. *Aslib Proceedings*, 41, 1989. 119–25. p.119.
2. Parker, J.S. *Unesco and Library Development Planning.* London, Library Association, 1985.
3. Unesco. *Final Report of the Expert Meeting on National Planning of Documentation and Library Services in Africa. Kampala, Uganda, 7–15 December, 1970.* Paris, Unesco, 1971.
4. Kaungamno, E.E. and Ilomo, C.S. *Books Build Nations.* 2 vols. London, Transafrica, 1979. Vol 2. pp.24–5.
5. Parker, J.S. op.cit. p.230.
6. Conference on Information Networks in East Africa, 1973. *Unesco Bulletin for Libraries*, 28, 1974. p.52.
7. Unesco. *Final Report of the Meeting of Experts on Planning Documentation and Library Networks in Africa (NATIS). Brazzaville, People's Republic of Congo, 5–10 July, 1976.* Paris, Unesco, 1976. p.1.
8. Harrison, K.C. *Republic of the Seychelles: Libraries, Documentation and Archives Services.* Paris, Unesco, 1978.
9. Mphundi, B.G. A conceptual framework towards a National Information System for Malawi. *MALA Bulletin*, 2, 1981. 16–33. p.26.
10. Ngaunje, M.A. NATIS in Malawi. *MALA Bulletin*, 4, 1986. 37–43. p.41.
11. Shio, M.J. and Musana, A. *Evaluation of User Seminars Conducted in Tanzania, Zambia, Malawi, Lesotho, Swaziland, Botswana.* Bonn, DES, 1981.
12. Hutteman, L. (ed.) *Establishment, Function and Management of a National Library and Documentation Service* (Harare Workshop Papers). Bonn. DES, 1985.
13. Hutteman, L. (ed.) *Establishment and Management of a National Information Service in Botswana.* (Gaborone Workshop Papers). Bonn/Gaborone, DSE/Botswana National Library Service, 1987.
14. Saracevic, T. Perception of the needs for scientific and technical information in less developed countries. *Journal of Documentation*, 36, 1980. 214–67.
15. Ibid. p.216.
16. Gehrke, U. Information for development. Some problems of national

coordination, regional coordination and international assistance. *INSPEL*, 19, 1985. 166–75.

17. Mchombu, K.J. and Miti, K. Formulation of National Information Policies in Africa: some unlearnt lessons. *International Information and Library Review*, 24, 1992. 139–71.
18. Davies, S. Information, knowledge and power. *IDS Bulletin*, 25, 1994. 1–13.
19. Plumbe, W.J. British librarianship overseas. *Library Association Record*, 62, 1960. 272.
20. Benge, R.C. An expatriate in an emergent country. *Library Association Record*, 63, 1961. 333.
21. Benge, R.C. *Cultural Crisis and Libraries in the Third World*. London, Bingley, 1979.
22. Amadi, A.O. *African Libraries: Western Tradition and Colonial Brainwashing*. Metuchen, NJ, Scarecrow Press, 1981.
23. Durrani, S. Rural information in Kenya. *Information Development*, 1, 1985. 149–57.
24. Mchombu, K.J. On the librarianship of poverty. *Libri*, 32, 1982. 241–50.
25. Opubor, A.E. (ed.) *Rural Africana* (Issue on communication for rural development), 27, 1975.
26. *Rural Africana* (New Series), 1, 1978.
27. Adimorah, E.N.O. Information and documentation for integrated rural development in Africa. *Quarterly Bulletin of the International Association of Agricultural Librarians and Documentalists*, 29, 1984. p.25.
28. Adimorah, E.N.O. An analysis of progress made by public libraries as social institutions in Nigeria. *UNESCO Journal of Information Science Librarianship and Archives Administration*, 5, 1983. p.162.
29. Aboyade, B.O. Communication potentials of the library for non-literates: an experiment in providing information services in a rural setting. *Libri*, 34, 1984. 243–62.
30. Amaratunga, C. and Shute, J. Extension and adult learning in a Ghanaian community. *Canadian Journal of African Studies*, 16, 1982. 549–66.
31. Oladele, B.A. Toward an integrated agricultural information consolidation scheme for farmers in the Nigerian rural areas. *Quarterly Bulletin of the International Association of Agricultural Librarians and Documentalists*, 32, 1987. 98–101.
32. Adimorah, E.N.O. Users and their information needs in Nigeria. *Nigerian Library and Information Science Review*, 1, 1983. 137–48.
33. Aina, L.O. Information needs and information-seeking involvement of farmers in six rural communities in Nigeria. *Quarterly Bulletin of the International Association of Agricultural Librarians and Documentalists*, 30, 1985. 35–40.
34. Nwagha, G.K.N. Information needs of rural women in Nigeria. *Information Development*, 8, 1992. 76–82.
35. Mchombu, K.J. Information needs for rural development: the case study of Malawi. *African Journal of Library, Archives and Information Science*, 2, 1992. 17–32.

36. Sturges, P. and Chimseu, G. Qualitative research in information studies: a Malawian study. *Education for Information*, 14, 1996. 117–26.
37. Ogunsheye, F.A. Education and training for library and information service to rural communities. In: Aboyade, B.O. (ed.) *Education and Training for Library and Information Services in a Predominantly Non-literate Society.* The Hague, FID, 1981. 87–103.
38. Kukobo, R.J. Serving the rural communities: the role of the branch/ area libraries in the organisation and preservation of local records and archives. Paper presented at IFLA pre-sessional Seminar on Education for Librarianship at the Grassroots Level, Nairobi, 13–18 August, 1984.
39. Asamani, J.O. et al. (eds) *Libraries and Literacy. Proceedings of the 7th Standing Conference of the Eastern, Central and Southern African Librarians, Gaborone, 4–8 August, 1986.* Gaborone, Botswana Library Association, 1987.
40. Aboyade, B.O. *Provision of Information for Rural Development.* Ibadan, Fountain Publications, 1987.
41. Chijioke, M.E. Public libraries as information networks: Nigeria in the twenty-first century. *Journal of Librarianship*, 21, 1989. 174–85.
42. Kedem, K.A. Libraries as partners in the fight to eradicate illiteracy in sub-Saharan Africa. *Journal of Library and Information Science*, 16, 1991. 87–101.
43. Kantumoya, A. Public libraries and community information services in Africa. *African Journal of Library, Archives and Information Science*, 2, 1992. 33–8.
44. Dawha, E.M.K. and Makinta, Y. Future rural information services in Nigeria: further thoughts on the role of libraries and their staff. *New Library World*, 94, 1993. 17–22.
45. Zaaiman, R.B., Roux, P.J.A. and Rykheer, J.H. *The Use of Libraries for the Development of South Africa* (Final report on an investigation for the South African Institute for Librarianship and Information Science). Pretoria, Unisa, 1988.
46. Mgoqi, W.A. Looking back in order to look forward. *Cape Librarian*, Feb., 1995. 30–1.
47. Lor, P.J. Africanisation of South African libraries: a response to some recent literature. Paper delivered at the Info Africa Nova Conference, Pretoria, 4 May 1993.
48. Mchombu, K.J. On the librarianship of poverty. *Libri*, 32, 1982. 241–50.
49. Mazrui, A. Challenge to a duel of words. *Sunday Nation* (Kenya), 18 August 1996.
50. Sturges, P. International transfer of information and national self-sufficiency: the case of Botswana. In: *Proceedings of the 49th Annual Meeting of the American Society for Information Science.* Medford, NJ, ASIS, 1986. 320–5.
51. Olden, A. *Libraries in Africa: Pioneers, Policies, Problems.* Lanham, MD, Scarecrow Press, 1995.
52. Rosenberg, D. Can libraries in Africa ever be sustainable? *Information Development*, 10, 1994. 247–51.

53. Empowerment of rural people. *RLRDP News Bulletin*, 1, 1995. p.5.
54. Mchombu, K.J. Information support for democratization in Africa. In: Feather, J. (ed.) *Transforming Libraries and Educating Librarians*. London, Taylor Graham, 1997. 41–56.
55. Olden, A. Sub-Saharan Africa and the paperless society. *Journal of the American Society for Information Science*, 38. 1987. 298–304.
56. Chambers, R. All power deceives. *IDS Bulletin*, 25, 1994. 14–26.
57. Ndiaye, A.R. *Communication à la base: enraciner et épanouir*. Dakar, ENDA, 1994.
58. Saracevic, T. Consolidation of information: a concept of needed information products and services for developing countries. In: *Proceedings of the 48th Annual Meeting of the American Society for Information Science*. Medford, NJ, ASIS, 1985. 150-4.

Chapter Five

A Foundation for the Future

When the principles set out at the end of the last chapter are used as a set of criteria for assessing the achievements of African national and public library services, the reasons why so much of the content of this book is written in a spirit of scepticism about the usefulness of these services should be clear.

National and Public Libraries

The national library tends to be almost entirely an irrelevance in African terms. Globally the national library building can be nearly as much a symbol of national identity as the national theatre, the national stadium or the national airport. In fact, while many African countries have most parts of the full national prestige set, in comparatively few cases does this include the national library building. It is questionable whether any of these symbols are worth the immense sums lavished on them by nations painfully deprived of basic facilities for the bulk of their population. This scepticism extends not merely to the idea of a national library building but also to some of its services. The national library can seem like an irony as repository of the nation's written output, where that output is tiny; as the creator of a national bibliography, when the listings are in the service of non-existent scholarly enterprises; as a central focus for library activity, when library activity is moribund. The effect would not be enhanced if it were to occupy the kind of building that makes a capital city a little more like Paris or London.

The idea is often proposed that if there were such an institution as a national library (where there is none), or if it could be funded sufficiently to perform a full set of functions (where it manifestly achieves little), then things would begin to improve. This idea is a divergence from the hard path of actually bringing services to the people. It places faith in a mechanism that never has operated and can never operate in the future. A bureaucracy at the centre, or a service to a highly-educated elite, will not of itself generate an all-pervasive service to the nation. Only a multiplicity of local initiatives can do that. Zimbabwe has some of the best library services at all levels in the whole of Africa despite, rather than because of, its almost wholly ineffective National Library and Documentation Service. A national library service in the context of Africa is only much use as a facilitator and funder of local projects. In fact, the best African national library services tend to approximate to this function, as their role is almost entirely that of provider of public library services.

Yet the public library, whether provided as part of a national library service or by local administration, or by some NGO, has not been a notable success. Rosenberg's query about the sustainability of public libraries in Africa is almost, but not entirely, unanswerable. The public library was an implant which African governments have virtually never financed to levels at which it could function effectively. It tends to survive on donations and the minimal financial support which will keep a building open and some salaried staff at their posts. As Nzotta has put it:

> The branch libraries in Nigeria are grossly inadequate to achieve their major objective of making public library services easily accessible to a wide cross-section of the populace. There are very few branch libraries relative to the areas and populations of the states they serve. These branch libraries are poorly staffed and funded. Their collections are very small in size and could hardly meet the needs of the clients.[1]

Its resources are generally pathetic and not at all nourishing for the minds of the few adult users. In fact, the libraries are not usually empty because as Chijioke explains:

> The largest category of individuals visiting our libraries remains the private students seeking a quiet place to study their own textbooks with no interest in the stated purpose of the facilities.[2]

Only in South Africa, where the city libraries compare favourably with those of any developed country and branch libraries are to be found in every small town, and in one or two other exceptions to this generalization in other parts of Africa, are there good public libraries.

When one looks at an exception, one finds that it usually serves a rather more sophisticated and demanding community, and is managed in an energetic and innovatory manner. The Public Library of Bulawayo, Zimbabwe, for instance, celebrated its centenary in 1996 and until independence served only the white community of the city. Today its doors are open to all and it thrives despite unfavourable financial circumstances. The grant from a City Council with many calls on its purse has been small for some time and reduced in recent years, but the library has defied this with an expansionist and entrepreneurial policy. It has opened new branches and acquired a new mobile library. It has a large, and much used, reading room for students in the basement, with a textbook collection. It loans videos, cassettes, talking books and braille books. Its services to children make full use of story hours and competitions, attracting high levels of use. All of this has encouraged record levels of loans and a rising membership, in excess of 17,000. Virtually all of the well-publicized 'extra' services cost the user directly, and it has a 'Red Carpet Service' providing new bestsellers for subscribers, and a similar 'Super Text Service' for the best new textbooks. Its bookbindery sells its services to the public, and about the only alternative the library does not contemplate, is lying down to die. Bulawayo Public Library has a strong claim to being the best public library between South Africa and the Mediterranean fringe, and it proves that success is possible. The tragedy is that it is such an exception.

Despite the existence of this good example, it is hard to see most existing public libraries as viable in current African circumstances. This does not mean that public libraries should be done away with willy nilly, although there may be a few so far from being functional that they might be closed down with little loss. Libraries which are definitely meeting some community needs should be consolidated and those that are not should be used as the base for new and practical programmes of services, devised to fit the finances available. Successful libraries presuppose not merely satisfied users, but the political will to sustain a service. No one in their right mind would interfere unduly with this. However, even libraries that are successful might usefully re-examine their priorities. This is particularly true of those in South Africa, which have built their success on service to highly literate and bibliographically sophisticated users (principally white, or educated in a European tradition).

The presence of large numbers of schoolchildren and college students doing their homework and making limited use of the collections and services is sometimes regarded with distaste by librarians expecting more demanding users. This is a considerable mistake, as discouraging this unsophisticated type of use would tend to choke off the potential sophisticated users of the next generation. Attachment to the library, even attachment of a somewhat tenuous kind, is not to be rejected. The hold of the public library over its clientele is being challenged everywhere in the world (even Iceland has seen its truly exceptional rates of use decline slightly with the impact of local television stations and the availability of videos). Where readers are less committed, the challenge is obviously much greater. The fiction loans at Bulawayo Public Library fell noticeably during the six months immediately following the availability of MNet TV reception dishes. Although the extent to which the reading habit and the television habit are interchangeable is certainly limited, it is enough to make a difference to library systems which desperately need to be able to demonstrate reader loyalty.

The one thing that would offer most encouragement for the future of public libraries is the spontaneous creation of new ones as a result of community action. Such occurrences are to be found, but more commonly in some countries than others. In Senegal, tiny *bibliothèques du quartier* can be found quite frequently in the high density suburbs of Dakar. They are usually part of a community centre, such as the Centre de Lecture et d'Animation Publique (CLAP) in Guediawaye. This particular example is funded from a number of sources: the local society Action en Développement provides the basic funds; donor organizations like Bibliothèque Lecture Développement (BLD) give small contributions; and the 205 current members pay a monthly subscription which is small but not insignificant in relation to local incomes. The library is a smallish room in an unpretentious main street building, which contains other facilities like a kindergarten, in an area inhabited by the poor of Dakar. It has a volunteer librarian, and novels, children's books and information leaflets (on topics like AIDS) on home-made shelving around a small table for readers. It is extremely humble from any point of view, but it is a community initiative, managed from within the community.

What the CLAP represents is just one manifestation of what Ndiaye calls *les nouveaux phénomènes associatifs*.[3] By this he means the community organizations which are tending to supplement, and even replace, both official structures and the more traditional forms of local social organizations. Ndiaye is able to draw attention to a considerable range of such organizations, with numbers of members between them totalling hundreds of thousands in each of several francophone West African countries. He draws the conclusion that this movement is so significant that,

> *L'information et la communication à la base doivent etre repensées relativement au nouveau contexte ainsi crée, marqué par la présence déterminante de ces structures associatives paysannes.*[4] [Grassroots information and communication must be thought through afresh in the new context established by the dominant influence of this peasant associative movement.]

A similar spirit is to be found elsewhere, represented in South Africa, for instance, by street committees, women's groups and leagues, burial societies and a host of other semi-formal groupings. Again this popular associative spirit can show itself in the form of a library. In 1985, a youth group in Kwathema township obtained assistance from the NGO READ (Read, Educate and Develop) to set up a library.[5] They also obtained funds from local companies, and accommodation from the Catholic Church. The library they created was run by a management committee from the youth group, who began to develop it into a broader cultural and educational centre. An unusually high concentration of such small community libraries is to be found in and around Bulawayo, many, but not all, owing to the initiative of Obadiah Moyo, a local citizen with a strong sense of mission regarding libraries.[6] Although scattered, the examples of spontaneous creation of libraries are there, albeit in a form slightly different from the fully-fledged 'official' public library. It is surely out of them that a new stronger African public library movement will emerge.

Services to the Young

Africa is often described as a continent where reading is an alien and unpopular activity. The colonial education system, inherited by Africa and expanded since independence, seems to have presented reading as something to be learned, rather than a means to enjoyment. The skill of reading is still taught in a mechanical and inflexible way, so that people tend to associate books with the hard grind of study, rather than the luxury of leisure. What is more, both the content of the books and the solitude required to read them conflict with traditional values, making them at once less comprehensible and less acceptable. Some parents who cannot read themselves, and who are uneasy about what their children are learning, do not provide the necessary home support and encouragement, and the homes themselves are overcrowded, noisy and, after sunset, too dark for the printed word to be seen. Even many of Africa's educated elite are non-readers, content only to use the printed word to pass exams and acquire certificates, but once free from the tyranny of books, reluctant to read again.

The conclusion which some commentators tend to draw from all this is that Africa presents a hostile environment to library development and that only after such obstacles have been overcome, and the preconditions for a reading society have been set in place, will the library start to fulfil its true potential. This line of argument has consoled librarians who are anxious about the poor reaction of the community to the services they provide. Indeed, it has become such a standard formula that its recitation tends to blind those who adopt it to causes for optimism. Yet many years ago Chakava pointed out that:

> Readership surveys conducted during the last five years in countries like Nigeria, Kenya, Benin, Ghana, and Uganda have shown that more and more people, especially the young, are reading for pleasure.[7]

As an example of such survey evidence, the Kenya National Academy for Advancement of Arts and Science's survey of reading habits and preferences,[8] which was published as long ago as 1980, found 91 per cent of children claiming to read for pleasure. The supporting information, such as the expressed preference for comics over story books, lends credibility to the findings. The children also expressed a stronger preference for stories with distant rather than local settings. This runs directly counter to the accepted wisdom that lack of local content is the main disincentive to reading among African children. More recent work in Nigeria tends to shift support back towards local content, but not so strongly as to devalue the exotic themes and content of imported books.[9] Taken as a whole, these surveys do emphasize the need for fostering publications with genuine local content. A further interesting finding from the Nigerian study is that the importance of illustrations and print quality may be overestimated by commentators on children's literature.

What no survey has denied is that young people's taste for comic books is very strong. In the British tradition of attitudes towards literature for children, there is a clear desire to forget this fact. Comics are regarded as vulgar items, probably American, which, when not actually harmful, are educationally useless. The French have no such inhibitions, granting the *bandes dessinées* the status of art or literature, and comfortably accepting their value to both young and adult readers. The same is true in francophone Africa, where *bandes dessinées* are published by the most reputable of publishing houses, alongside their academic lists. For instance, NEA, the most prestigious house in Senegal has published a history of the country in comic book form, *Le Senegal et Leopold Sedar Senghor*, various adventures of Moussa le Vagabond by Saliou Sene, and Samba Fall's *L'ombre de Boy Melakh.*

That we are not just talking about children and their reading in some kind of isolation from the rest of society should be clear. Young people are effectively changing the balance of society in a way that makes their abilities and preferences an immediate key to the future needs of society. The population of sub-Saharan Africa is growing at an annual average rate of over 3 per cent. The cumulative effect of this sort of growth in recent decades is that half of the population is under the age of 15. The majority of these young people receive formal schooling and are gaining the basic skills of literacy, which their parents less commonly had available to them. The trend of population growth alone is reason to believe that a reading society is in the process of emerging in Africa.

The rapidly growing and, proportionately, very young population has a desperate thirst for education. Africa's governments have long recognized this by devoting extremely large percentages, often as much as one-third of their total expenditure, to education. What governments and ministries of education seem less frequently to accept, or even consider, is that book and library provision should form an essential component of this investment. The library profession also has not recognized the full significance of the information dimension in education. The neglect of this sector is extremely unfortunate, when its potential demand for library services is greatest and its need strongest. In this, African librarians are following a precedent set too often in the past in other continents. Public library service to children has frequently been comparatively undervalued, and school library service has been relegated to the last place on a scale of priorities.

Such biases have a particularly unfortunate effect when transferred to Africa. It is not uncommon to find a public library swarming with school children but devoid of adult readers. The collection may even have what appears to be an impressive stock of adult material, well organized and representative of the type of materials to be found in good branch libraries anywhere in the Northern countries. Set alongside this might well be a children's section, comprising a few tattered and filthy books, hidden away in some corner of the library, uninviting, badly organized and clearly forming a marginal part of the librarian's concern. Public libraries quite simply find it hard to accept that they are, and will be for some decades, institutions where the demand is from children, and where the response needs to be directed at children. It may be a hard pill to swallow for librarians trained for an idealized Northern version of the public library, but swallowed it should be. After all, where is the shame in serving the youth of the country, and doing it well?

The continuing debate on the future of libraries reflects only the barest appreciation of the vital importance of service to Africa's young people. The services provided for them do sometimes include the menu of story hours, play readings, film shows, painting competitions, quizzes and talks that one would expect to find in Northern countries, but not frequently. Book box schemes to remote rural areas, usually involving schools, represent a typical response of library systems. As a beginning they are important, but the size of the collection and the frequency of its exchange are seldom sufficient to satisfy or nurture a demand for books and reading.

Instances of responsive approaches can be found, but are extremely rare. For example, when in 1975 a user survey of three new branch libraries in Lusaka, Zambia, showed that 60 per cent of users were children who did not attend school, the bulk of the funds for purchasing additional material for the libraries was directed towards their needs. The kind of evidence that was used to justify this shift in emphasis is available in many other places. Analysis of users of community libraries set up for adults shows that the overwhelming majority of actual patrons are school children

(70–90 per cent of users in such centres in countries as diverse as Botswana, Mali, Mozambique and Zimbabwe).

One can also cite isolated examples of similar reactions elsewhere. In Zimbabwe a Children's Literature Foundation was set up to encourage Zimbabwean writing for children, and story sessions in children's own languages have been organized by libraries. Small collections of books suitable for parents and children to read together have been distributed via the Adult Literacy Association of Zimbabwe, and it was intended to make these as widely available as possible, even to the extent of lodging them in private houses where no formal library structure existed. These initiatives have, sadly, had little impact, and a more typical situation was that in Kenya in 1978, when a 75 per cent cut in the Kenya National Library Service budget resulted in the cessation of all purchases of children's material. Even the excellent township libraries of Bulawayo, Zimbabwe, have sometimes been forced by lack of sufficient books to withdraw the lending service to children. As recently as 1986 it was possible to find it stated that 'Library service to children is a virgin area in Nigerian librarianship'.[10]

School libraries are also neglected. Even where some semblance of a school library exists, it is frequently inadequately staffed, with an appallingly sparse collection, and is thus marginal in terms of its impact on the teaching–learning process. As Ojiambo points out, surveys show overwhelming problems, including: lack of government policy for school libraries, shortages of finance, staff, equipment and library materials.[11] The majority of schools possess no library and no librarian, just a few books which are locked away from the prying fingers of eager and clamorous children anxious to acquire fresh knowledge. The story is told of a visitor to a school in South Africa being ceremoniously shown the jealously guarded school library, which consisted of three books (two of which were the Bible and the Koran). Even a seemingly well-stocked library may be a disappointment on closer examination. In one example, for instance:

> The donations of books that had been received from embassies, government sources etc., were hardly a riveting read for children from this part of the world. They included the lives of American presidents, histories of the UK's Royal Family and Parliamentary system, and a whole row of books in Russian. There was one small shelf devoted to African literature; well thumbed and ragged copies indicated the popularity of this section. But as the librarian pointed out, 'We have no funds to

expand our purchase of books and at commercial outlets they are too expensive.'[12]

It is not just the swiftly growing number of young people that calls for a more positive response to the library and information needs of children; there are also compelling arguments within Africa's educational system which call for a greater library involvement. To the casual observer, the education of its citizens since independence can be counted as one of Africa's success stories. From extremely inauspicious beginnings, when education was the preserve of a tiny minority, primary education is now no longer a dream for most children, the doors of secondary schools are opening to a growing majority, and increasing opportunities for tertiary level education and training are becoming available. Yet education in Africa is in deep crisis, a crisis of similar proportions to that in which librarianship finds itself, but one of far greater consequence.

From colonial times up until the present day, education in Africa has been criticized as a system whose purpose is examination rather than education. The whole focus of attention tends to be on the final examination, which can be passed only by strictly following the prescribed curriculum, which must be taught in the prescribed way, usually following a single prescribed textbook. Rote learning is the norm, with good books and good teachers generally in short supply. A large number of the primary level teachers are ill-equipped to teach effectively, the secondary teaching force is overstretched and undermotivated, while the university sector is disenchanted, lacking the essential research resources upon which good university-level teaching depends. As a result, children and students are taught, rather than being encouraged to learn, and what is worse, they are often all taught the same facts, at the same time and in the same way, regardless of their abilities.[13]

The 'book famine' or 'book hunger' which we have referred to before does not merely mean an absence of libraries in schools but, more crucially, a dire shortage of textbooks. Pupils share books that were designed to be studied individually, books are passed on from year to year, getting more and more tattered with each new group of users, and parents who can ill-afford it are required to contribute money for the purchase of essential books that the state cannot provide. This is despite a large number of very highly funded textbook projects, supported by organizations like the World Bank. These projects seem to have been like a drop in the ocean of demand, and have only alleviated the situation temporarily in some places. What exist are educational systems which do not generally even seek to provide the type of resource environment in which innovation and creative ideas can flourish.

To make things worse, the faith in education as a means for both the salvation of the individual and the nation, which inspired the leaders of African independence and convinced them to invest a considerable financial outlay, has been severely tested in recent years. The modern employment sector, which witnessed a boom after independence, has for many years stagnated and declined, with insufficient jobs being created to satisfy the aspirations of a potential workforce with plentiful paper qualifications. Unemployment began to emerge among primary school leavers in the 1960s, among secondary school leavers in the 1970s, and has subsequently affected university graduates. Although shortage of suitably qualified personnel is still described as one of Africa's more persistent problems, the educational system's achievements have generally not been in the direction of providing those personnel, but instead in producing a better qualified cadre of the unemployed.

This has led to a serious crisis of confidence in education, which in the past has generally been regarded as a vital component of successful economic performance. Although some writers still reaffirm the 'profound beneficial implications of education in development',[14] there is no longer unanimity on this. The counter view is that education cannot simply be treated as a contributor to economic success, but may, on the contrary, be a luxury to be enjoyed when that economic success has been achieved. As one writer puts it,

> Independence raised the expectations of the ordinary man in Africa. He asked for the good things of life which had been promised before independence. One of these good things was education.[15]

In the early 1970s some economists openly questioned the entire premise that education in abundance beyond literacy is an unmitigated social good and an engine for development. They argued that, on the contrary, education was capable of being an investment in idle human resources. They suggested that, while in the 1950s and 1960s there was a genuine need for educated personnel, by the end of the 1960s this was not matched by a real increase in new jobs. This had not been noticed immediately because the demand for workers generated by localization and the ambitious projects of new governments was not seen as a temporary phase, but rather as a normal condition. But gradually it began to emerge that education and employment creation were not marching in step. Suggestions as to why this happened, apart from the general economic climate, include the import of labour-saving technology; the comparatively high wages being paid to modern sector employees, which forced employers to limit staffing levels; the continuing dependence on expatriate staff and, paradoxically, the success, over the previous three decades, in opening up educational opportunities.

The argument will probably never be satisfactorily resolved, and there is some evidence to support a reassertion of the more optimistic view of education.[16] The World Bank, for instance, which has preferred its involvement to be confined to areas where a quantifiable outcome can be guaranteed, generally seems to accept the view that countries which invest heavily in schooling have measurable advantages over those that do not. Some countries which have substantially improved their ranking in economic indicators (Togo and the Congo Republic, for instance) have a correspondingly strong commitment to educational investment, while others (such as Niger, Burkina Faso) which have a poor or declining record of schooling, have not improved economically in a comparable way. What the figures seem to show is that where education, particularly primary education, is more readily available there tend to be higher levels of personal income and associated improvements in nutrition and health. The sequence of causation is open to question, and it would be easy to argue that the improvements do not arise from the benefits of education, but at least this line of argument is some relief from the pessimism about education that has prevailed recently.

Gloomy views of education may seem to suggest that the prospects for library services to education are gloomy too. In practice the opposite ought to be true: the crises in education ought to offer opportunities for library and information work. Various new approaches, for which the guiding principle is 'pedagogical decentralization',[17] amount to a move away from centralized curricula towards learning that is better matched to the needs of the individual and the community. This has led to a different view of formal schooling in Africa, which suggests that:

Formal schooling is essentially complementary in nature to less formal systems that impart vocational skills and the weaknesses of many earlier educational strategies lay in their disregard of the existence of highly efficient informal educational structures. Perhaps formal schooling largely through the provision of literacy, numeracy, and general education generates a basic 'ability to learn' that is vital in the innovatory development process.[18]

A reduced emphasis on formal schooling and a shift towards informal structures presents opportunities for a revitalized information service.

The systems being referred to include 'education with production'. This is probably best known through the work of Patrick van Rensberg in Botswana.[19] This reasserts the values of traditional education by imparting useful skills through practical experience, alongside more conventional schooling. Other new curricula which are broadly conceived and more adaptive to Africa's educational needs are being developed, tested and revised. All these approaches start from a perception of the needs of citizens in society as it presently is and as it might be in the immediate future. Moreover, all emphasize an enhanced interaction between the teacher and the taught, and lay particular stress on the importance of the teaching and learning materials that are part of that process.

The implications for libraries, although seemingly quite obvious, have not been taken up by Africa's librarians. Their response has seldom gone beyond a half-hearted plea for governments to provide more school libraries. Ocholla has described some policy formation activities taking place in Kenya which amount to the first steps towards a useful response by government.[20] Yet it is clear that for the most part, the struggle to provide a sufficient number of textbooks is more than enough for governments to handle. School libraries will have to wait quite some time before they can hope for wholehearted government support.

This is a big problem when African librarians themselves are still only half convinced of the importance of librarianship for young people. School libraries are particularly likely to be neglected or ignored while this mentality persists, for their librarians work largely alone and have difficulty in finding means to present a collective case for their specialization. Teachers, as distinct from educational theorists, are even harder to convince of the value of libraries. Too many of them are content to persist with the rigid and sterile teaching methods which they themselves experienced as children. Such attitudes contribute to a very unfavourable environment for the improvement of school libraries and the practice of school librarianship.

Parents, encouragingly enough, can be found taking a more positive attitude. In Zimbabwe there are numerous examples of parent groups building school libraries with their own hands, in the expectation of government funding for the materials to go in them. In Kenya there are good numbers of parent-promoted school libraries, funded on the *harambee* basis, or using the usual repertoire of sponsored walks and other fund raising techniques. Charging a small fee for library use, or requiring the donation of a book by each pupil-user are other methods used to supply what official funding neglects. When there is such clear evidence of parent commitment there is real hope that this vital sector can be developed in some countries at least.

For the situation to be improved radically, it is important for librarians to be as engaged as, or more so than, the parents. For this to happen, the education of librarians needs to place a much stronger emphasis on the rationale for school libraries and the techniques of school librarianship. African information and library schools can make a major contribution by striving to ensure that their graduates meet these requirements. There is also the need for those responsible for library services in their countries to promote the inclusion of a more positive approach towards school libraries in the courses provided by institutions of teacher training. When both librarians and teachers are more firmly convinced of the case for libraries in schools there will be scope for a better case to be made to ministries of education than is done at present. This is no easy programme but it is a vital one if, as is essential, school libraries are to be an effective part of a new approach to librarianship in Africa.

Services to Higher Education

No programme for the improvement of information service to education would be complete unless it took proper account of higher education. Yet the problems in this sector are also acute. The central problem when one turns to higher education is no longer lack of recognition of the importance of library and information services, but one of the sheer expense of providing such services properly. When one looks at higher education in Africa, one finds a story of aspirations blunted by deteriorating financial reality. Academic libraries are inevitably expensive to provide. Wherever they are in the world, they need to stock large quantities of costly publications, many of them imported, and they are likely to require elaborate bibliographic and related support services. Their staff must necessarily be highly trained. Because academic libraries are so costly, it is arguable that they are the type of library which suffers most damagingly from the poverty of African countries.

The many fine library buildings illustrated by Sitzman[21] include a high proportion of university libraries, but in the 1990s it has been a depressing experience to walk through the echoing public areas and the dusty stacks of these buildings. Deterioration of collections has been considerable. The situation can be utterly catastrophic, as for Makere University, Uganda, during the worst of the Amin years. There,

> The existing holdings had to be defended with barbed wire because the Librarian and his colleagues found pages of scientific journals being used to wrap groundnuts in the local market. Library attendants had sold off the books for the value of the paper to supplement their abysmally low wages.[22]

Even in a wealthier country such as Nigeria, low wages are a problem, with many librarians and other university employees needing a second source of income to support themselves and their families. Librarians returning to their homes from Europe have been known to use the residue of travel grants to buy and take with them machines that might help them earn money through means as diverse as photocopying and popcorn making. An examination of the collections of academic libraries in Nigeria showed that, before 1979, 80 per cent of total collections consisted of imported material (with the figure for journals taken alone reaching 90 per cent).[23] Import restrictions and exchange controls have subsequently reduced imports to virtually nothing, and collections are much diminished in size and scope.

Nations saw their universities as leading them to further stages in development through investment in human resources and through the beneficial effects of the research they could support. Such has been their decline that when the World Bank published its report on *Education in Sub-Saharan Africa* in 1988,[24] it identified the revitalization of university education as a major priority. Various international agencies have sought to provide guidance and assistance, and a good proportion of this has gone towards helping university libraries acquire books, continue journal subscriptions and incorporate information technology into their systems.

This donor support has been vital because most African universities are able to allocate barely 1 per cent of their budgets to the library. While a donor may sometimes take on the responsibility of financially shoring up the library of an institution across the range of its needs, it is much more common for help to take the form of intervention in a specific area of need, most commonly in the form of book donations, help with information technology implementation or staff training. Just looking at book donations, it becomes clear that even when donors are willing and able to meet expressed need, rather than merely passing on material that is conveniently available for donation, a coherent collection development process of the kind essential to a good university library becomes more or less impossible. For a university library the receipt of study or research material, however interesting in its own right, is not of much value if it is not very specifically relevant to the institution's own programmes.

In practice donations often relate to a donor organization's subject interests, do not always come on a regular basis, may be available only over a period too short to make exploitation worthwhile, and do not offer much hope for long-term sustainability of collections.[25] On the last point, it is quite common to find that at the termination of a donor programme none of the necessary continuing expenditure on journal subscriptions, training or information technology is continued by the recipient institution. This leaves the library to revert very swiftly to its previous state.

The starting point for improvement must be good planning and a vigorous management of limited resources. Unfortunately, a survey of African university libraries carried out by Rosenberg in 1995 shows that there is little sign of these at present. She discovered that:

> There is little evaluation of performance or investigation of library decisions. Statistics are collected, but do not form the basis of future decision-making. Librarians said that they were not being asked to be accountable or prove their value to the education process . . . . They are not in control of their own destinies and do not plan ahead to meet the challenges of decreasing funds. Rather they react when crisis occurs.[26]

Evidence of libraries taking some control of their own destinies is rare. Financial crisis has been alleviated to a very limited extent by acquisition tactics such as buying from local suppliers whenever possible, developing exchange programmes, the use of Unesco coupons and resource sharing schemes. More rigorous management of stock, to ensure that what is bought and kept on the shelves is really needed and will be used, is to some extent a positive consequence of the difficulties. Moves to stimulate local academic publishing, fraught with difficulties though they may be, are also very positive.

None of these ideas, however, answer the need for more income than is generally available. To provide funds for the library Alemna suggests alumni appeals, the setting up of offices to pursue donors, and twinning with libraries in industrialized countries.[27] This, however, is just a slightly more systematic application of the begging bowl, which has provided useful immediate help, but which offers nothing for the long-term future. In just one or two cases, librarians have asked why they should not assume more responsibility for income generating, so that the library might have more command of its own destiny. Moi University, in Kenya, has actually allowed the librarian to raise income and retain control of it for library purposes. Given this opportunity, a set of library charges has been developed (rental for study carrels, fees for certain kinds of searches, etc.) and the income has been devoted to replacing cuts in the library budget. This may be anathema to defenders of the free library principle, but at least it offers the prospect of a library which is more than a series of empty rooms.

There is also scope to use the idea of information consolidation.[28] This involves some agency, based in an industrialized country which has access to the whole range of literature, evaluating and condensing information materials (books, reports, serials or whatever) for distribution to institutions serving specific user groups. Condensing means selecting, summarizing and, possibly, physically reducing material in size by the use of forms such as microfiche or CD-ROM. The groups served might be any group of specialists such as medical students or civil engineers, and the institutions involved would frequently be academic libraries. The crucial feature of this process is that it should be done by specialists, in the closest touch with the user community.[29] It is not an activity for generalist librarians.

Examples of consolidation programmes set up with developing

countries in mind are the Rockefeller Foundation's CISmed and CIShealth, both aimed at improving access to biomedical and health literature.[30] CISmed provided a core collection of high quality biomedical journals, initially on microfiche, but potentially on CD-ROM, supported by a workstation for searching purposes, and a link with a document delivery organization. The technology could be varied according to developments in the market, but the essential features stayed constant. The collections were selected on the basis of quality and evidence of wide use. Costs were kept to the minimum in all aspects of the service. The orientation was towards users rather than librarians. It was intended as a way of providing a genuine core information service in the subject area at a cost significantly cheaper than running a conventional library or information centre. It has to be noted that such services can never be free: either a donor pays for them, or they are paid for by the beneficiaries. The important thing is that they bring high quality service into a cost range which a developing country institution could afford if it were serious in its information-providing intentions.

A strict realism over the role that the academic library can hope to play in the immediate future is essential. This means that the comprehensive university library, accumulating materials speculatively, on the grounds that future teachers and researchers may obtain value from them, is an unrealistic concept in most African countries. All but a few university libraries need to accept a role much more directly tied to immediate teaching requirements. Recognition of this principle is implicit in the book bank system applied in Uganda. In 1989 the Ugandan government purchased multiple copies of textbooks on the recommendation of departments at Makerere University. These are administered by the university library, but kept in departments, from where they are loaned to students, if necessary for the whole academic year. This system recognizes that students will be largely restricted to a textbook-centred approach to learning, but regards this as superior to the previous situation in which the library scarcely functioned and students could not afford to buy books for themselves. It is an approach which may horrify librarians and progressive educationalists, but it has the virtue of guaranteeing a solid minimum of provision, as opposed to continuing to espouse high principles while providing virtually nothing.

There is also a strong case for suggesting that African university librarians should recognize that the treasured goal of providing a general research library needs to be abandoned, at least for the foreseeable future. Most research collecting is probably more appropriately handled at this stage of development by specialized institutes which collect in very specific and well-defined fields. These may be administered by the university itself in some cases, but they may also be the special libraries which provide a focus for the next section of this chapter. If the university library is to provide research materials, it too should specialize.

None of this is a particularly comfortable vision for services to higher education, but at least it offers opportunities for action. A stunned acceptance of catastrophe, and a prayer that some outside force will retrieve the situation, has been the normal response for too long. Academic librarians owe it to their clientele to adopt unpalatable but realistic alternatives so that a better service than is currently offered can be put in place.

Services to Research

Naturally some of the issues dealt with under the previous heading apply here too, but there is a whole sector of government research stations, and a research need in ministries, parastatals and NGOs, which are served by special libraries and information units. Despite almost overwhelming difficulties, research does go on in Africa and there has been a certain attention to it at the policy level. In 1964 in Lagos, the International Conference on the Organisation of Research and Training recommended that each country should allocate 0.5 per cent of GNP to research and development expenditure. Two Unesco Conferences of the Ministers of Science and Technology in Africa (CASTAFRICA) met in 1974 and 1987. The former made many policy recommendations which the latter more or less reiterated, with additions, since so little had been achieved. CASTAFRICA II's recommendations can be summed up as a call for better policy and planning, institutional structures and financial resources. Between these, the Lagos Plan of Action had been adopted by the OAU in 1980, and this had also called for investment of sufficient resources to promote science and technology. Virtually none of this exhortation has had a significant effect. Even when a country such as Ivory Coast does manage to exceed the 1964 recommended level of expenditure, of the 0.6 per cent it spends, two-thirds goes to pay administrative costs.[31]

Research is an expensive activity, requiring highly qualified research staff and technician support. A ratio between these two categories of 1:2 was suggested by CASTAFRICA I. There is also frequently a need for sensitive equipment, powerful computer capacity and a continuing maintenance budget. All of these types of expenditure are needed over long periods of time and, because science is essentially a speculative activity, do not actually guarantee useful results. As measured by the patenting of inventions, African science is not productive. In the 1970s, 400–500 patent applications per year were filed in Nigeria, of which only about 20 or 25 were generated from within the country itself. Most member states of the francophone African Organisation of Intellectual Property (AOPI) could only generate patents in ones and twos. Over the years research has tended to be concentrated on basic problems, despite the desperate need for applicable research in African economies.

This is fortunately not true everywhere, and good examples of research with practical applications can be found. The Department of Applied Biology and Biochemistry at the National University of Science and Technology in Bulawayo, Zimbabwe, had nine or ten projects and groups of projects in simultaneous progress in the early 1990s, for instance. Much of the work has direct application to the food production industries of the country. An extensive study of the biology of amphistomes, endoparasites which infect cattle, goats and sheep in Zimbabwe, tackles the lack of knowledge on the pathogenesis of a chronic disease which causes loss of weight and anaemia in ruminants. Another group of projects has undertaken quantitative determination of proteins, lipids and ascorbic acid in indigenous Zimbabwean legumes and fruits. A method for the determination of lactic acid in ostrich meat was developed in the department for use by the Cold Storage Commission in the storage and packing of this increasingly popular foodstuff. Work on the fruit of the marula tree examined the retention of vitamin C in marula wine, and the pectin content of the skin and pulp of the fruit was investigated to aid jam production. Yet another project investigated the occurrence of aflatoxins in Zimbabwean agricultural projects, because of their association with high levels of liver cancer in neighbouring Mozambique. All of this was done without particularly generous financial allocations and while the department was still in shared laboratory space. A good flow of conference papers and publications has resulted, while at the same time the research is directly benefiting the country.

Unfortunately, even when scientists are producing useful results, they are not always given the encouragement to persist. At a conference in Nairobi, over 200 of Africa's leading scientists, from 40 countries, complained that their research efforts, which were producing results that in many instances had global implications, were being frustrated by government neglect. Professor Samson Gombe, secretary of the African Academy of Science, cited an example from Kenya:

> where a special lamp was designed to detect inferior coffee berries before processing, an important function for high-quality blends and one that is hard to perform by eye alone.[32]

Because of the lack of interest from the Kenyan coffee industry, as well as the absence of any effective form of legislation to protect research and intellectual property, the lamp was patented in Europe, and was likely to be re-exported back to Kenya, with considerable loss of face and foreign exchange. Singh indicates that the problem is endemic, as:

> At a symposium organised in Yaounde in 1980 by the African Organisa-tion of Intellectual Property (AOPI), it was pointed out that a great many exploitable patents covering African products were gathering dust in files; technical information does not circulate properly, nor is it used to good effect. Little is known about the advantages of patents and the need to exploit them for purposes of technical development.[33]

Documentation of African research is generally inadequate. Much very high quality work actually takes place outside the continent, by African scholars on attachment to, or in collaboration with, foreign universities or research institutions. There are also high numbers of theses on Africa written by students of European and North Amer-ican universities. There are many thousands of theses on Africa available from University Microfilms International (UMI), but it has been suggested that:

> Organisations like UMI provide a vital service by making much com-pleted work accessible, but it is plain that the vast bulk of research conducted in Africa has been effectively lost in that it is not reasonably accessible to other students. It may be, for various reasons, incomplete, or it may be lying unreferenced in any one of a thousand small colleges or research institutions.[34]

The role of special libraries in Africa in attempting to draw together as much of this documentation as possible is a vital one. In fact, it is arguable that special libraries and information services are the sector of librarianship which shows the most positive signs of vitality in many parts of the continent. The special library, whether it be in a government department or a research institute, is often small and may be able to function to a reasonable level without too much imported literature. It is comparatively easy for some agency to begin to accumulate a few publications and files, subscribe to some journals or information services, and find that it has begun to provide a special library facility without realizing that anything of the kind was happening. The formalization of a budget for such service and the employment of suitably trained personnel is a later and sometimes rather more difficult stage. In this formative stage, which is the situation in many cases in Africa, the service may not be particularly elaborate. Indeed, Alemna takes a bleak view of the sector in Ghana for this reason. He suggests that:

> The special collections serving public establishments and private concerns are indisputably the weakest sector of our library system. Many important information generating groups, particularly in the private sector, have no libraries or depositories.[35]

This neglects the presence of good numbers of well-established special libraries throughout the continent. Some of the very first were libraries of national geological surveys. As long ago as 1967 an account of more than twenty of these was published.[36] Few had professional librarians, but several had qualified geologists as information officers. Their collections had few books, but many reprints, pamphlets, maps, microforms and photographs. These libraries were originally a response to colonial perceptions of the importance of the mineral wealth of African countries, but subsequently they have become a means by which independent nations seek to assemble the information they need to cope with the prospecting activities of multinational companies. The vast financial resources of these companies enable them to use modern techniques like remote sensing to detect the significant variations of the earth's surface which might indicate the presence of valuable mineral resources. Faced with the ability of organizations from outside the nation's boundaries to accumulate information of the most crucial commercial and strategic importance, the state has to ensure that its ability to insist on the deposit of full prospecting documentation is as effective as possible. Well-run geological survey libraries and records centres are a means to this end.

Agriculture is nowadays the most common subject area for the provision of special libraries. Of the more than twenty government research institutes in Nigeria, the majority are concerned with agriculture.[37] Despite the fact that a survey of their libraries in 1983 suggested that all of these were inadequately funded and had serious deficiencies in their buildings, collections and services, their very existence is significant.[38] What is more, there is a case for claiming that the agricultural information sector is the most lively of any to be found in developing countries.

It is vital that the special library has clearly defined objectives so that its financial resources can be spent to the best advantage. Baldwin and Varady show how one such unit, the Documentation Service of the Ministry of Planning in Niger, was analysed to facilitate such definition.[39] At the end of this exercise, the Service had a clearly identified position within the Ministry, an internal organization scheme and job descriptions for the staff. The users are naturally of central importance, and the small numbers of the clientele of almost any special library permit closer acquaintance and more complete understanding of them than in almost any other form of library. It is not even necessary to carry out a survey so as to understand them better. Records of transactions kept by the Documentation Unit of the Pan-African Institute for Development in the Sahelian Region of West Africa, in Ougadougou, Burkina Faso, are unusually full and explicit.[40] This has enabled the staff to develop a typology of users, which in turn has influenced the management of the unit and patterns of service provision.

In providing service, the most significant category of information source tends to be elusive because it is not formally published, but appears in a variety of non-conventional forms usually referred to as grey literature. In addition to research and consultancy reports, this type of material can be made up of a variety of items which are not available through the normal publication channels, and includes reports, minutes of meetings, data collections, conference papers, reprints, theses, technical rules, and so on.[41] The material, although not formally published and marketed for sale, does have more than temporary significance, and represents a vast potential store of knowledge about Africa.

A study of grey literature in Lesotho, based on the acquisitions of the documentation centre of the Institute of Southern African

Studies, at Roma, has revealed a considerable amount of detail about this type of material.[42] In a three-year period of intensive collecting effort, the institute managed to acquire just under 3000 documents, including 180 (often rather irregular) annuals and more than 100 periodicals. These figures are worthy of note, for Lesotho is a very small country, and the facilities and resources available to the Institute are far from lavish. A proportionate volume and a similar effort from larger and better-endowed countries would no doubt confirm that grey literature forms a very bulky category of documentation, as well as one with a very significant content. Indeed, estimates that grey literature represents something like 70 per cent of the publishing in Nigeria, or 60 per cent of publishing in Africa, very probably underestimate the proportion by a sizeable factor.[43]

The situation in Lesotho is, however, rather better than that in many other countries. The comments of the economist Balabkins illustrate the problems any researcher can face when trying to access this type of material. Most grey literature is thought to be inaccessible because nobody, including most librarians, pays much attention to it. Quite the opposite can be the case, as these comments show:

> Nigerian military government officials particularly hoarded the grey literature. This practice served to increase their power vis-a-vis other groups in society, and, to judge by the complaints of the Nigerian and expatriate business community about the difficulty of obtaining information, it did so effectively. The practice also served to increase the income of officials, for they did make the grey literature available in exchange for bribes.[44]

This renders a large part of discussions of acquisitions and bibliographical control distinctly marginal. The majority of African countries do have a national bibliography, which, often after some time, succeeds in listing the bulk of the conventional output of the country. However, it should be remembered that some countries like Burundi, Djibouti or Somalia, are considered by the Library of Congress's East African Field Office in Nairobi to have virtually no commercial publishing sector at all. It is also the case that even Nigeria, the giant of African publishing, lists an average of only about 1000 titles a year. Such figures place the significance of conventionally published literature in clearer proportion to the more numerous products of the grey sector.

The virtual absence of grey literature, not only from Africa's national bibliographies, but also from her library shelves, is an issue that has been insufficiently discussed by librarians. They have tended to avert their gaze from it because it is obviously difficult to cope with, and have been able to justify themselves because it does not fall within the traditional scope of the librarian's task. Fortunately, other institutions, in particular archives, which have a strong proprietary interest in information at this embryonic stage, are taking up the challenge. Archives are too frequently regarded as guardians of historical material, which might be of interest to the academic researcher, or have some value to the nation's educational system, but which has no relevance to more urgent issues related to national development. This, however, is far from being the case, and the National Archives of Zimbabwe, for example, has an explicit policy 'to intensify its efforts to encourage the maximum use of semi-current records by government officials'.[45] This is based on the conviction that a considerable amount of archival information can be used for national development planning purposes.

Semi-published reports of the grey literature kind consistently form part of archival holdings, and are particularly useful in this context. Statistical information is a major example of material that can be acquired from archival sources. The Zanzibar Archives, which began taking in records from the Ministry of Agriculture in the early 1980s, encouraged use by advisers working on the decline of clove and coconut production and possible diversification.

> The agricultural advisers, initially sceptical, were delighted to find that once the files were processed and stored in the Archives they could quickly retrieve information on the coir fibre industry, cocoa planting, citrus fruits, or chillies. British and German aid officers working on clove and coconut research were also enthusiastic about the accessibility of past investigations and trials. Moreover the Zanzibar government was now in a position to link the planning of any new agricultural development initiative to past policy and its results, while aid officers working in Zanzibar in the future would be able to assess the background to the Ministry's operations.[46]

The challenge of providing a comprehensive collection of grey literature which not only has the depth of coverage to respond to the shifts in priorities and interest of researchers, but is also easily accessible to those who need to use it, is one that Africa's librarians need to face. In response, Raseroka has suggested a rearrangement of priorities, with the acquisition of local material, in particular grey literature, being given central importance for the collections of most libraries.[47] The short-term implications of such a policy shift would be very hard to accept for many librarians who are used to regarding the output of the most famous international publishers as their standard of excellence. Such is the importance of the capture of this material, however, and so great the need to make it available, that Africa's librarians have little choice in the matter.

The use of grey literature as a means of delivering information to the user is frequently advocated,[48] but there are a host of reasons why such documents, prepared with a specific and quite limited purpose in mind, are not welcomed by more than a few very committed searchers. Despite this, an analysis of the citations in a number of African research theses in agriculture suggested that as much as 14 per cent of the material used was grey literature, mainly consisting of technical reports and conference proceedings.[49] As suggested earlier, this material is hard to acquire, but it has the advantage of frequently being free (in the sense of not having to be paid for directly), and not calling for great resources of foreign currency. A special library with a well-organized acquisitions pro-gramme can realistically hope to build good collections of grey literature by hard work rather than the expenditure of large sums of money. The more extensive use of the content of grey literature rests on the extent to which it can be consolidated or repackaged. The difficulty is that for librarians the tasks involved in consolida-tion are unfamiliar. As one writer put it,

> Some libraries and information centres in less developed countries found themselves in the position of writers, rewriters, popularisers and publishers of literature, a role for which they are not well suited.[50]

Fully developed ideas on how to exploit grey literature through repackaging are not too readily available, but an example from Malawi does suggest that with a little imagination, ways can be found.[51] In the Ministry of Health Library and Documentation Centre the inter-reaction between acquisition and dissemination, through the repackaging process, is of particular interest. The library had considerable difficulty in acquiring reports, research findings, conference and seminar proceedings generated within Malawi itself. A desktop publishing unit was established to publish the institution's own research reports. This opened the way to publishing on behalf of other health personnel and because the library was more noticeable as a publisher it began to attract more deposits of report literature. A repackaging element was then feasible within this programme. Abstracts and reviews of material in the library, which by now had a strong grey literature element, were included in a newsletter, *Malawi Drug Bulletin*. The content of this is intended to be relevant and useful to those providing health care at all levels in Malawi, and it is distributed to health workers in the villages.

A local database was also created, including the whole range of grey literature which the library was now receiving. This database was published in hard copy as *A Select Bibliography of Health Information in Malawi 1980–1991*. Publication resulted in the receipt of further large quantities of reports, articles, conference papers and theses, sent in by authors because they had not been included. This improved the library's holdings once again, both upgrading the database and providing further potential content for *Malawi Drug Bulletin*. The significance of this is the mutual benefit which publishing, repackaging, acquisitions and library services derive from each other when combined within the one institution. Each activity benefits the others and, indeed, it might be argued that some could not exist without the others. Certainly this complex of activities provides a platform for effective dissemination of health care information from both published and grey literature to every relevant level.

It is not easy to be this imaginative, but when money and other resources are short, the need for more original input is clear. It is also obvious that falling back on hackneyed solutions, such as cooperative and interlending schemes, as some sort of a panacea, just will not do. Boadi, after examining the effectiveness of such schemes in the African context, rightly points out that:

> Cooperative acquisition schemes have been tried with disappointing results and interlending programmes have in most cases proved equally unsuccessful.[52]

Yet the special library cannot truly function effectively in isolation from other holdings of research material. In particular, the resources held in the industrialized countries of the North are indispensable to a complete coverage of a given topic. Here information technology becomes inescapably relevant. There are literally hundreds of computerized databases which list these resources. To take just one, the FRANCIS data file, which is a general database produced by the French Centre National de la Recherche Scientifique (CNRS), contains over 1,000,000 items and inputs 90,000 new items per year, including much about Africa.[53] It includes research from all over the world, on a broad range of subjects from ethnology through to administrative science. It is available on-line from anywhere in the world, and aims to be easy to use by non-French speaking countries. As of March 1986, it contained over 36,000 items of African relevance. These were dominated by articles from journals, comprising 86 per cent of the total. Of these, 60 per cent were published in Western Europe, 7 per cent in Eastern Europe and less than 1 per cent in Africa. An African-based user of this, or many other such databases which might have been cited, is being offered what is essentially a menu of documentation that is unlikely to be available in any easily accessible institution. Only document delivery services, most of which are highly expensive, can supply it, and the researcher is more likely to suffer frustration than satisfaction from using remote databases.

Availability is obviously more likely if the material listed in a database contains a higher proportion of bibliographic records originating in the countries the documents concern. The intervention of various agencies, in particular those associated with the United Nations, has resulted in the design of some international information systems with the developing world in mind. Perhaps the best example is the Agricultural Research Information System (AGRIS) set up in 1975 by the United Nations Food and Agriculture Organization (FAO). It is in essence a decentralized bibliographic system for agricultural information which has been very effective in providing both on-line and conventionally published information. Although criticized on some grounds, for instance for the quality of its indexing, AGRIS has performed well in developing countries.[54] The main reason for this is that countries contribute their own bibliographic records to the system and are therefore in a strong position to influence the content of the service. It is true that this influence is only a relative one, since developing countries input only 25 per cent of AGRIS content, but this is positive in a context where most bibliographic databases are overwhelmingly dominated by the developed world. As a consequence of this, not only is the content of AGRIS of relevance to Africa, but the participatory element of the AGRIS scheme has stimulated some local activity and assisted in the development of a locally-based information workforce.

There is other database activity which is, arguably, even more positive for Africa, because its content is controlled from within Africa. The Réseau sahélien de documentation (RESADOC) is one such example.[55] RESADOC was begun in 1979, and has been a function of the Institut du Sahel (INSAH) since 1988 when it was brought together with INSAH's documentation centre. Regional coordination takes place in Bamako, Mali, and each member state has a participant centre, reporting material so as to create a database. By the end of 1991 this held 20,000 references. The system also has specialized databases, such as the CD-ROM Sesame on tropical agronomy, with 66,500 references, to which RESADOC contributes, and others on topics such as appropriate technology, agroforestry and desertification. These are supported by a documentary resource of over 11,000 documents, plus periodicals, microforms and CD-ROMs. There is particular emphasis on collecting grey literature, particularly by microfilming, repatriating dispersed documents and encouraging local documentation centres to supply copies.

No bibliographic database is entirely satisfactory for the researcher if the documents it lists cannot be obtained easily. What seems to be the best option for the delivery of documents is the use of the same CD-ROMs and other forms of optical disc that are used for bibliographical databases. Experimentation with the use of CD-ROM for many purposes has been under way since the mid-1980s in many African countries.[56] Surveys in the early 1990s suggested that 10 to 20 per cent of African academic and special libraries had the technology.[57] It is still a comparatively expensive, vulnerable technology, but it has the enormous virtue that it is not dependent on telecommunications links. Comments by Nkhata on CD-ROM bring us back to issues already discussed here.[58] He recognizes the technical appropriateness of CD-ROM for Africa, but he has fundamental doubts about the content, which largely originates in the industrialized countries. What is needed is for African documentalists to take control of the technology for themselves. Isolated examples of this do already occur. For instance in Zimbabwe, a tourism information CD-ROM, *MuZimbabwe*, has been created by the company IDATA Systems Incorporated to publicize the country's attractions in interactive form. From such beginnings a major flowering of documentation developments is needed. If they were to occur, then much light would be introduced into the comparative darkness of the African research information scene.

References

1. Nzotta, B.C. The administration of branch libraries in a developing country: a case study. *Public Library Quarterly*, 9, 1989. 47–60. p.60.
2. Chijioke, M.E. Public library services as information networks: Nigeria in the twenty-first century. *Journal of Librarianship*, 21, 1989. 174–85. p.175.
3. Ndiaye, A.R. *Communication à la base: enraciner et épanouir.* Dakar, ENDA, 1994. p.206.
4. Ibid. p.212.
5. Zaaiman, R.B., Roux, P.J.A., and Rykher, J.H. *The Use of Libraries for the Development of South Africa.* Final report on an investigation for the South African Institute for Librarianship and Information Science. Pretoria, Unisa, 1988. p.47.
6. Atherton, L. Community libraries in Zimbabwe. *Information Development*, 9, 1993. 36–43.
7. Chakava, H. Reading in Africa: some obstacles. *IFLA Journal*, 10, 1984. p.351.
8. Kenya National Academy for Advancement of Arts and Sciences. *A Survey of Reading Habits and Preferences among Nairobi Primary and Lower Secondary School Children.* Nairobi, KNAAAS, 1980. p.13.
9. Osiobe, S.A., Osiobe, A.E. and Okoh, J.D. Theme and illustrations as correlates of literature preferences among Nigerian primary school pupils. *Library Review*, 38, 1989. 45–52.
10. Adeniji, A. and Issah, M.S. National Library of Nigeria; functions and achievements. *Libri*, 36, 1986. 136–45. p.143.
11. Ojiambo, J.B. School library services in sub-Saharan Africa. *International Library Review*, 20, 1988. 143–55.
12. MacIvor, C. African mind starved of books. *New African*, Feb. 1993. p.32.
13. Fafunwe, A.B. and Aisiku, J.U. (eds) *Education in Africa: A Comparative Study.* London, Allen & Unwin, 1982.
14. Court, D. and Kinyanjui, K. African education: problems in a high growth sector. In: Berg, R.J. and Whitaker, J.S. (eds) *Strategies for African Development.* Berkeley, CA, University of California Press, 1986. 361–92.
15. NEIDA (Network of Educational Innovation for Development in Africa). *Education and Productive Work in Africa: A Regional Survey.* Dakar, Unesco Regional Office for Education in Africa, 1982.
16. Behrman, J.R. Schooling in developing countries. *Economics of Education Review*, 6, 1987. 111–27.
17. Williams, P. African education under siege. In: Hawes, H. *et al.* (eds) *Educational Priorities and Aid Responses in Sub-Saharan Africa.* London, ODA, 1986. 91–105.

18. Foster, P. The contribution of education to development. In: Psacharopoulos, G. (ed.) *Economics of Education: Research and Studies.* London, Pergamon, 1987. 93–100. p.100.
19. NEIDA. op. cit.
20. Ocholla, D.N. Essentials for school library development. *New Library World,* 93, 1992. 9–15.
21. Sitzman, G.L. *African Libraries.* Metuchen, NJ, Scarecrow Press, 1988.
22. Crowder, M. The book crisis: Africa's other famine. *African Research and Documentation,* 41, 1986. p.5.
23. Obiagwu, M.C. Foreign exchange and library collections in Nigeria. *Information Development,* 3, 1987. 154–60.
24. World Bank. *Education in Sub-Saharan Africa.* Washington, DC, World Bank, 1988.
25. Lundu, M.C. and Lungu, C.B.M. Acquisition of scientific literature in developing countries: Zambia. *Information Development,* 5, 1989. 99–106.
26. Rosenberg, D. A review of university libraries in Africa. *Development in Practice,* 6, 1996. 77–80. p.80.
27. Alemna, A. Alternative approaches to funding university libraries in Africa. *New Library World,* 95. 1994. 15–17.
28. Saracevic, T. Consolidation of information: a concept of needed information products and services for developing countries. In: *Proceedings of the 48th Annual Meeting of the American Society for Information Science.* Medford, NJ, ASIS, 1985. 150–4.
29. Sturges, P. Using grey literature in informal information services in Africa. *Journal of Documentation,* 50, 1994. 273–90.
30. Saracevic, T. Experiences with providing a low-cost high-quality collection of journals in medicine for developing countries. *INSPEL,* 25, 1991. 69–98.
31. Singh, K. Managing science and technology development in Africa: policy tasks ahead. *Africa Quarterly,* 30, 1990. 65–88.
32. Matheson, A. African scientists thwarted at home. *Observer.* 28 August 1988. p.27.
33. Singh, K. op. cit. p.75.
34. Robertson, A.F. Perspectives on African Studies in the United Kingdom: the social sciences. In Sternberg, I. and Larby, P.M. (eds) *African Studies. Papers Presented at a Colloquium at the British Library, 7–9 January, 1985.* London, British Library, 1986. p.19.
35. Alemna, A.A. Libraries and the economic development of Ghana. *Aslib Proceedings,* 41, 1989. 119–25. p.121.
36. Kennington, D. Geological survey libraries. *Unesco Bulletin for Libraries,* 22, 1967. 17–21.
37. Oladele, B.A. Toward an integrated agricultural information consolidated scheme for farmers in the Nigerian rural areas. *Quarterly Bulletin of the International Association of Agricultural Librarians and Documentalists,* 32, 1987. 98–101.
38. Nzotta, B.C. Providing information for research: Federal Research Institute Libraries in Nigeria. *Information Development,* 1, 1985. 223–8.

39. Baldwin, C.M. and Varady, R.G. Information access in Niger: development of a West African special library. *Special Libraries*, 1989. 31–8.
40. Diop, A. Attitudes of information users in the Sahel. *Information Development*, 4, 1988. 21–7.
41. Balabkins, N.W. Collecting information in a developing country. *Harvard Library Bulletin*, 32, 1984. p.67.
42. Ambrose, D. Collection and bibliographic control of grey literature of Lesotho. *African Research and Documentation*, 36, 1984. 11–24.
43. Obasi, J. Bibliographical control of Nigerian publications: social science primary materials. *Journal of Documentation*, 38, 1982. 107–24.
44. Balabkins, N.W. op. cit.
45. Kamba, A.S. Archives and national development in the Third World. *Information Development*, 3, 1987. 108–13.
46. Thurston, A. The Zanzibar Archives Project. *Information Development*, 2, 1986. 223–6.
47. Raseroka, K.H. Relevant library services in developing countries. *IFLA Journal*, 12, 1986. 288–91.
48. Aina, L.O. The problem of organising and disseminating grey literature in Africa. In: *Proceedings of the First International Conference on Grey Literature, Amsterdam, 13–15 Dec., 1993*. Amsterdam, Transatlantic, 1994. 169–74.
49. Aina, L.O. Grey literature and agricultural research in Nigeria. *Quarterly Bulletin of the International Association of Agricultural Librarians and Documentalists*, 32, 1987. 47–50.
50. Saracevic, T. Progress in documentation: perception of the needs for scientific and technical information in less developed countries. *Journal of Documentation*, 36, 1980. 214–67. p.235.
51. Lippman, M.J. The library as information producer: the case of the Ministry of Health Library and Documentation Centre in Malawi. *Journal of Documentation*, 49, 1993. 55–9.
52. Boadi, B.Y. The information sector in the economic development of Africa: the potential role for libraries. *IFLA Journal*, 10, 1984. 139–44.
53. Rahard, M. and Bourdin, J.F. FRANCIS can inform you on Africa. *African Research and Documentation*, 42, 1985. 8–19.
54. Samaha, E.K. Document delivery: the AGRIS cooperative solution. *Information Development*, 3, 1987. 103–7. p.103.
55. Aw, S. Les acquis du Réseau sahélien de documentation. *Documentaliste – Sciences de l'information*, 29, 1992. 285–9.
56. Kinney, J. Agricultural information services and the new technology. In: Asamani, J.O. *et al.* (eds) *Libraries and Literacy. Proceedings of the Seventh Meeting of the Standing Conference of Eastern, Central and Southern African Librarians, Gaborone, 4–8 Aug 1986*. Gaborone, Botswana Library Association, 1987. 23–33.
57. Compton, A.W. Opportunities for CD-ROM information services in Africa. *Information Services and Use*, 12, 1992. 283–90.
58. Nkhata, B.W.M. CD-ROM in developing countries: is it a technology for the distribution of information? *Electronic Library*, 11, 1993. 295–7.

Chapter Six

New Information Services for the Whole Community

The last chapter offered thoughts on the future of the library in Africa, proposing a better-defined role in the total scheme of information provision. That done, it is possible to turn to the question of information needs for which the conventional library is definitely not the answer. It is quite clear that the majority of the population of African countries live in ways which for the immediately foreseeable future are unlikely to be touched by libraries. Yet an alternative service providing information, in the broadest possible sense of the word, to the inadequately-served majority does not exist, except in a bewildering range of incomplete prototypes, experiments and ideas. These tentative beginnings, taken with lessons learned from many other types of communication can, however, suggest how a new type of service might look.

Because any attempt to do justice to this topic must discuss a mix of functioning services, pilot projects and experiments, and also ideas which have not actually been tested, it is necessary to issue a warning here. Africa is too big, and the relevant examples too thoroughly scattered throughout the continent, for the authors to have seen and inspected everything that will be discussed. We have tried as hard as possible to say what is real and what is an idea, but we have been dependent on those who have written and talked about things we have not seen. It is perfectly legitimate to discuss all of this in one connected argument, but it is important to remember that we are dealing with a fluid and evolving area, not a set of practices that have fixity and permanence.

Since none of this is in a fixed state, it makes sense to discuss it in relation to questions, presenting answers to each which are as congruent as possible with the six guiding principles outlined at the end of Chapter 4. The questions that need to be asked about a new form of information service are:

- for whom should it be provided?
- what should it deliver?
- where should it be provided?
- by whom should it be provided?
- in what forms should it deliver information?
- how should it deliver information?

The first two of these questions will only require brief restatements of the case which has been developed in the earlier chapters, but the remaining four questions require thorough examination.

For Whom?

As the subtitle of this book indicates, a new type of information service is required for the people of Africa, urban or rural, of whatever race, religion, culture or background, but particularly for those disadvantaged by illiteracy and inadequate education, official neglect, isolation, membership of a minority, gender, age (whether young or old). The people are served at present mainly from their own resources of indigenous information and by traditional and informal types of communication. Although such resources and methods answer many needs, they are not sufficient unaided to meet the challenges created by a world where change touches even those in the furthest and most isolated village, or in the deepest recesses of some urban slum maze. The question at the head of this section is deliberately put as 'for whom' rather than 'to whom', because it is envisaged as not merely directed at the people, but provided so that they can obtain a response from it according to their needs.

What?

The service is intended to deliver as complete a range of response to the information needs of the people as can be achieved. It is clear that because of their pressing physical needs, for food and the means of producing food, clothing, shelter and health care, that people need information to help them find assistance, judge what alternatives to choose and understand how to pursue opportunities that might exist. When asked, they express their need for information on income generating activities, agriculture, health and hygiene, education, domestic skills. They also express their need for spiritual sustenance, entertainment and mental stimulation. Any information service which confined itself entirely to the practical would be performing a major role, but it would be falling short of satisfying the whole scope of need. Because of the urgency of practical needs, and because of the shortage of funds to provide for such needs, let alone for information connected with them, any service must seek to deliver practical information first and foremost. It should nevertheless not neglect the whole human being when there is any possibility of providing mental fare even more satisfying and enriching.

Where?

This is perhaps the question on which most attention has centred, and the answers to it that have been offered suggest a big range of options. To make it worse, many projects are distinguished by sets of initials, potentially turning any account of them into a kind of alphabet soup. Some existing services and some ideas which have been suggested embody part only of a complete answer to the questions which are being asked here. Nevertheless, this is the point at which such projects should be outlined. For this purpose, five main types of answer can be identified to the question 'where?'. Some we will discuss at length in this section, others will be dealt with mainly under other questions. The five main types of answer are:

- reading facilities;
- services still called library and resource centres;
- cultural centres;
- technology-based services;
- itinerant services not attached to any one place.

Reading facilities

The idea of the reading room has been lurking around in Africa for many years. In Nigeria, village reading rooms were set up by the

British colonial administration to publicize the Allied war effort during the Second World War. They originally contained radios, newspapers, maps, pamphlets and a few books. They were allowed to decline and disappear after the war, although some efforts were made to revive them during the 1950s. To librarians they were generally a source of annoyance, despite evidence that they had been useful in relation to literacy programmes. The usual library response to them was summed up by a Nigerian librarian who said that:

> Their administration made it impossible for us to convert them to libraries. The functions they were created to serve are in direct conflict with our ideas of a public library service.[1]

In other parts of the continent the reading room idea has been revived and reconstituted in a modern equivalent, explicitly in connection with literacy programmes. Indeed, an important point about such schemes is that they do arise much more from the activities of adult education organizations than from library services. To librarians the idea seems less like an innovation and more like a retreat from full library provision to an inferior level of service. We do not believe that the idea has to be seen in this way. When existing resources patently do not permit full library service to be delivered to more than a small number of communities, there is a strong case for providing the much less expensive reading rooms to a much larger number of communities. This can ensure both a more effective and a fairer distribution of available resources. Even more important is the fact that the reading room concept is very appropriate to the present needs of many communities.

Reading institutions, which respond directly to African circumstances, may often need to be much simpler than their Northern counterparts. Both formal schooling and literacy programmes, for instance, create certain straightforward needs. One is for a quiet place, away from the bustle of family life, where it is possible to concentrate on reading. Although this book is called *The Quiet Struggle*, for many people it is the struggle for quiet that is most important. A letter in the Bulawayo press drew attention to this in a very direct manner. People were playing loud music near the library in the Pumula high density suburb. The writer upbraided them:

> It is really unbearable in there because of your noise. I wonder whether there are no council by-laws to control such a bad practice. Can the

relevant authorities please do something because the situation is pathetic to say the very least. If I may pose this question to you, how many houses have study rooms, let alone individual bedrooms for children where they can do their homework and study quietly? The answer is probably one percent, that is why these young men and women and students from surrounding schools use the library facility for studying. Please think about the library users when you next turn on your sets.[2]

Although the writer talks of library users, the word that applies to them best of all is readers. It is not people selecting books to borrow, or others asking the librarians for information, that are talked of, but those sitting for long periods of time studying.

The African climate usually comfortably permits sitting out of doors, but this provides only limited opportunities for the reader. The evenings are short, and the very brief period of fading light which is all that may be available after a full day in school, or of work in the fields, the factory, or domestic service, dictates the need for a reading room with artificial, preferably electric, light. Readers can frequently be found in homes with no electrical connection poring over their books and newspapers by the light of a paraffin lamp, but this is far from ideal.

Other facilities can be quite unpretentious: a few tables, chairs and shelves are all the furniture that is needed. Catalogue drawers, date stamps and the usual paraphernalia associated with libraries are not essential. Indeed a reading room may not actually provide any reading material itself, but still be useful to readers who have nowhere to read their own textbooks or study materials. The concept does, however, invariably include the provision of some basic reading matter. Because they are usually more than just a room, they are often referred to as village libraries, but this dignifies them unnecessarily. The large number of reading rooms in Tanzania (maybe 3000 if figures are to be trusted) are generally called village libraries, because each is supposed to hold about 400 items of reading material.[3] They are under the supervision of the local adult education coordinators, part of whose job it is to encourage the local authorities to provide standardized buildings. At present they are often to be found in a variety of premises, such as primary schools, clinics, court houses, the offices of cooperatives, and even private houses.

The difficulty of actually establishing this type of system at village level, as opposed to conceptualizing it from the desk of a ministry building in the capital, can be seen from experience in Botswana, where such a system has been under development since the mid-1980s.[4] Government commitment to the initial provision of over 300 reading rooms by the Department of Non-Formal Education in small village communities throughout the country was achieved with comparative ease. The translation of this approval into effective practice is where the difficulties occurred. A pilot project in the Kgatleng District was tried first. Local institutions gave some early encouragement by agreeing to provide premises, but changes of mind on the part of Village Development Committees or Land Board officials led to the eventual use of a primary school, and a Botswana National Library Service branch library as the first sites. Schools, as the most widely distributed public facilities, are frequently hosts to reading rooms, although their function in educating children may incline some adult new literates, sensitive of their status, to avoid them. The use of a National Library Service branch is ironical, since reading rooms are essentially intended to be alternative or complementary to libraries. It is indicative of the level of difficulty in the practical implementation of something even as simple as the reading room idea.

Shortage of reading materials has been an obstacle to the reading rooms in Tanzania advancing beyond the rudimentary stage of merely providing space. The bulk of the material supplied to the village libraries is supposed to be in Kiswahili, the language in which people learn to read. Despite this intention, an increasing proportion now tends to be the English language product of foreign-owned commercial publishers. No reliable way seems to have been found, in Tanzania or elsewhere, to produce enough material in the people's mother tongues to meet the need. The consequence of this is to limit the number of publications which are comprehensible to new literates. This means that the most enthusiastic readers among them can easily exhaust all the material made available to them and then have little incentive to visit the village library. Renewable collections offer a possible answer to this problem. In Botswana, the National Library Service's book box scheme, originally provided for schools, has been seen as a means of providing reading rooms with small collections of reading material that can be renewed at regular intervals. A similar idea was included in the Malian Five Year Plan, 1984–8, with public library services decentralized through the provision of collections of 50 books to rural communities.

A thorough evaluation of the Botswana reading rooms, carried out in 1994, provides a good idea of what they can do, and what they cannot.[5] The results of a survey of nearly 1000 people suggested that school work and recreational reading were the main reasons for their use. When asked if the reading rooms met their needs, respondents mainly gave the obliging response that they did (57 per cent) or that they weren't sure if they did (22 per cent). The interesting thing, however, is that 21 per cent were clear enough in their own minds to say directly that they weren't satisfied. This last category consisted mainly of people who were not very competent readers, or who had just been involved in some sort of non-formal education. They, and many other respondents, had some quite specific criticisms of the rooms. High among these (from 42 per cent of all respondents) was the need to move them out of primary schools into somewhere not associated with children's learning activities. This discontent indicates very clearly the limitations of the reading room.

The situation is that the reading room, given basic administrative support, is capable of meeting many of the needs of school children and other learners. With a certain supply of suitable reading material, it is also capable of providing some useful support for some of the immediate needs of new readers. When the readers are much more numerous and their demand for reading material and information is sufficiently intense and varied, there is scope for expansion of the reading room concept to meet their requirements. An assessment of the Tanzanian reading rooms in 1992 did, in fact, suggest that they should be assisted to mature into community information centres with a wider scope. Kedem talks of a very similar evolution when he advises that:

> Adult literacy libraries should be built upon the concept that new literates should have cheap and suitable reading materials easily at their disposal. These libraries should be equipped and managed in such a way that they can sustain literacy in the society. They should also be used by the governments as a basis for achieving the policy of 'one man one book'.[6]

Whether or not a national or district system of reading rooms, as such, is contemplated, the reading facility, as described above, is an essential feature of any complete concept of a new service.

Library and resource centres

As illustrated in the last section, those who organize this type of service find it very hard to abandon the word library, even when much of what they are talking about is hardly recognisable as the usual form of library service. Hickwa explains the use of the word by the Zimbabwean Rural Libraries and Resources Development Project (RLRDP) thus:

> We tend to use the term Community Libraries concerning the holistic use of information resources in a community. These resources, we always emphasize, go beyond the printed matter ordinarily associated with libraries. Our idea of a library is inclusive of print and non-print materials, and people that volunteer to dispense wide categories of information by whatever means. All our programmes have elements of drama, song and dance as 'barefoot' means of exhaustively putting information across to the people we serve.[7]

The word is used of something as rudimentary as the home library, which uses an individual's home as a community centre for reading and exchange of material from a small collection. Such arrangements can be found in various parts of Zimbabwe, and the Bulawayo Home Library Project has been supported by the Swedish International Development Agency.[8] In fact the Bulawayo groups first of all met in the literacy centres which gave them birth.[9] Subsequently the project expanded to other centres where groups of various kinds meet. The collections of material used consist of about 100 books. They correspond quite closely to the book boxes conventionally used by library systems to spread services to points where the availability of a room enables them to reach people not served in any other way.

A humble collection of this kind is also known by terms such as suitcase library or, in francophone Africa, as *une valise de brousse*. Sam Nikoi, a Ghanaian librarian, even claims to have run a wheelbarrow library, by regularly using one of these conveyances to take books to a point at which they could be used. The idea is currently being used to restore some kind of simple library service in the Nampula province of Mozambique, devastated by years of war.[10] Lockable cases of books (disconcertingly, for English-speakers, known as mobiles) provided by Nampula Province Library are moved by bicycle between the administrative centres of the *bairros* of Nampula. The books are made available to readers during the day, often on the verandah of the building and moved to the home of the 'librarian' for safekeeping at night. During the rainy season the service is suspended and the time used for working on the collections (and the bicycles).

The best evidence for positive community reaction to initiatives providing rudimentary library service, is that a home for the service is often built by community members themselves. Sadly, this may not always be enough to obtain a partner able to put a service in place within the four walls. The Zimbabwean National Library and Documentation Service (NLDS), for instance, which does have about 30 school/community libraries in Matabeleland, acknowledges that

> Most of the communities are willing to mould bricks and construct libraries if they can be assisted with building materials. It is, however, difficult for the underfunded NLDS to provide such assistance.[11]

Many services with a fixed base which is owned, leased or borrowed, can be found throughout the continent under names which include Resource and Study Centre (in South Africa, with networking through Resource Centre Fora), Rural Libraries and Resources (Zimbabwe, under the direction of the Rural Libraries and Resources Development Project), Rural Community Information Centres (Malawi, run by the National Library Service), Rural Community Resource Centres (Sierra Leone and elsewhere in Africa), Rural Community Library and Information Centres (anglophone West Africa), Centres de Documentation Communitaire (francophone West Africa). Of these, Rural Community Resource Centre is probably the most used in anglophone Africa. The word 'rural' in this term and all the others is superfluous because such centres are just as valid in urban areas, which share many of the same forms of deprivation and have certain more acute needs arising from the disruptive effects of migration to the cities. A definition of what a rural community resource centre should be is provided in the widely available manual prepared by Shirley Giggey.

> A resource centre is a place where members of a community can: find information about subjects of interest to them; take part in learning activities; discuss and share knowledge, information and concerns with extension and other community workers, planners and administrators; find materials to help them to retain their literacy and numeracy skills; meet to organise and work together on community projects; use equipment to produce their own informational materials; enjoy culture and leisure activities.[12]

One of the objectives of Obadiah Moyo's RLRDP organization expands this somewhat by placing it in a clearer context of community activity. It refers to

> promoting and strengthening socio-economic, cultural and recreational activities, pre-school, adult literacy and other mass-oriented learning programmes in the rural areas, by providing relevant and appropriate reading materials.[13]

The RLRDP also has its manual for those setting up and working in centres, and it says that

> The library in a rural area is expected to provide a service to the community and not just be a storehouse of books. It must be a dynamic social agency, providing a wide range of information to the community.[14]

This emphasis on dynamism is intended to distinguish the idea from traditional visions of the library. It is expressed particularly clearly in relation to Rural Community Resources Centres in Sierra Leone. These are being set up as pilot projects with support from the British Council and UNESCO. The organizers say of them that:

> The challenge is to move into a more dynamic-interactive mode suitable for dealing with rural communities, to serve not only as repositories of 'stored knowledge' but also as centres of 'knowledge in the making' and, finally, to adopt a diversified approach to the media/technologies used for collecting as well as for storing, retrieving and disseminating information.[15]

The cumulative effect of these statements is to give a clear idea of what is intended for such centres, whether existing or proposed. However, it must be pointed out that while these versions of the idea may seem to stay fairly close to the library concept in that they provide for a fixed information point with resource holdings of some kind, the important thing is that they stress the centre as the focus of information-related activities, not merely a repository to which people may come for reading material. An Ndebele phrase for library is *isiphala solwazi*, which translates directly as 'granary of knowledge'. The granary not only provides a supply of nourishment for the coming years, but it contains seed corn for future crops. It is a store in the most positive sense. The term has a marvellous way of expressing the fruitfulness and life-giving qualities for which the RLRDP's rural libraries and resource centres aim.

As an indication of the RLRDP's interest in dynamic, information-based interaction with the community, it organized a malaria awareness campaign from its library at Nkayi in 1995. The library had been supplying material on health matters, but realized that a particularly intense outbreak of malaria in the area called for a more intensive programme. Funded by the Save a Baby Save a Zimbabwean Association (SABSAZA) it cooperated with health personnel in holding sessions to pass on messages verbally and with the backing of written materials. In particular, the campaign was successful in encouraging more people to recognize that the symptoms they experienced actually were malaria, so as to obtain treatment earlier, and then follow courses of medication through more consistently. As Moyo puts it:

> Relevant information is the key to the development of our communities. All development starts with information. Once bad information is provided, it should not be surprising that the results of using such information are bad. Rural areas lack most of the basic necessities which are essential for a better life. The best way to achieve and sustain this development is to start providing appropriate and accessible libraries, which relate well with what goes on in the village.[16]

The library and resource centre idea has attracted good support from funding and coordinating bodies. RLRDP, for instance, has received funding from the Canadian Organisation for Development through Education (CODE), the Norwegian Agency for Development Cooperation (NORAD), the Danish International Development Agency (DANIDA) and other agencies. There have also been a number of very useful workshop meetings devoted to the organization of such services. The German Foundation for International Development (DSE) promoted such a meeting in 1984, and published the proceedings.[17] There was a national seminar in Nigeria in 1989 on Rural Library Development,[18] and in 1991, the Commonwealth Library Association (COMLA) organized a Regional Workshop for West Africa on Rural Community Library and Information Centres.[19] IFLA's Advancement of Librarianship in the Third World Programme (ALP) has also been much involved. It was responsible for a major seminar in Botswana in 1994, which reviewed developments throughout most of Africa.[20]

Cultural centres

The discussion of library and resource centres blends almost imperceptibly into discussion of cultural centres as a focus for information activity. Iwuji in 1989 envisaged a community information resource with a much wider range of involvement:

> This civic centre would be pulsating with community activities like work-based adult education, such as agricultural extension instructions on new ways of doing old things, generation of reading materials for new literates, art and cultural exhibitions and festivals, viewing of recorded oral literature and tradition, meetings and workshops organised by the various interest groups in the community, and a whole range of other activities aimed at enhancing the social craft of the people.[21]

It is more common to refer to such an idea as a cultural centre, and the explicit mention of culture in the title of an organization or centre almost always identifies it as originating in the French sphere of interest. Culture and reading are naturally spoken of in the same breath in countries like Mali, where planning in the 1980s linked

> the organisation of cultural tours, including shows in local languages, as well as the setting up of reading areas in the six villages of the Bamako district.[22]

This is not exclusively so, as one of the best-articulated versions of a wide-reaching cultural institution with information service among its interests came from Zimbabwe. The Culture House idea was launched in the 1980s, but unfortunately it was only a tentative beginning, which disappeared into the sands of financial under-provision. The one Culture House which was opened, at Murehwa, stands as a monument to the idea. As Made and Motsi put it,

> Every culture house will have a library, a museum and an oral archive, an all-purpose hall, a theatre, arts and crafts and printing workshops.[23]

The idea seems to have been too ambitious to be sustainable. When Atherton visited Murehwa some years later she found:

> Despite having the hall available, no literacy classes take place at

Murehwa and the radio and television are not used for instructional purposes. There is no oral archive at Murehwa, although this is a project that the library could initiate and develop.[24]

A humbler version of part of the same idea was the Culture Hut that Atherton found at the Nyajezi community library.

> It contains artefacts and items of daily use such as hoes, pots and mats. The intention is to help children learn about their own culture and past, and they too make sculptures and pots to add to the collection. Samples of the local crops are also exhibited and labelled with information about use and growing conditions. Adults are encouraged to share their traditional skills with the children. Books in the library give further details about African traditions.[25]

This shows something of what the culture centre might achieve in relation to material culture, but for a fuller examination of the potential of the idea it is necessary to look to francophone Africa.

An ambitious network of centres, conceived in the context of an internationally fostered programme, is to be found throughout the French-speaking countries. The Centres de Lecture et d'Animation Culturelle en Milieu Rurale (CLAC) have been set up with technical and financial support from l'Agence de Coopération culturelle et technique (ACCT). The first CLACs were set up in 1986 in Benin, and there are now more 100 in 11 countries including Mali and Senegal, and others have been planned for the Central Africa Republic, Chad, Guinea and Togo.[26] Their objectives are to create better access to modern information media, stimulate activity in education and training in subjects like health, agriculture and literacy, and encourage local culture and tradition to flourish. To realize these intentions,

> Various activities take place in the CLACs. The principal ones are the lending of books, use of the library for reference, the lending of educational games and toys, the watching of documentary or fiction films, group activities and activities with schools or associations such as reading and debating clubs, and cultural activities such as theatre, music and dance.[27]

It is important to remember that this is the intention, and that the reality may be a little less expansive. In Senegal there are seventeen CLACs, which have libraries and audiovisual centres. They are managed locally, have furniture and fittings made by local craftsmen and, although much basic stock comes from donors, they raise income from their activities to pay the expenses of the centre. For example, the CLAC at Joal Fadiouth has a comparatively large library for adults and children with about 4000 books, and five newspapers are taken. A small monthly subscription is charged and there are approaching 100 active members. Regular public showings of videos (hired for the occasion), for which a charge is made, attract about 20 or 30 people, but the centre has virtually no video stock, and there is little evidence of an ability to create audiovisual materials. Further activities, such as a theatre group, are planned, but were not established in 1996. The centre is run by volunteer *animateurs*, and although it is far from luxurious and the range of activities is not as wide as intended, there are, nevertheless, the indications of a certain basic vitality.

In discussing the CLACs, it is important to recognize that while this is a fairly new programme, the cultural centre as focus for information activity is a well-established concept in the francophone West African region. Senegal is a very fruitful example and Dakar must rank as one of the cities with the highest number of library service points for the public in Africa. Each administrative region of the country has a major cultural centre provided by the Ministry of Culture. The Centre Culturel Blaise Senghor in Dakar has a gallery space, theatre, music rehearsal and performance facilities, workshops and children's activity areas, as well as large children's and adult libraries. The Ministry of Youth and Sport also provides many cultural and educational centres (the CDEPS). That at Pikine-Guediawaye among Dakar's high density suburbs has a theatre and meeting hall used by popular theatre groups and a kindergarten, rooms which provide a home for literacy classes and craft education, and youth activities. There is also a small, well cared-for library, provided in cooperation with the Ministry of Culture and BLD, a Senegalese NGO which promotes library activity.

The municipality of Dakar also provides socio-cultural centres which include libraries. A particularly attractive example is at Derkle, where health centre, kindergarten, training centre, theatre and meeting rooms and library share a complex of buildings set in well-kept gardens. The centre at Ngor has similar facilities, also in an attractive modern building, but including in addition outdoor sports areas. In 1996 there were twelve centres, all fairly recently established, but a total of 40 is planned. The various activities vary in popularity between different centres, with the library the most popular in some cases. Total membership registrations for the libraries in the municipality's centres have been very high, with tens of thousands of names on the lists (although it should be remembered that such lists tend to retain very high numbers of 'members' whose interest was only temporary).

The difference between information activity in Dakar and many cities in anglophone Africa is striking. Library activity, as such, has a weak tradition in francophone Africa and until comparatively recently there has not been much information work aimed at the whole community. The upsurge of activity has been generally associated with the general concept of cultural promotion and has undoubtedly gained in vitality from its association with a complex of other cultural activities. Personnel, committee members and political backers exchange ideas, resources are directed towards cooperative projects, and there are few preconceptions about how the information-related aspects of centres should be provided. In contrast, the separate and independent library systems of the anglophone countries fail to benefit from the energies generated by the symbiotic relationships that are developed within the cultural centre. The Kaloleni branch library of Nairobi City Libraries, for instance, shares a roof with a community centre which contains meeting hall, kindergarten, cafeteria, workshops and sports rooms. Sadly the roof is all it shares: the library shows absolutely no sign of cooperation with its neighbours to promote their mutual interests and enhance their impact on the community.

Technology-based services

The exciting possibilities offered by technology have spawned good numbers of proposals and experiments. Some of these originated in the perception that audio-tape offers great possibilities in communities with low rates of literacy. Some discussion focused on the capture by a conventional library or archive service of material from the oral tradition and its repackaging in audio-visual formats. As long ago as 1973, in a contribution to a conference on publishing in Africa, K.K. Oyeoku suggested that,

> The initial emphasis of African libraries need not be on the printed word. It is quite feasible and more meaningful to start a library in a rural community with miles of tapes of the people's folklore, music and culture.[28]

He proposed experimentation with a new institution in a rural village, which would collect oral material from the villagers into a community library of tapes. The institution would gradually transcribe the material for use in connection with literacy teaching, so that new readers could have familiar and well-loved material available to them in print form. Second and third stages would involve local preparation and informal publishing of primary and vocational education materials developed from the oral materials and using the skills acquired during that stage of the programme. A final fourth stage, of publishing for secondary and higher education and for other purposes, including recreation, could then be explored.

By 1982 Mali was at the forefront in exploring such possibilities, with a joint UNDP/Malian government project (joined in 1990 by IDRC), to establish a headquarters sound library at Bamako and branches in the villages which would collect on tape the local communities' oral heritage. The operation was then to be extended to remoter rural areas through the use of a mobile sound library service. Village sound libraries were to be

> designed as autonomous centres of living culture in which information can be collected and exchanged, primarily for the large majority who are still illiterate. Thus instead of being isolated in their illiteracy, they will, by means of recorded items, be able to acquire vivifying information on their own culture, as well as that of neighbouring socio-cultural communities and other countries throughout the world. They will be a new kind of library equipped with the basic technical means for making and storing tape-recordings, so that anyone can come and obtain information on a variety of subjects such as the history of the village, general history, traditional technical skills, appropriate technology, elementary health care, agriculture, animal husbandry, etc. They will function like ordinary libraries but with sound recordings in the place of books, and will have facilities for borrowing, listening to and copying tapes.[29]

This idea has subsequently taken root as the Audiothèques rurales du Mali.[30] In nearly 150 villages, Committees for Oral Knowledge consisting of local dignitaries, traditional healers, extension workers and volunteer audiolibrarians, administer a service. The national structure is intended both to disseminate information on hygiene, health, farming, environmental protection and other practical matters, and to give wider access to traditional knowledge in the forms of local history, stories, songs, medical and agricultural knowledge.

The more recent thinking on technology naturally looks towards the computer and telecommunications to provide information to the whole community. Also, as might be expected, a good deal of the thinking and experimentation on this has been done in South Africa. Here they tend to be referred to as resource and study centres, and a good definition of what is meant by this suggests that,

> Human and other resources in a variety of media and equipment are arranged or made accessible in an appropriate manner for the purpose of empowering people through information dissemination, production, skills and resource sharing.[31]

They originate in centres set up throughout South Africa as part of the struggle against apartheid, which are largely organized into regional networks, known as forums.[32] The significance of these centres in the struggle has undoubtedly contributed to the popularity of the resource centre idea in official circles in South Africa, as is indicated by the frequent references to information services for the community in the Reconstruction and Development Programme (RDP). The National Telecommunications Forum has a project to develop the infrastructure for multi-purpose community centres (MPCCs) which are intended to serve local community information needs. The South African police have obtained funding for 'community safety centres', the Welfare department is building community centres in the Western Cape, Eskom has donated computers to an MPCC in Rabie Ridge, the Communications Task Team of the RDP is obtaining aid from the USA to set up ten pilot MPCCs, and the IDRC has a project to assess MPCCs generally. The information technology industries, not surprisingly, see this as a business opportunity.

> By providing computers and information centres to a largely illiterate population, we should be realising that we are in fact opening up a market in iconic program development, and touch screen specialisation.[33]

The MACIS project, set up in Pretoria's Mamelodi township in September 1995, by the information section of the CSIR (South Africa's national scientific and industrial research centre), is reasonably typical of the thinking behind this type of development. The project began by creating a local information database and making it available, both in printed form and through a work-station at the Mamelodi Public Library. The idea is to develop an independent service which will offer citizens access to computer information resources, using touch screen to promote ease of use. Other technical facilities (telephone, fax, photocopying) will be offered both to support this information facility and to raise income for what is intended to become a financially self-sufficient organization. A media facility for community use completes the basic vision of what is intended to become Mamelodi Information Bureau (MIB).

It is an attractive vision, but vision it largely remains at present. In South Africa there is a good chance that technology-based services can succeed, at least in some communities. Their validity through-out most of the rest of the continent is more questionable. The wisdom of committing too much effort to trying to begin with a technology-based service in countries without South Africa's infra-structure should be considered very carefully. After all, there is no reason why technology should not eventually be grafted on to a service which initially employs more mundane, but proven meth-ods.

Itinerant services

The idea that information service should not be tied to a fixed place, or centre, is strongly argued by, among others, Ndiaye. He suggests that the term Centre de Documentation communitaire (CDC) which has been used to describe information services for the community should be abandoned in favour of Points d'Informa-tion et de Communication à la Base (PICB).[34] The word 'communication' is an explicit shift in emphasis, and the use of 'point' is intended as a substitute for 'centre', which has too much of the context of a physical structure or building. If communication is the aim, then this must be done where the people are. Travel to a centre is time- and energy-consuming for people who have no transport but their own legs, and who, in rural areas, may live at considerable distances from each other. The difficult question is what form a 'point' might actually take.

There has long been an answer to this in the concept of the mobile library (and, indeed, in the itinerating collections repre-sented by the book box and home library services of various kinds described above). Service from a vehicle can link a whole series of points, chosen to bring information to where people live and congregate. The mobile library using trucks and other vehicles with internal combustion engines has, however, generally been a problem in African conditions. It has not stood up well to the rigours of dirt roads, and the maintenance expenses have generally been well beyond the financial means of African library and information services. When it does work well, as does the Bulawayo Public Library, it is in the outskirts of a community with good roads, which can somehow or other assemble finance for the running expenses.

The idea has not generally been domesticated to good effect in Africa, although there are exceptions to this. Booksellers have experimented successfully with taking services out into the community. A Zimbabwean company, Grassroots Books, did literature outreach in the years 1993–5, taking writers and a car boot full of books to rural centres. Seventy or so such visits in a two-year period drew good crowds (as many as a thousand on one occasion) and sold out the book supplies at discounted prices. What is more, this took place in poor rural communities. Grassroots Books planned to begin a regular mobile bookshop in 1997, selling affordable books to people who did not have easy access to conventional bookshops. Lake Books of Kenya have sold books in a similar way; one of Dakar's major bookshops is well known for its yellow bookshop truck; and a *librairie-bus* tours cultural centres, schools and hotels in the environs of Bamako, and visits events like conferences and seminars, selling and publicizing books.[35]

Unusual forms of mobile library service are also to be found. Mali has a library in a railway carriage.[36] The *wagon-bibliothèque* serves ten communities along the railway line, for two days each. A railway carriage avoids many of the maintenance problems experienced by road vehicles, and is well suited to the needs of a country where many settlements cluster along a railway line. The Zimbabwean RLRDP provides a mobile service of a very different sort from its Nkayi library. This uses a donkey cart as its means of conveyance. The cart was manufactured by a local artisan to RLRDP's specification, and can carry up to 400 books. It serves communities in a 5-kilometre radius from its base, and its debut in 1995 was something of a local sensation. The cart combines a number of virtues in addition to its ability to catch the imagination of local people, and overseas visitors. As a physical product of the community, it encourages a sense of ownership, and maintenance depends on materials and skills easily available locally. Outside the local community, its greatest significance is to draw attention to the validity of low-tech solutions to problems like transport. Pack mules have been used in South America to transport collections of books to remote communities; bicycles can move information workers, and small quantities of materials, at low cost in difficult terrain; and other variants can, no doubt, be developed if they are encouraged and supported.

The contemplation of the mobile library tends, however, to direct the emphasis towards modes of transport, and away from the points at which information might be delivered. The idea is that the information worker should move through the community, meeting individuals or groups, either in their homes or at agreed meeting places. This is not new. Aboyade's RUDIS experiment involved information workers regularly coming to an agreed point in the village they sought to serve. Villagers were encouraged to come with questions to be answered, or to hear readings from materials of their choice.[37] Travelling to the people is also precisely what the agricultural and other extension workers already do. In the Training and Visit system of organizing extension work, the agent has a demonstration plot in each village or hamlet, where his presence is expected at an agreed time each fortnight. The agent can also visit farms, homes, community centres and other public places as needed, either to pass on a formal message or advise on some plan or difficulty. The agents are essentially communicators who bring their essential stores of information in their own heads, or in very portable forms (a few leaflets and magazines, or some seeds and other agricultural samples). An itinerant information service would need to move more materials around, but the quantity should not be so great that it could not be contained in a pack or manageable box.

As to the points to be visited, Rosenberg makes suggestions in a passage where she says that:

> One of my (maybe) utopian visions for rural Africa is an information centre without four walls: instead the information worker uses traditional centres of information transfer as his/her library – the village market place, the beer hall, the health clinic, the clothes washing area. The librarian can have a role as information intermediary in a number of contexts; skills in information handling are not only useful within the confines of libraries or information centres.[38]

The places she mentions are indeed the natural points for the communication of information. The indigenous knowledge and communication systems continue to be manifest at such places, and if a new information system is to recommend itself to people, it is there that its presence should be felt.

Probably the best of all is the market, which provides a commercial meeting point for people living within a radius which is traditionally defined by distances that could be walked by people and their livestock within the hours of a market day.[39] The market also connects the people it serves with a broader world through the agency of traders who visit from other market towns and the cities. Brieger and Kendall identified the market as the prime means of setting up a mechanism of health surveillance, and it also offers marvellous scope for information dissemination and response.[40] The market ethos is dominated by exchange, not only of goods but also of information, and there are established and valued standards of trustworthiness attached to markets and all the types of transactions that take place there. An information stall in a market-place, preferably staffed by a known and trusted local resident, could conceivably have exceptionally good levels of contact with a client community and could develop high credibility.

Unfortunately, formal markets, so closely spaced and effective in West Africa, are not to be found at quite the same levels of development in the rest of the continent. Good alternative potential information points can be found, even if many of them have drawbacks which cause them to be less appropriate than the market. Official meeting places and traditional courts, like the chief's *kgotla* in Botswana, where announcements and debates take place, have a certain value for the communication of self-contained packages of information, but are less useful for interactive purposes. Churches and mosques exclude non-believers. Beer halls and informal beer brewing and drinking events offer a receptive atmosphere, but high probability of serious message-distortion through hangover clouds. Clothes washing areas are good for communication by a female information worker, but when a river or lake is used, women also wash their bodies there, and modesty excludes men from such places. Men have their own washing places at points discreetly separate.

One of the most interesting suggestions on a good information point is Durrani's identification of the communication virtues of the ubiquitous food kiosks in Kenya.[41] He points out that, in addition to the discussion that takes place between owners and customers, information posters already decorate their walls, customers read aloud to others from newspapers, and they frequently have radios, cassette players and even TV sets in use. A regular visit from an information worker, using the kiosk as the point for an information clinic, would only need to build on and confirm some of its existing character.

Rosenberg's list of points of information transfer actually includes one non-traditional point, and that is the health clinic. Along with this it is necessary to remember educational establishments, and other government and local government premises, some of which actually function to an extent as advisory or social welfare centres. The providers of a new information service would be well advised to visit, and if possible leave information materials at, points like this where people already come for information connected with their health, educational and other needs. Health advisory workers, school teachers, village development workers and others already communicate extensively with the community.

One could also suggest links with a variety of institutions, for example, self-help housing agencies, financial and mutual aid institutions such as burial societies, and village cooperatives. Working in conjunction with such groups gives the information worker potential access to community members precisely at their time of need. It also enables the information service to communicate with people through the proxy of a health worker, other community worker or society officer who has been provided with information, either for dissemination or as a response to a specific instance of need.

Perhaps the most attractive option of this kind was identified by Sturges and Chimseu when they looked at rural communication in Malawi.[42] The extension services are the prime institutional means of communication with the rural community. The agents are supposed to visit every village, and agriculture is their chief focus of interest, as it is that of the rural citizen. Despite some community suspicion and disillusion concerning their performance of their role, their opportunities to build up local knowledge and networks of personal connection and trust are almost unique. They have information in abundance to communicate, but what they lack are means to perfect their comprehension of some of this material, and to respond to client queries on topics which are beyond the scope of their immediate knowledge. If information service of quite a rudimentary kind were to be provided for the extension agents they could become the most effective proxies for a general community information service. Such service to extension would need to take the form of some basic reference materials at their local administrative headquarters, and a means whereby the queries they received from their clients could be answered within the fortnightly cycle of their travels. Little attention has been paid to this need, although Bernardo suggests a central depository agency to support extension workers by collecting,

> primers, extension pamphlets, farmers' bulletins, and training material for extension [which] are produced by colleges and universities, research centers and other government agencies.[43]

Finally, in this discussion of itinerant services, there is the possible association of information provision with literacy classes and follow-up activity groups. The scope for work in conjunction with literacy programmes is immense. A literacy class brings together a group of people who have made a conscious decision to learn. They want to have access to reading matter and they also have questions on a host of matters to which they want answers. Visits to classes in progress and liaison with tutors and group leaders offer enormous scope to the information worker. The involvement of learners with the literacy programme can be one which extends over quite a long period. A major national literacy programme, such as that in Ethiopia, had to adjust to the realization that nearly 40 per cent of literacy course participants failed to gain their certificate, and required one or more subsequent courses of training. A post-literacy phase also had to be introduced, linked to the community education services, so as to support those who had successfully completed the course, and those who were still learning.

To support this type of need there were proposed: village reading rooms; community skills training centres; regional radio stations with educational programming; information bulletins in the vernaculars; and a network of district centres to bring together educational personnel, representatives of popular associations, and the general public for the encouragement of community involvement in all types of educational institutions and programmes. Such a set of programmes offers endless opportunities for information service involvement of one kind or another. An account of the Malawian Functional Literacy Programme suggests that:

> A high level of illiteracy hinders information exchange and the transfer of skills. Illiterate farmers, for example, have limited access to information that could help them to increase their agricultural output through

the adoption of modern agricultural techniques, since the dissemination of these techniques is mostly through the print media.[44]

While this is intended as purely an argument for literacy education, it also draws attention to the scope for informing rural people through provision of information services along with instruction in reading and writing.

By Whom?

If the answer to the question 'Where?' seems to be 'Everywhere', the answer to 'By whom?' is probably 'By everyone', and sometimes even, 'By everyone, except me'. The ideal people to run new kinds of information service are not easy to identify, because the role presents a daunting mix of the difficult and the unattractive. It is genuinely difficult because it is new and involves grappling with the intractable problems of the less privileged part of society. It is considered unattractive in that it involves a great amount of time spent in the neglected rural and urban areas. Existing information professionals have not generally shown much relish for work of this kind. As suggested in Chapter 3, they have often retreated from challenges into sterile preoccupation with routine, and have resisted taking posts away from the attractions of the cities.

The first issue to deal with is whether information service to the community is a professional, para-professional or non-professional activity. One simple answer to this is that there is a need for trained people at all of these levels. This does rather assume a hierarchical or pyramidal structure, using different types of personnel for different tasks and responsibilities. In such a structure, there might be a core group of professionally qualified people managing the service. Para-professionals would then provide the skills for the organization of materials that they had acquired in gaining their diplomas and certificates in librarianship. Such skills tend to be more than adequate for the requirements of small, informal collections. At the same time there would be scope for the use of non-professional staff at the point of delivery of the service. Such non-professional staff can bring considerable local credibility and even a missionary enthusiasm which is invaluable in face-to-face contact with the community.

In practice, some systems have a rather flat pyramidal structure, and are staffed more or less entirely by non-professionals. The RLRDP in Zimbabwe, for instance, staffs its library and resource centres from the local community. Perhaps not entirely typical, but a marvellous example, is Mrs Jester Moyo who re-enrolled at school at the age of 48 to catch up with the primary education she had missed. Since then she has worked as a librarian with RLRDP, and has coordinated the network of Sizanani Clubs, also promoted by RLRDP, which bring together women in income generating projects, such as soap-making, basket weaving and pottery. All this has been achieved against the background of a struggle to exist and bring up a family in a demanding rural environment. Despite what was said in Chapter 3 about the problems of bringing the barefoot principle into information service, the advantages should not be ignored.

Certainly there should be little trouble in accepting that there is genuine scope for non-professional staff at the more rudimentary service points like reading rooms. The problem sometimes comes in the way this is implemented. The Tanzanian reading rooms are staffed by someone who is referred to as a 'village librarian'.[45] This village librarian is selected from the community, with no more than a primary level standard of education. The same person often also performs the functions of a literacy group tutor. In return for the payment of an honorarium equal to one-eighth of the national minimum wage, the village librarian is expected to open the reading room and supervise its use, as well as organizing discussion groups around what is currently being read. Irregular arrival of the honorarium, imprecise lines of responsibility, lack of helpful contact with the central administration, all tend to act as a disincentive to the village librarian to become a committed proselytizer of the reading room concept. This is unfortunate, because where non-professional staff are used, it cannot be as a cheap substitute for better-educated people. Their genuine virtues for this type of work need to be used and rewarded.

There must be a temptation when proposing a service which attempts something substantially beyond provision of a reading facility, to think that para-professional staffing would be a good compromise solution. Since community members recruited and trained on the barefoot principle need administrative and technical back up, and since well-qualified professionals are very expensive to hire, it might be asked who could be better to provide the back up than people who are rigorously trained in the routine aspects of librarianship technique? Such a conclusion could seriously underestimate the demands that really effective information service places on the provider. There is no valid escape into routine where activities like information repackaging, community profiling, referral and networking are concerned. They all require informed judgement and knowledge beyond the normal librarianship curriculum. Good para-professionals frequently take on such tasks and do them well, but they do so without the levels of recognition and reward that the tasks deserve. There is a role for the para-professional on the administrative and technical side, but not as a substitute for professional input, and probably not as a substitute for the community service-deliverer either.

The role of the professional is mainly at the administrative heart of things in this hierarchical version of the idea. Adimorah puts probably the boldest case for professional input, when he suggests that every information centre could need as many as five professional staff with specialized knowledge and skills.[46] A good service of any kind certainly calls for management skills. Finances, personnel and other resources require informed attention and positive decisions, especially in a climate of shortages and limitations.

It is also impossible to envisage worthwhile information flows without specialists monitoring published and other information with a view to repackaging it for use at community level. The grey literature which ought to provide raw material for information service cannot simply be handed over to unsophisticated users in the hope that they will be able to interpret it and obtain value from it. Identifying what it contains that is of use for this purpose and presenting it in new forms is a task that requires knowledge of both the subject matter and the potential users.[47] The professional should also have, or easily acquire, the social science research techniques needed to profile the community, and the horizons of knowledge useful in building up contact with the subject experts who will be able to answer difficult queries or prepare very specialized materials. Liaison with experts in information technology, media and the performance arts is also a highly professional function.

It is genuinely doubtful that all of this can, as a matter of course, be expected of one individual. A professional team with each of its members specializing would definitely be needed. Setting aside this matter of just how many areas of professional expertise need to be covered, it must be remembered that this is all part of a discussion of a hierarchical type of structure. It relates to a vision of a system managed by professionals, administered by para-professionals and delivered by non-professionals.

A second rather different approach would be to suggest that a hierarchical structure totally misses the scope for innovative professional information work in direct contact with the community. If, for instance, an itinerant service of some kind were to be planned, it could involve information clinics at markets, churches, food kiosks or other suitable points. These might indeed be staffed by local volunteers or by para-professionals, but the likelihood is that to make them most effective a considerable level of professional input would be needed at the service point. This may be a little difficult to envisage, but it is very much the type of immersion in the community practised in francophone countries by the *animateur*. The adoption of the concept of the *animateur*, in the form of some kind of information animator, could actually permit a better definition of many of the functions of a new information service.

The information animator could be the kind of enabler, or facilitator, mentioned in many proposals for new services, that a librarian seldom tends to be. The main task of the animator, would be that of mediating between the content of print and other formal resources and the oral medium in which the material would mainly be delivered. The animator would not only contribute to the repackaging of information, but act as an interpreter of the information, aiding the individual in absorbing and using it. In the reverse direction the animator should be able to contribute to the repackaging of traditional content, in forms such as audio- or videotape, and print, as discussed later in this chapter. In this way the messages of oral society would be made open to a wider audience, and the voice of the underprivileged made audible outside the immediate community. The animator would also be available to advise other agencies and services on the delivery of their information and obtain feedback from their clientele.

At present, as the previous section of this chapter shows, information services appear under many names, but the balance between library and communication activities is skewed towards a document-based approach and to employment of people who are recognizably librarians. New types of personnel, comparatively free from the library preoccupation, could take service out of the four walls of the information store, deliver it to new people in new places, using new forms and methods. They would have to have a distinctly different professional education, but the prototypes of a curriculum for such an education do already exist in the educational institutions of the francophone countries, which have been turning out *animateurs* in numbers for years. There are also a few precedents elsewhere, such as the systems of cooperative learning for rural development, created with this kind of service in mind, at Hawkesbury College, Western Australia.[48]

If information animators were to be educated on such models, they could be employed by government agencies, such as national library services or departments of adult education, by NGOs of various kinds, or by a new and distinct information service. Recruiting for such services would certainly not be easy unless there were an educational programme to produce them. If there were no such programme, animators might need to be recruited from young professionals in adult education or the existing information professions. Their training for the job would then be the issue. So far, training of para- and non-professionals for information service provides most of the experience that can be examined for guidance as to how it should be done.

Training for a service intended to be radically different from existing services calls for a radically different approach. This point was well taken by the Zimbabwean Ministry of Community, Cooperative Development and Women's Affairs when it set up the cadre of village community workers (VCWs).[49] They chose to adopt the 'problem-posing education' ideas and methods of adult education and community development of Paulo Freire, using his principles of conscientization and empowerment, to underpin the programme that was created.[50] The intention was to encourage open and flexible attitudes, in recognition that the VCWs would need to analyse and reflect on the situations they met, if they were to come up with constructive and democratic solutions. Training took place in the very community halls, school premises or churches where the VCWs' work would take place. The actual trainers were district teams consisting of the Ward Community Coordinators who were at the step immediately above the VCWs in the personnel hierarchy. The content and methods of the training came down to the trainers from a national training team at the Ministry, through eight provincial teams, in a cascade training strategy which thus involved the Ministry staff at all levels.

The curriculum had three parts: a core, a local element, and a health-related element. Training booklets were developed for each element, embodying the same philosophy of empowerment and involvement for the training which the VCWs were expected to use in their day-to-day work. If the need for community decision making, popular power and people's participation were to be stressed in the field activities, then the training needed to use the same principles. Freire's methods involve the use of pictures, drama, song, dance and poetry as means to enable people to identify, analyse and develop plans for their own life situations. Their use in the training process may seem to compromise the dignity of the trainers, but anyone who has observed training of this type in practice will have been caught up by the sheer fun and enthusiasm it generates. It is ideal in method and, to a great extent, in content for training the community information worker.

The problem with most training specifically for information service is that the burden of librarianship technique tends to lie heavily upon it. Rosenberg points out that in a whole series of schemes, the training for the non-professional service deliverers has been aimed merely at keeping records and the maintenance of stock.[51] The training is sometimes not very extensive or regularly refreshed. The staff of the Botswana reading rooms when surveyed in the early 1990s, for instance, had only had a course of three days to a week's duration, and virtually no refreshers appeared to have taken place over a ten-year period.[52] Most of the staff were desperate for more training, and about one-quarter of them would have liked to take a certificate in librarianship.

Training has been a slightly more positive experience elsewhere. For Tanzanian village librarians it consisted of a one-month course at a Folk Development College.[53] The courses had their drawbacks. They were said to suffer from a dearth of instructional material in Swahili and insufficient follow-up. A very positive feature, however, was that the village librarians studied alongside people taking similar courses on health, agriculture or building. The very fact that the courses placed them in a broader learning context was a potential contribution to better motivation and morale. The basic problem may also be exacerbated, rather than solved, by manuals for community libraries and information centres. These tend to look uncomfortably like primers in library administration.

The lesson has, however, been learned in some cases. RLRDP holds workshops in Integrated Rural Library and Information Services to train its personnel in which the programme does include basic librarianship, but also has coverage of: gender and development studies; environment and cultural studies; popular education methods; and networking. Workshop participants are encouraged to identify specific community information needs, and the skills of community profiling are taught. Ways in which the trainees can direct library and information service towards the needs of their own community are developed out of discussion. Until there are education programmes producing a cadre of professional information animators, it is to training programmes that we must look for the development of personnel, and it is at least encouraging that some examples of appropriate practice can be found.

In What Forms?

The nature of the packages into which information is placed for the benefit of users is crucial in provision of information services to the whole community. Information consolidation, or repackaging, has already been mentioned a number of times previously, and it is a key to success in this type of provision. The production of good quality packages containing what people want to know in ways they are capable and willing to accept is a demanding assignment. No service is likely to be fully effective if it confines itself to one medium of communication, but the production of information packages in a variety of media calls for a wide range of skills. The choice of whether to use text, audio and visual means, and to use them singly or in combination, can make all the difference between success and failure. Almost all of the media available also have inherent drawbacks which call for caution in their use.

Print materials are definitely important, even in the most resolutely non-library type of service. People want print information, even when it must be read to them by some more literate friend or relation. Print on paper is actually in many ways a very good medium for use in less developed countries. It is very portable, little dependent on technology for its use, its content acquires an aura of authority from the form, and it is good to refer back to after a first reading. Where people are used to receiving print, as in the case of the Malawian Ministry of Agriculture's magazine *Za Achikumbe*, and then find themselves deprived of access to it because of some difficulty of distribution, they complain bitterly.

Reading materials for new literates on topics such as agriculture, health and nutrition, child care, and the skills of local traditional industry, have been prepared to good effect in many countries. For example, a series of pamphlets produced by the National Adult Literacy Programme in Malawi each provide about twenty pages of text in Chichewa, with some simple but effective line drawings as illustrations. Thus a pamphlet on temperance has suitably disgusting depictions of drunkenness, and one on ox-ploughing has good clear drawings of various types of harness and ploughs. The text of the pamphlets is written by a team of carefully selected and instructed writers, often educators, but sometimes librarians. They are made available to the public in the Rural Community Information Centres administered by the National Library Service. Some of them have on the back cover a charming drawing of villagers selecting pamphlets to borrow from the display in a tricycle-borne delivery cart.

Other countries, such as Tanzania, also have considerable experience of publishing to support literacy work, which is relevant to this discussion of print for information services. Tanzania launched its National Literacy Campaign as long ago as 1970 and immediately recognized the need for reading materials appropriate to the needs of new literates. Rural newspapers in Swahili formed a major part of the response to the problem.[54] Unesco and the Norwegian Agency for Development (NORAD) provided the initial funding in 1974 for a programme to produce newspapers. Eventually, a four-page newspaper containing both information and entertainment was provided in most of the areas of rural Tanzania. All the papers had a standard format, with page one covering national news, page two local news, page three a miscellany including letters, and page four a collection of practical material on topics such as 'How to grow better cotton' or 'How to make a wheelbarrow'.

Each newspaper office was run by a team consisting of an editor assisted by six people: a journalist/assistant editor, photolithographer, typist-compositor, messenger, watchman and driver. In addition each paper had its own news-gathering network, using officers at the regional education headquarters, and in the districts and wards the education coordinators. The offices for the newspapers were based in the communities they served, but production was contracted to outside printers. It must be admitted that distribution, as is often the case in rural areas, was a source of difficulties. Even if the editorial and production processes went smoothly there was still the problem of getting the newspaper out to its readers each month. From the regional headquarters the papers were sent by four-wheel drive vehicle to the districts, from where they were further redistributed to individual readers via adult education field staff, using book bags fitted to bicycles. This extended and vulnerable chain of delivery often resulted in newspapers not reaching their readers. The most important thing, however, was that there was a dedicated editorial facility for the creation of reading material for the previously neglected rural population.

The creation and acquisition of audio materials for a sound library, or audiotheque, has been discussed earlier in this chapter, but it should be remembered that audio packages should also be offered by other non media-specialized services. Indeed, it is arguable that the sound library concept, as a distinct form of information service, may not be the best option. The idea offers immediate benefits in that it communicates in a familiar way to people who then need not feel disadvantaged by their poor or nonexistent reading ability. In the long term it may seem to offer them the choice of opting out of literacy altogether, which would be a sad limitation of their horizons. This is not to say that information tapes created for dissemination of information to rural communities, and the products of the commercial recording industry, should not be exploited with enthusiasm by information services. Despite the concerns expressed above, they most certainly should be used whenever appropriate, but in conjunction with other materials. There are, however, more fundamental worries about the sound library and the way it uses audio materials derived from the oral tradition.

One such is the fear that the sound library threatens the oral medium itself by enmeshing it in technological limitations that are not intrinsic to it. The essence of the oral tradition is that it does not deal in fixed packages, but that its content lives and breathes, changing as does a living organism. Recording technology may ultimately inhibit its growth and development by freezing performances in a way which is profoundly untraditional. Once committed to tape, or even worse transcribed to form a written record, many of the added nuances and the adaptability of the forms that are an essential part of the oral medium disappear and thus much of the original message is lost. It is worth noting that the emphasis in writings on the oral medium in information journals has been largely on collection, with little real exploration of the methods let alone the implications of re-dissemination of content.[55] It would be a great pity if, because of a lack of sensitivity to the problems that might be caused by the creation of information delivery packages of material from the oral tradition, the actual foundations of a sophisticated orality were undermined.

A second concern is that, as the content of the oral tradition is in some way the intellectual property of the people, its security could well be violated by fixation and distribution in another medium. The interest of international big business in the pharmaceutical, cosmetic, nutritional and other content of traditional knowledge was discussed in Chapter 2, but that is not quite the full scope of the concern. The dairy industry of Nigeria provides an illustration of the point. The industry is dominated by the informal sector, and in particular by large numbers of Fulani women who produce a variety of milk products suited to local tastes, human physiology and climatic conditions. The sector operates successfully despite government attempts at intervention, and the competition of formal businesses. It is rooted in complex relations between consumers, farmers and the Fulani dairywomen, involving networks of obligation and communication which, in turn, bring a host of side benefits to the community. Researchers have contemplated circulation of documentation of their knowledge of the processes in a whole range of media, so as to enrich the dairying community's business capabilities. However, they have held back for reasons including the possibility that:

> Better-quality information about rural people's knowledge could strengthen the position of urban-biased macro-planners and large-scale entrepreneurs in an extractive economic system, allowing them to better manipulate market conditions.[56]

The researchers had looked at communicating information from the Fulani dairying industry not only by audio methods, but by using visual materials such as photographs, drawings and slides. The use of other visual forms such as posters and film strips is also practiced in rural communication. There are two reasons why this is an essential element of the information delivery package spectrum. The first is that, in societies with low levels of literacy, the visual has the potential to communicate where written text cannot. The second is that some essentially practical matters are infinitely better communicated via visual media than they are by either the spoken or written word. Both of these assume, however, standards of 'visual literacy' which may not be found in communities which have almost no regular access to pictures. Visiting homes in deprived rural areas, and also in the poorer urban areas, it becomes clear that most people possess virtually no pictures of any kind, and that they consequently treasure the occasional old calendar or poster which might have come their way.

Educational researchers have explored the precise implications of this deprivation, which amounts to an unfamiliarity with the pictorial and graphic conventions of line, space, scale, form, tone, texture and colour.[57] This can have what may seem surprising consequences. For instance, a bilharzia awareness poster widely used in Eastern Africa included, among a series of other images, a picture of the tiny snail which transmits the disease to those unwary in using water from lakes and streams. Because of the crucial importance of the snail it was depicted many times magnified, alongside quite small pictures of people. Villagers shown this poster by health education workers are said to have claimed that they had no problem because there were no enormous snails like that in their area, and if such snails arrived they would be noticed immediately and could easily be avoided.

To awareness of the difficulties of visual communication as such, should be added a similar consciousness of the layers of cultural assumptions that are contained in all pictures. Sophia Kaane's work on the use of posters in Kenyan health education showed that people were frequently disturbed and distracted by aspects portrayed which were alien to their local culture.[58] Also, they often focused on the decorative aspect of a poster, to the detriment of their understanding of its message. These and other communication problems were experienced less strongly by viewers who had received higher levels of schooling. The Kenyan health education posters were generally sent into the community with little care to ascertain whether their messages could be comprehended. This rather counters a common fear that the use of posters and other visual images by marketing companies to manipulate popular tastes and consumption makes the medium particularly prone to exploitive communication. It does not, however, remove the anxiety that they are generally used for one-way, top–down communication. This anxiety provides the energy for an excellent manual on the creation by Linney of people-centred visual aids for development purposes.[59]

The creator of images for development communication does need to work very closely with the community in which those images will be used. Alioune Diouf, a Senegalese artist, was trained at the École nationale des Beaux Arts in Dakar, and chose there a communication option usually favoured by students intending to go into advertising. He has, instead, specialized in development communication posters for the Ministries of Health and Education. This has involved both single posters and sequences of posters in a display case (*boite d'images*) to be used by communication workers while giving talks. He always works on the principle of testing his visual ideas in the target community, so as to enable him to use appropriate cultural detail in his depiction of people and places. This also makes it possible to find ways of avoiding offence to people's susceptibilities, when dealing with delicate matters such as AIDS transmission. Diouf, and his methods, are precisely what is needed in the creation of not only visual but all other materials for use by information services.

The need for highly specialized judgement and skill in the creation of information materials is felt even more strongly when the audio and visual are used in combination. Audio-visual communication is undoubtedly popular. The Malawian Ministry of Agriculture's yellow vehicles which take film shows to the villages, for instance, are eagerly anticipated and the infrequency of their visits bemoaned. There is, however, every reason to doubt whether it is the content of their information documentaries which is the attraction or the sheer entertainment value of a film show. Film and video are such seductive media that there is an ever-present danger that they overshadow any message they are supposed to carry. Such is the technical sophistication of their production, that it is also debatable whether information institutions themselves can ever create substantial film or video packages satisfactorily. The expense of creating worthwhile products is considerable, and the risk of miscommunication much higher than with other materials.

Multimedia, which go several stages further by offering juxtapositions of text, sound, graphics and the moving image, present much the same problem. It is easy to argue the case that multimedia offer the ideal means of development communication. They contain information accessible at various levels, whether to the literate, the semi-literate or the wholly oral user, with one source reinforcing the other so as to consolidate learning. What is more, they are interactive, encouraging users to assemble and compare materials in different forms and from different sources, according to their own preferences. Since they are generally delivered in optical disk form, all the arguments used to justify CD-ROM as a practical information delivery mechanism in developing countries also apply to them. Unfortunately, all this array of virtues is undermined by precisely the arguments about expense and the technical difficulties of production that have been outlined in relation to film and video. It needs to be noted that these difficulties did, in fact, lead to a much slower take-up of multimedia than predicted even in the industrialized countries where they were developed.

If this account of the packages in which information can be delivered to the people seems to concentrate overmuch on the problems, this is deliberate. It is common to dismiss the question of the forms in which information might be delivered by a cheerful recitation of the various forms that are available, as if this is all the answer that is needed. It is not that simple. As was stressed at the start of this section, good choices of forms, and the combinations in which to use forms, are vital. When making such choices it is vital to remember that all forms are not equal, and that what is appropriate varies according to the relationship between the characteristics of a particular form and the circumstances in which it is proposed to use it.

How?

It is absolutely clear that the delivery method employed by any innovative information service of the kind proposed in this chapter must be essentially oral. It can incorporate drama, puppetry, song or any other valid communication method, and the package presented to the user may certainly include the written word, graphic illustration, audio-tape or even more sophisticated technology, but all of this must either serve, or be served by, oral communication. An appreciation of the ways in which the oral and the written interrelate is not a simple thing to develop, but as Ndiaye suggests,

> The librarian's job is to try to gain in-depth knowledge of orality in order to mark out the areas where there is conflict and those where orality and libraries are really compatible. The needs of both must be brought into harmony.[60]

The conclusion that the traditional oral medium should play a major part in information systems has been reached from other directions. People working in the discipline of communication studies, such as Kwame Boafo, have advocated ideas of precisely this type. He, for instance, argues that,

> An optimal information utilisation in rural development in Africa is dependent on communication strategies which consistently amalgamate the traditional media and the modern media technologies.[61]

Delivery through traditional media would not only involve the passing on of answers to specific questions, but also contributing to the incorporation of information of general interest, on such topics as health and hygiene, farming, child-rearing or education, into the framework of traditional narrative, song, drama and festivals, as suggested by Aboyade.[62]

The question immediately occurs as to how this might relate to existing community practices and preferences. We do, in fact, have occasional insights into how oral communication has been spontaneously used in association with other forms to achieve particular purposes. For instance, a fascinating variety of ways in which traditional styles of communication were used, first as a means to generate informed debate, and then as a means of more widespread dissemination of information, are illustrated by the story of Odi Weavers in Botswana.[63] The small rural factory called Lentswe la Odi Weavers has produced woven tapestries, wall hangings and carpets since the early 1970s. The artistic content of the tapestries is the product of a communal discussion process.

> Themes are drawn from real incidents in the women's lives, current events in the newspaper or radio, traditional stories, arguments or issues which come up in their daily work and topics of conversation in the village.[64]

To watch the weavers creating their large and colourful tapestries without any blueprint, using strands of wool to express their visions in unique and personal form, is an exciting experience. Each completed tapestry has content which can provide a focus for more discussion, debate and dialogue in the factory. In this way, a purely productive activity has taken on a role in a wider communal life. The weavers are more than just contributors to a productive process, and the tapestries are more than just a product.

Similar processes of debate and the artistic expression of ideas and opinions have been used in solving problems in the factory.

Originally it was a cooperative with full sharing of the whole range of tasks, but as the factory grew a management committee took firmer control. The weavers began to resent their loss of control, and expressed this in songs and a drama which depicted the change in worker–management relationships. The resulting discussions brought an acceptable resolution of the difficulties. Subsequently, as the profits from the weaving factory grew, so the weavers decided to establish a development fund, which they called *Sethunya sa Dithabololo* (Flower of Development). This was to provide loans and grants to other groups and individuals to help them establish small-scale productive projects. Once again, the weavers used a variety of forms of communication to promote the fund. The traditional village court, the *kgotla*, was exploited as a forum for publicity. Tapestry exhibitions and the presentation of dramas were used to explain the fund in nearby villages. Gradually takers emerged, and new businesses were set up using funds from Odi.

The extent to which a spontaneous process like this can, or even should, be simulated by external information providers is an important question. The oral medium can be seen as the one authentic voice of the community, through which various strategies and options for development should be allowed to emerge without any outside interference.[65] This is a valid viewpoint, but it is really not possible for those who live in a predominantly oral society to avoid the need to absorb and, if possible, benefit from modern ideas. Likewise, those who wish to communicate with them cannot ignore the opportunities offered by traditional media. While we have argued earlier that the recording of content from the oral culture tends to fix such content in a way that is alien to the spirit of oral society, the contrary is true of the introduction of fresh themes and messages. This actually accords very well with the mutability of oral culture. Traditional media can, in this light, be seen as a wholly suitable vehicle for modern messages.

Experiments conducted in Nigeria in the early 1970s by Fiofori showed that people happily accepted the use of oral narratives to convey modern messages, adjusting easily to new content in old forms. The familiarity of the narrator and the form of the narration, in conjunction with the potential for dialogue, were the strengths of this technique, which he referred to (more than slightly inelegantly) as 'communoraldition'.[66] Another relevant term, applied to the medium rather than the process, is 'oramedia'.[67] What should be remembered in looking at oramedia, is that they tend to be

talked about in the context of what might be called 'official communication', where accurate passing on and absorption of messages,
rather than the dialogue suggested by communoraldition, has been
the main issue. This is rather the way it is used by bodies such as the
Malawian Ministry of Health. The Ministry's Katemera Band, a
nine-strong touring ensemble, performs songs and playlets containing health messages as part of an overall communication strategy.
Use of oramedia can be at heart a one-way, and even top–down,
type of communication, passing a message from a professional to
community members.

What is important is always to provide for two-way communication, so that the information that people receive is what they truly
desire. An information surgery, held at some information institution, or at one of the informal meeting places where people gather
to talk over the business of the day, might well use oral narrative to
pass on detail concerning matters of general interest. But at such
surgeries the animator, or other information professional, would
need to spend time in dialogue which explored the information
needs of individuals and groups. Such occasions could also be
opportunities to discuss and interpret the content of broadcasting
and newspapers. All this should ideally be done in close relationship with, and to a certain extent through the agency of, established
community practices and institutions.

First of all, traditional beliefs must not merely be respected, but
can also be incorporated into the content of communication. A
project for the encouragement of tree planting in rural Zimbabwe,
for instance, needed to build on the extensive and detailed local
knowledge about the viability and usefulness of planting certain
varieties. It also needed to take into account the existing structures
of local leadership and consultation. But, more than that, it had to
show an awareness that the protection of trees could have a religious dimension in matters such as rain making.

> Big trees should be conserved because the cuckoo bird sings for rain
> and it likes to rest in such trees. Ancestral spirits also come and rest in
> these trees when they attend rain making ceremonies. People also
> protect trees for fear of retribution. For example, if they cut down trees
> they can be punished by the high god *Zame* who does it by stopping
> rains.[68]

The reverse process of including themes of current concern in
traditional instruction is also important. Initiation systems for

young men and women have been neglected in recent years in most African countries, seemingly on the grounds that they are a relic of a superstitious past. Their association with male circumcision (and sometimes the equivalent practice for women) has also discredited them. Their neglect has been recognized as a loss by chiefs and elders, and the revival of systems such as *bogwera* among the Bakgatla in Botswana has been a deliberate move to restate old educational and cultural values. Revival of such ceremonial can easily incorporate modern information. The Society for Women and AIDS in Zambia (SWAAZ), for instance, has, with finance from United Nations agencies and Norwegian and Irish government aid agencies, begun to make use of traditional education practices called *imbusa*.[69] These involve instructing young people who are about to get married in sexual matters, the dangers of promiscuity and, now, how to avoid AIDS. The instruction, given by trained traditional counsellors called *banafimbusa*, takes place in classrooms with symbolic pictures on the walls, and makes use of songs and dance. The principle behind this combination of the current and the traditional is precisely that which needs to inspire a new form of information service.

Information service needs to work through a host of existing societies and organizations. Social, sporting, financial and other mutual aid societies have, as noted earlier, blossomed in recent years. Extension services have also turned, in many cases, to working through groups. In Botswana, rural people were encouraged to form groups to help design technology improvement projects, by the Agricultural Technology Improvement Project (ATIP).[70] The idea appealed to the participants, and other groups emerged to tackle issues such as control of livestock parasites, fencing and provision of water.[71] Where such groups exist, extension workers can provide information support and seek to direct resources their way. What is more, their community credibility and experience in dealing with outside advisors makes them ideal contact and communication foci for an information service.

Most significant of all, in dealing with communities where tradition is particularly strong, the elected or hereditary leaders are an indispensable piece in the jigsaw puzzle. To illustrate this, attempts to assist the Boran pastoralists of northern Kenya in managing the natural resources available to them, started with an assessment of customary institutions and resource management rules.[72] The elected clan leaders, the *jalaba*, were found to have an extensive capacity for mediation and conciliation, even though their decision-making powers were limited. In particular, the *jalaba* were capable of playing a major role in clan redistribution of livestock. The movement of herds to make best use of scarce water and fodder was also vitally important. This was dealt with by groups called *deda*, in which any herd owner could speak, which met and took decisions by consensus. In their task of designing means to improve resource management, the researchers found that their task was part done already through the agency of these customary institutions. The need was to work with them, strengthening and redirecting them in the process. The importance for information service of such roles and institutions, and their equivalents in other societies, is obvious. In conjunction with statutory councils and committees they define the limitations within which a well-organized information service can work, and indicate the channels through which information can be passed most effectively.

The information worker can, in some communities, call on traditional institutions expressly intended for the transmission of information. In many West African societies the town crier, an individual known only as a colourful relic in Europe, still shouts messages around the village. As Odi explains:

> The message the town crier delivers may vary according to need and circumstance: it could be informing the people of a vital meeting with the village head, or a decision by the elders concerning a particular event in the village, or it may be merely to announce the visit of an important government official.[73]

An institution more apt for the announcement of information surgeries or the transmission of information of general interest would be hard to invent. Where such practices survive, or where they could be revived, or introduced, information service could develop a close and mutually supportive relationship with them.

If ways of working through existing structures can be established, the most natural idea to follow next is using the performance arts in information service. There is a strong case for this approach, which rests on the fact that performance of many kinds is ubiquitous in traditional African society. Indeed, a living culture naturally renews the content of its own traditional forms. Thus, a study of the role of Ethiopian oral poetry in rural communities reveals that food shortages and their consequences provided thematic material for performers. This occurred sufficiently early in the famine cycle as to constitute something of an indigenous early warning system.[74] At the other end of the scale, in the cities, theatre groups whose work contains a strong political and social content are increasingly to be found. Bulawayo is particularly rich in such groups: for example, Iluba Elimnyama, which tackled women's issues ignored by other groups.[75] Other, possibly less familiar, forms can also be acceptable means to pass on important messages. For instance, an evaluation of the use of puppets in South African AIDS education programmes showed that it improved knowledge, and even influenced behaviour, at least in the short term.[76]

Just exactly how an information service can pass on its messages and responses in performance mode is a question that has yet to be thoroughly answered. Does the information worker need to be a performer too, or is liaison with creators and performers the only answer? The solution is probably a compromise, with performance-oriented information delivery linked with close relationships with individual performers and groups who might accept suggestions as to content for their work. Recruitment of uninhibited information workers who could use song, story and perhaps some other types of performance would certainly be a worthwhile aim for any community-directed service. There is a little guidance on how to do this. As pointed out earlier, Aboyade illustrates some ways in which current content can be introduced in traditional festivals and songs,[77] and Nwagha even presents some songs and jingles (?of her own composition) as an indication of how it might be done.[78] For the most part, however, the integration of performance with information delivery is a technique that has yet to be developed.

A more established practice is the delivery of information at a distance, direct or mediated through performance, by radio. The impact of 'development messages', whether in the form of short advertisement-type slots, or full-length broadcast programmes is debatable. It probably works best in the guise of entertainment, as with a programme such as *Ndinga Nacio* on Kenyan radio, which drew very high audiences with its presentation of real issues in a serial drama about rural life. To achieve the best effect with radio material which is intended to inform the general public, it is best if radio is not used in isolation from other means. Radio listening clubs are an approach to integrating radio communication with local indigenous communication, which complements the work of a community information service very well. Such clubs are found in Niger, where interaction between programme producers and groups of listeners has continued since the foundation of the Association des Radios-Clubs du Niger in 1962.[79]

The Federation of African Media Women in Zimbabwe developed a programme of Development Through Radio in 1985 to try to ensure that women in rural areas had access to the Radio Four channel which broadcast educational material.[80] For many reasons, including the high cost of radios, batteries and spares, such access was somewhat constrained. Funds were obtained to link up with the Association of Women's Clubs (which runs over 20,000 clubs throughout the country) to form Radio Listening Clubs. These meet regularly to debate current issues. They tape material arising from the meetings, and the material is sent to a coordinator who compiles programmes on subjects chosen from it, using the listeners' own recordings where possible. Pressure on official bodies resulting from programmes has been shown to result in swift solutions, and members' heightened consciousness of the potential for community action has led to the setting up of numerous successful self-help projects by clubs. A tribute to their effectiveness is a certain suspicion on the part of village leaders who feel their own role in an established top–down communication system to be threatened. Certainly, listening clubs are precisely the kind of link to radio communication that an information service could foster and benefit from.

It is also the case that information service needs to give a very significant role to other forms of telecommunication. The paucity of rural telephone services has been mentioned earlier. It is a serious hindrance to people's communication with distant friends and relations and with official bodies. Shortage of telephones also limits one of the most effective means of delivering responses to information needs. It can be observed that when people, however deprived their circumstances, have access to a telephone, they will use it to try to obtain information that they need. If they have the number of the headquarters or local service point of an information service, there are occasions when they will use this. If an information service were to be provided on an itinerant basis, it would be quite deficient if there were no number that could be used to obtain responses between the times of information surgeries. Programmes for the expansion of telephone service are crucial to the functioning of good information services.

Fixed information service points could provide a major community benefit if they had telephones for public use. Private enterprise telephone centres can be found on almost every street corner in Dakar, and the often unreliable telephone booths in other African cities have constant queues of ordinary people waiting to use them. Morris and Stavrou show that rural people travel long distances to use public telephones, but only use private phone services reluctantly, because of the cost.[81] Their experiments with telephone agencies in private premises showed that they were popular with agents, who drew a small but useful income from them. The agencies also pleased users, who got help with telephone use, information on numbers and, often, an informal message-taking service. It is easy to envisage ways in which an information service could benefit from, and give value through, some version of such a scheme.

Telecommunications connection is also, of course, absolutely necessary for any information service that intends to make use of information technology. Schemes for electronic information kiosks using touch screen, or whatever new and improved means the industry develops, require connection to a system. While we are sceptical about the immediate practicability and utility of technology-based services, the provision of telecommunications infrastructure is important and it is needed as early as possible. Information may be delivered to large numbers of African communities by electronic means sooner than the authors anticipate. Any system of information points ought at least, for this reason if no other, to include basic telephone connection. A more sophisticated fibre-optic type of link should then be added whenever the opportunity arises.

To advocate, as we have done, that an information service needs to start from affordable basics of human communication does not mean that the possibility of technological solutions should be wholly neglected. Information technology is the delivery mechanism of the present in many parts of the world, and it is also expected by many to be the paradigm for the delivery of information in Africa at some stage in the future. It is reasonable to anticipate a growing synergy between an immediately achievable paradigm of oral delivery and an 'exotic' paradigm of information technology-mediated delivery in a more long-term future. Karlsson suggests that such synergistic systems are already emerging in South Africa, and they are based on:

• the realization that neither indigenous nor exotic systems are necessarily mutually exclusive and neither is more 'correct' than the other;

- a willingness to explore beyond the traditional limitations of indigenous and exotic systems;
- a critical awareness of the strengths and inadequacies of both the indigenous and the exotic paradigms for contemporary contextual realities; and
- the understanding that rural communities exercise an influence far beyond the extent of indigenous systems and rural areas.[82]

Before such a synergy can develop, however, there is an immediate need to establish information services that work well in the context of a predominantly oral society. Everything that has been discussed in this chapter is intended to assist those who seek to set up such information services. The argument is that their efforts need to be given precedence over those eager to introduce information technology. This is first of all because the people are ready for oral delivery in a way that they are not for technology-based services. It is also because information service delivered by technology surely cannot thrive unless it is introduced into societies already prepared for the idea that they can expect information service provided for their welfare, by its delivery in a much more familiar and acceptable mode.

References

1. Olden, A. Constraints on the development of public library service in Nigeria. *Library Quarterly*, 55, 1985. p.418.
2. Ncube, S. Letter. *The Chronicle* (Bulawayo), 28 October 1996.
3. Nindi, J. Some constraints for production, publication, and distribution of reading materials, especially rural newspapers, for new readers: Tanzania case study. In: Asamani, J.O. *et al.* (eds) *Libraries and Literacy. Proceedings of the 7th Standing Conference of the Eastern, Central and Southern African Librarians (SCECSAL). Gaborone, 4–8 August, 1986.* Gaborone, Botswana Library Association, 1987. 79–87.
4. Botswana Library Association. *Report of the Conference on Libraries and Literacy, Kanye, April, 1985.* Gaborone, Botswana Library Association, 1985.
5. Mutanyatta, J.N.S. and Mchombu, K.J. *The Village Reading Room Services in Botswana: Final Report of an Evaluative Study.* Gaborone, Botswana National Library Service, 1995.
6. Kedem, K.A. Libraries as partners in the fight to eradicate illiteracy in

sub-Saharan Africa. *Journal of Library and Information Science*, 16. 1991. 87–101. p.97.

7. Hickwa, L. Editorial. *RLRDP News Bulletin*, 2, 1996. p.1.
8. Patte, G. and Geradts, A. Home libraries in Zimbabwe. *IFLA Journal*, 11, 1985.
9. Atherton, L. Community libraries in Zimbabwe. *Information Development*, 9, 1993. 36–43.
10. Pilale, A. The project to re-establish the network of libraries in Nampula Province. In: Johansson, E. (ed.) *Seminar on Information Provision to Rural Communities in Africa, Gaborone, Botswana, 22–25 June 1994.* IFLA APL Project report 3. Uppsala, Uppsala University Library, 1995. 82–4.
11. National Library and Documentation Service, Zimbabwe. *Rural Libraries – Matabeleland Region.* Bulawayo, NLDS, 1996. p.1.
12. Giggey, S. *Rural Community Resource Centres: A Guide for Developing Countries.* London, Macmillan, 1988. p.viii.
13. Rural Libraries and Resources Development Programme. *An Introduction to the RLRDP.* Bulawayo, RLRDP, n.d. p.1.
14. Rural Libraries and Resources Development Programme. *A Manual for Rural Libraries in Zimbabwe.* Bulawayo, RLRDP, 1992. p.5.
15. *UNISIST Newsletter*, 20, 1992. p.31.
16. Moyo, O. Empowerment of rural people. *RLRDP News Bulletin*, 1, 1995. p.4.
17. Huttemann, L. and Musana, A. *Information Services for Rural Development and Industry.* Bonn: DSE, 1984.
18. NATCOM/UNESCO National Seminar on Rural Library Development, Owerri, Nigeria, 27–29 September, 1989.
19. Addo, D.B. Workshop on Rural Community Library and Information Centres. *COMLA Newsletter*, 74, 1991. 32–3.
20. Johansson, E. (ed.) *Seminar on Information Provision to Rural Communities in Africa, Gaborone, Botswana, 22–25 June 1994.* IFLA APL Project report 3. Uppsala, Uppsala University Library, 1995.
21. Iwuji, H.O.M. Librarianship and oral tradition in Africa. *International Library Review*, 21, 1989. 201–7. p.206.
22. Danset, F. Public reading in French-speaking Africa. *International Library Review*, 21, 1989. 245–8. p.247.
23. Made, S.M. and Motsi, G.C. Alternative ways of providing rural information. Culture houses: the Zimbabwean experience. *Zimbabwe Librarian*, 18, 1986. 4–6.
24. Atherton, L. Community libraries in Zimbabwe. *Information Development*, 9, 1993. 36–43. p.41.
25. Ibid. p.38.
26. Sagny, R. Popular reading in francophone sub-Saharan Africa. In: Johansson, E. (ed.) op. cit. 17–20.
27. Lebry, R.B. The Centres de Lecture et d'Animation Culturelle, Ivory Coast. In: Johansson, E. (ed.) op. cit. 80–1.
28. Oyeoku, K.K. Publishing in Africa: breaking the development barrier. In: Oluwasanmi, E., McLean, E. and Zell, H. (eds) *Publishing in Africa in the Seventies.* Ife, University of Ife Press, 1975. p.280.

29. Rahnema, M. The sound library, a simple but revolutionary tool for development. *Unesco Journal of Information Science, Librarianship and Archives Administration*, 4, 1982. 151–8. pp.156–7.

30. Diakite, F. The dissemination of information in a rural environment: the public library services and the rural audiolibraries of Mali. In: Johansson, E. (ed.) op. cit. 71–9.

31. Karlsson, J. Methods of information provision to rural communities in South Africa. In: Johansson, E. (ed.) op. cit. 47–57.

32. Stilwell, C. Towards transformation? An update on the Resource Centre Fora of South Africa. *International Information and Library Review*, 26, 1994. 303–13.

33. Kahn, M. Head of Gauteng Information Technology Department, quoted in the *Star* newspaper, 14 September 1996.

34. Ndiaye, A.R. *Communication à la base: enraciner et épanouir*. Dakar, ENDA, 1994. p.240.

35. Fofana, M. Une démarche novatrice pour la diffusion de livre: la librairie-bus. *Takam Tikou*, 5, 1995. 17–18.

36. Cuzin, J. Mali: le wagon-bibliothèque est sur les rails. *Takam Tikou*, 5, 1995. 19–20.

37. Aboyade, B.O. Communication potentials of the library for the non-literates – an experiment in providing information services in a rural setting. *Libri*, 34, 1984. 243–62.

38. Rosenberg, D. Information provision to rural communities in Africa – summary and conclusions. In Johansson, E. (ed.) op. cit. 134–9. p.137.

39. Hill, P. *Rural Hausa: A Village and a Setting*. London, Cambridge University Press, 1972.

40. Brieger, W.R. and Kendall, C. The Yoruba farm market as a communication channel in guinea worm disease surveillance. *Social Science and Medicine*, 42, 1996. 233–43.

41. Durrani, S. Rural information in Kenya. *Information Development*, 1, 1985. 149–57.

42. Sturges, P. and Chimseu, G. The chain of information provision in the villages of Malawi: a rapid rural appraisal. *International Information and Library Review*, 28, 1996. 135–56.

43. Bernardo, F.A. Catering to the information needs of extension workers. In: *Agricultural Information to Hasten Development: Proceedings of the VIth World Congress of the International Association of Agricultural Librarians and Documentalists, Manila, March 1980*. Manila, Agricultural Libraries Association of the Philippines, 1981. 13–19. p.18.

44. Kishindo, P. The Functional Literacy Programme in Malawi: educating adults for improved standards of living. *Journal of Social Development in Africa*, 9, 1994. 19–26. p.20.

45. Nindi, J. op. cit.

46. Adimorah, E.N.O. Establishing community libraries and information resource centres: facilities and resources. In: *Proceedings of the Workshop on Rural Community Library and Information Resource Centres*. Accra, Ghana Library Association, 1992. 53–61.

47. Sturges, P. Using grey literature in informal information services in Africa. *Journal of Documentation*, 50, 1994. 273–90.
48. Bawden, R. Creating learning systems: a metaphor for institutional reform for development. In: Scoones, I. and Thompson, J. (eds) *Beyond Farmer First: Rural People's Knowledge, Agricultural Research and Extension Practice.* London, Intermediate Technology Publications, 1994. 258–63.
49. Higgins, K.M. and Mazula, A. Community development: a national strategy in Zimbabwe. *Community Development Journal*, 28, 1993. 19–30.
50. Freire, P. *Pedagogy of the Oppressed.* London, Penguin Books, 1972.
51. Rosenberg, D. Rural community resource centres: a sustainable option for Africa? *Information Development*, 9, 1993. 29–35. p.33.
52. Mutanyatta, J.N.S. and Mchombu, K.J. op. cit.
53. Nindi, J. op. cit.
54. Ibid.
55. Alemna, A.A. Towards a new emphasis on oral tradition as an information source in African libraries. *Journal of Documentation*, 48, 1992. 422–9.
56. Waters-Bayer, A. The ethics of documenting rural people's knowledge: investigating milk marketing among Fulani women in Nigeria. In: Scoones, I. and Thompson, J. (eds) op. cit. 144–7. p.146.
57. Holmes, A. *A Study of Understanding of Visual Systems in Kenya.* London, OVAC, 1963.
58. Kaane, S.I. A study of the effectiveness of visual media in the promotion of child immunization in Kakamega District, Kenya. Loughborough University, PhD thesis, 1995.
59. Linney, B. *Pictures, People and Power: People-centred Visual Aids for Development.* London, Macmillan, 1995.
60. Ndiaye, R. Oral culture and libraries. *IFLA Journal*, 14, 1988. 40–6.
61. Boafo, S. Utilising development communication strategies in African societies: a critical perspective. *Gazette. International Journal for Mass Communication*, 35, 1985. 83–92.
62. Aboyade, B.O. *The Provision of Information for Rural Development.* Ibadan, Fountain Publications, 1987. pp.57–68.
63. Lewycky, D. *Tapestry: Report from Odi Weavers.* Gaborone, National Institute of Research, 1977.
64. Byram, M.L. Odi Weavers: material culture, workers organization, and nonformal education in Botswana. In: Kidd, R. and Colletta, N. (eds) *Tradition for Development: Indigenous Structures and Folk Media in Nonformal Education.* Bonn, DSE, 1980. 207–44. p.230.
65. Hall, B. and Freyh, B. Foreword. In: Kidd, R. and Colletta, N. (eds) op. cit. 4–6.
66. Fiofori, D. Traditional media and modern messages: a Nigerian study. *Rural Africana*, 27, 1975. 43–52.
67. Ugboajah, F.O. Oramedia in Africa. In: Ugboajah, F.O. (ed.) *Mass Communication, Culture and Society in West Africa.* London, Hans Zell, 1985. 165–76.
68. Matose, F. and Mukamuri, B. Rural people's knowledge and extension

practice: trees, people and communities in Zimbabwe's communal lands. In: Scoones, I. and Thompson, J. (eds) op. cit. 69–75. p.71.

69. Mwansa, V. Sex dancers learn how to score bull's-eye in love and avoid AIDS. *The Chronicle* (Bulawayo), 12 October 1996.

70. Norman, D. *et al.* Farmer groups for technology development: experience in Botswana. In: Chambers, R., Pacey, A. and Thrupp, L.A. (eds) *Farmer First: Farmer Innovation and Agricultural Research.* London, Intermediate Technology Publications, 1989. 136–46.

71. Garforth, C. Reaching the rural poor: a review of extension strategies and methods. In: Jones, G.E. and Rolls, M.J. (eds) *Progress in Rural Extension and Community Development.* Chichester, John Wiley and Sons, 1982. 43–70. p.54.

72. Swift, J. Local customary institutions as the basis for natural resource management among Boran pastoralists in northern Kenya. *IDS Bulletin,* 22, 1991. 34–7.

73. Odi, A. Library and information dissemination in a traditional society: the Igbo of eastern Nigeria. *International Information and Library Review,* 26, 1994. 1–9. p.4.

74. Martin, A. Guided by those versed in the ways of famine. *Guardian* (UK), 23 August 1996.

75. Globerman, E. Backstage on the frontline: Iluba Elimnyama – a Bulawayo theatre collective. *Journal of Southern African Studies,* 16, 1990. 359–62.

76. Skinner, D. *et al.* An evaluation of an education programme on HIV infection using puppetry and street theatre. *AIDS Care,* 3, 1991. 317–29.

77. Aboyade, B.O. *The Provision of Information for Rural Development.* Ibadan, Fountain Publications, 1987.

78. Nwagha, G.K.N. Information needs of rural women in Nigeria. *Information Development,* 8, 1992. 76–82.

79. Ndiaye, A.R. op.cit. pp.169–74.

80. Moyo, M. Development through radio. *Community Development Journal,* 26, 1991. 227–32.

81. Morris, M.L. and Stavrou, S.E. Telecommunication needs and provision to underdeveloped black areas in South Africa. *Telecommunications Policy,* Sept/Oct 1993. 529–39.

82. Karlsson, J. op.cit. p.53.

Conclusion

A new paradigm for any aspect of human endeavour arises out of a time of practical confusion and dispute about ideas. Such a time of practical confusion has clearly existed for information and library service in Africa since the 1970s at least. The observer finds existing services which do not work, and a repetitive set of explanations for this which cluster around accusations of neglect, moral, administrative and financial, by those who hold power. The information and library studies literature worldwide has also contained disputes about ideas which are intended to relieve this confusion. Indeed, what might seem to be a disproportionately high number of writings offer some form of explanation, suggestion or proposal for the improvement of the African information situation.

The content of these writings, insofar as they appear in the accepted body of information and library studies literature, can be summed up as being effectively a debate between those who offer solutions based on what has worked elsewhere (principally the industrialized countries of the North) and those who seek some better solution from within Africa itself. At first the discussion of conventional panaceas (national information systems, library cooperation, etc.) dominated. Then, since the first radical critiques were offered in the early 1980s, the voices of those who call for a fresh approach have grown stronger. By the mid-1990s it could be argued that their message dominates. Yet their call for some kind of new direction in information and library work has nowhere contained a fully worked-out and justified set of proposals that could be considered as constituting a new paradigm.

This is, at least in part, because of a hole in the structure of the

debate. There is virtually no awareness among those who comment
and write for librarians and other related information workers that
there are other bodies of literature relevant to information in the
developing world. Once one explores the literatures of development and communication, it becomes quite obvious how
significant a gap this is. The writing is generally rooted in a very
much better knowledge of African societies and a willingness to
adopt much more radical approaches. If the present book does
nothing other than draw the attention of information and library
specialists to some of this literature, it will have advanced the debate
considerably. The intention has been to do rather more than that.
It has been to provide a more thorough analysis of the causes and
consequences of African information and library practices and
policies in the light of this richer literature.

A new paradigm is not, however, merely a better analysis of the
situation: it needs to contain proposals for changes. Because what is
reported in the literature inevitably lags behind the cutting edge of
practical innovation, we have sought evidence of initiatives in
various parts of Africa, and found them in encouraging quantity.
These have guided the synthesis of proposals for change which has
been offered here. It is to those who are actually trying fresh
approaches in the field that we really need to look for the emergence of the new paradigm. It is to these pioneers that this book is,
in effect, dedicated.

The argument of this book is that the evidence in the literature,
and in the experiments in the field, both point in the same
direction. They suggest a need not merely for new approaches to
librarianship, but also to the creation of parallel, and very different,
types of information service to complement and partially replace
library service. Creating an information service model that is less
formal, less book-oriented, more locally rooted and more precisely
targeted at Africa's real and potential information users is no small
assignment. The choice and presentation of the specific ideas on
just how a modified library service and a new community-wide
information service might look, which were offered in Chapters 5
and 6, arise from the principles for information service that were
outlined at the end of Chapter 4. These were that an information
service to meet Africa's needs should be based on financial realism,
self-reliance, sustainability, democracy, responsiveness and communication.

The employment of these principles points towards services

which must, first of all, be unpretentious and as free of waste as possible. They must not rely on fixed capital in the form of expensive buildings, large stocks of materials and revenue-depleting technology. Secondly, African information professionals need to find ways to move away from the status of importers not only of information materials and methods, but also of preconceptions and systems of ideas about information service. The information services they provide also need to be shown to be sustainable, although this principle must be treated with care. It is worth remembering that many great enterprises were begun with more faith than finance behind them. While it is certainly risky to begin a project without guaranteed long-term funding, fear should not inhibit enterprise where there is confidence that the enterprise is worthwhile.

Because information services are not currently serving the whole population anything like equally, the principle of democracy is of central importance. Yet it is one to which it is easy to accord lip-service, while everywhere it is neglected in practice. Democratic distribution of information is not only a just principle, it has positive economic consequences through its contribution to making a more productive population and to decreasing the eventual costs of caring for those disadvantaged by ignorance. A genuine responsiveness to expressed user need is also essential. This has long been a guiding principle of library practice, but following it has had the tendency to induce passivity. The important thing is the active seeking out of latent and unexpressed need. A truly responsive service can contribute to the empowerment and emancipation of the populace. Finally, an emphasis on communication is needed to counter the tendency to provide information in uninterpreted packages. A response is no use if it cannot be understood and used by the receiver.

The authors do not intend that the proposals made in Chapters 5 and 6 should be seen as dogmatic pronouncements. Using these suggested principles, readers can assess for themselves the extent to which they feel that the proposals are appropriate. The content of a new paradigm is not likely to be a matter of total unanimity, but if it can be based on agreed principles, it will take a sufficiently coherent shape. Total unanimity about what should be done would almost certainly be unhelpful, since different local circumstances can call for quite different solutions, all of which might be broadly consistent with principles such as those outlined here. The various ideas, plans, experiments and projects discussed here should, however, provide at least a sufficient indication of what is possible, and where further clues and guidelines can be found.

The last thing to say about what is proposed in this book is that it should be seen not just in terms of the geographical context (Africa) for which it was developed, but also in a proper time perspective. Peter Havard Williams (in joint authorship with Guy Marco) drew attention to this question of time in what may be the clearest way that it has been expressed in the information and library studies literature.[1] The argument is that Africa needs time to discover its own solutions to a host of questions relating to development, many of which result from the distortions produced by the experience of colonialism. Time will allow necessary stages to be passed through, and appropriate forms of development to be achieved. What is proposed in this book is intended as a contribution to a process in action and is therefore derived from a commentary on the stages it has reached.

This emphasis on time and the stages through which development needs to pass is not intended to mean that African countries should be expected to follow the same sequence of development stages as occurred in the industrialized countries, or that change should be expected to happen at similar speeds. For example, it is important to note that change in Africa is certainly likely to be faster than that which occurred in the North. It is also the case that the kind of proposals made in this book, particularly those relating to new forms of information service, can only relate to a fairly immediate future. In the long term, information work is entirely likely to take forms quite different from those suggested here. These more distant developments may, or may not, approximate to some kind of global standard.

Be that as it may, in the short term, careless application of a rationale derived from the experience of one continent to the case of another is to be avoided. In a profoundly sceptical paper given at the 1987 IFLA Conference, K.M. Aithnard drew attention to the way in which libraries are a concrete expression of the achievements and aspirations of the particular societies in which they have developed. He therefore found it difficult to comprehend

> the fact that people think it is essential to set up structures and infrastructures, deriving from a centuries old tradition, in other countries where the context is quite different. In other words, things are always presented as if all the changes necessary in the materially poor

countries should not only be modelled on the well-off countries but should also repeat a supposedly linear process having the same objectives.[2]

If we can avoid this kind of error, while trusting that vigorous and well-directed action can bring about appropriate forms of change over time, then there is hope for information service to Africa, parlous though its present position may seem.

References

1. Havard Williams, P. and Marco, G.A. Time, development, Africa. *Alexandria*, 3, 1991. 81–8.
2. Aithnard, K.M. Is the library a source of information in the developing countries? Paper presented at IFLA General Conference, Brighton, UK, August 1987.

Select Bibliography

Aboyade, B.O. Access to information in rural Nigeria. *International Library Review*, 17, 1985. 165–81.

Aboyade. B.O. Communications potentials of the library for non-literates: an experiment in providing information services in a rural setting. *Libri*, 34, 1984. 243–62.

Aboyade, B.O. *Provision of Information for Rural Development*. Ibadan, Fountain Publications, 1987.

Adam, L. Electronic communications technology and development in Africa. *FID News Bulletin*, 45, 1995. 298–306.

Adeniji, A. and Issah, M.S. National Library of Nigeria: functions and achievements. *Libri*, 36, 1986. 136–45.

Adimorah, E.N.O. An analysis of progress made by public libraries as social institutions in Nigeria. *UNESCO Journal of Information Science Librarianship and Archives Administration*, 5, 1983. 160–7.

Adimorah, E.N.O. Establishing community libraries and information resource centres: facilities and resources. In: *Proceedings of the Workshop on Rural Community Library and Information Resource Centres*. Accra, Ghana Library Association, 1992. 53–61.

Adimorah, E.N.O. Information and documentation for integrated rural development in Africa. *Quarterly Bulletin of the International Association of Agricultural Librarians and Documentalists*, 29, 1984. 21–8.

Adimorah, E.N.O. Users and their information needs in Nigeria. *Nigerian Library and Information Science Review*, 1, 1983. 137–48.

Aina, L.O. Grey literature and agricultural research in Nigeria. *Quarterly Bulletin of the International Association of Agricultural Librarians and Documentalists*, 32, 1987. 47–50.

Aina, L.O. Information needs and information-seeking involvement of farmers in six rural communities in Nigeria. *Quarterly Bulletin of the International Association of Agricultural Librarians and Documentalists*, 30, 1985. 35–40.

Aiyepeku, W.O. *International Socio-economic Information Systems: An Evaluation of DEVSIS-type Programs.* Ottawa, International Development Research Centre, 1983.

Alemna, A.A. Towards a new emphasis on oral tradition as an information source in African libraries. *Journal of Documentation,* 48, 1992. 422–9.

Amadi, A.O. *African Libraries: Western Tradition and Colonial Brainwashing.* Metuchen, NJ, Scarecrow Press, 1981.

Amaratunga, C. and Shute, J. Extension and adult learning in a Ghanaian community. *Canadian Journal of African Studies,* 16, 1982. 549–66.

Ambrose, D. Collection and bibliographic control of grey literature of Lesotho. *African Research and Documentation,* 36, 1984. 11–24.

Annis, S. Toward a pro-poor information agenda at the World Bank. *Development,* 2, 1990. 73–6.

Arap Tanui, T. Psychology and culture in information retrieval: with special reference to Moi University Library, Kenya. *Libri,* 39, 1989. 185–91.

Asamani, J.O. *et al.* (eds) *Libraries and Literacy. Proceedings of the 7th Meeting of the Standing Conference of Eastern, Central and Southern African Librarians, Gaborone, 4–8 August, 1986.* Gaborone, Botswana Library Association, 1987.

Atherton, L. Community libraries in Zimbabwe. *Information Development,* 9, 1993. 36–43.

Balabkins, N.W. Collecting information in a developing country. *Harvard Library Bulletin,* 32, 1984. 54–72.

Baldwin, C.M. and Varady, R.G. Information access in Niger: development of a West African special library. *Special Libraries,* 1989. 31–8.

Benge, R.C. *Cultural Crisis and Libraries in the Third World.* London, Bingley, 1979.

Boadi, B.Y. The information sector in the economic development of Africa: the potential role for libraries. *IFLA Journal,* 10, 1984. 139–44.

Boafo, S.T.K. Utilizing development communication strategies in African societies. *Gazette, International Journal for Mass Communication Studies,* 35, 1985. 83–92.

Brieger, W.R. and Kendall, C. The Yoruba farm market as a communication channel in guinea worm disease surveillance. *Social Science and Medicine,* 42, 1996. 233–43.

Brewster, B. *American Overseas Library Technical Assistance, 1940–1970.* Metuchen, NJ, Scarecrow Press, 1976.

Buchanan-Smith, M., Davies, S. and Petty, C. Food security: let them eat information. *IDS Bulletin,* 25, 1994. 69–80.

Chambers, R. All power deceives. *IDS Bulletin,* 25, 1994. 14–26.

Chambers, R., Pacey, A. and Thrupp, L.A. (eds) *Farmer First: Farmer Innovation and Agricultural Research.* London, Intermediate Technology Publications, 1989.

Chijioke, M.E. Public libraries as information networks: Nigeria in the twenty-first century. *Journal of Librarianship,* 21, 1989. 174–85.

Compton, A.W. Opportunities for CD-ROM information services in Africa. *Information Services and Use,* 12, 1992. 283–90.

Coombs, D. *Spreading the Word: The Library Work of the British Council.* London, Mansell, 1988.

Crowder, M. The book crisis: Africa's other famine. *African Research and Documentation,* 41, 1986. 1–6.

Danset, F. Public reading in French-speaking Africa. *International Library Review,* 21, 1989. 245–8.

Davies, S. Information, knowledge and power. *IDS Bulletin,* 25, 1994. 1–13.

De Boef, W. *et al.* (eds) *Cultivating Knowledge: Genetic Diversity, Farmer Experimentation and Crop Research.* London, Intermediate Technology Publications, 1993.

Dehne, K.L. and Hubley, J. Health education services in developing countries: the case of Zimbabwe. *Health Education Research,* 8, 1993. 525–36.

Diop, A. Attitudes of information users in the Sahel. *Information Development,* 4, 1988. 21–7.

Doob, L.W. *Communication in Africa.* New Haven, CT, Yale University Press, 1961.

Duces, B. World Bank activities in library and documentation services provision in developing countries. *Government Information Quarterly,* 8, 1991. 381–6.

Durrani, S. Rural information in Kenya. *Information Development,* 1, 1985. 149–57.

Garforth, C. Reaching the rural poor: a review of extension strategies and methods. In: Jones, G.E. and Rolls, M.J. (eds) *Progress in Rural Extension and Community Development.* Chichester, John Wiley and Sons, 1982. 43–70.

Gehrke, U. Information for development. Some problems of national coordination, regional coordination and international assistance. *INSPEL,* 19, 1985. 166–75.

Giggey, S. *Rural Community Resource Centres: A Guide for Developing Countries.* London, Macmillan, 1988.

Greaves, T. *Intellectual Property Rights for Indigenous Peoples.* Oklahoma City, Society for Applied Anthropology, 1994.

Havard Williams, P. and Jengo, J.E. Library design and planning in developing countries. *Libri,* 20, 1988. 160–76.

Havard Williams, P. and Marco, G.A. Time, development, Africa. *Alexandria,* 3, 1991. 81–8.

Higgins, K.M. and Mazula, A. Community development: a national strategy in Zimbabwe. *Community Development Journal,* 28, 1993. 19–30.

Hyden, G. The invisible economy of smallholder agriculture in Africa. In: Moock, J.L. (ed.) *Understanding Africa's Rural Households and Farming Systems.* Boulder, CO, Westview Press, 1986. 11–35.

Ifidon, S.E. Planning without facts: a comparative study of the uses and abuses of information and information technology. *Library Review,* 43, 1994. 27–36.

Iwuji, H.O.M. Africana in LC and DD classification schemes: a need for an Africana scheme? *Journal of Librarianship,* 21, 1989. 1–18.

Iwuji, H.O.M. Librarianship and oral tradition in Africa. *International Library Review*, 21, 1989. 201–7.

Johansson, E. (ed.) *Seminar on Information Provision to Rural Communities in Africa, Gaborone, Botswana, 22–25 June 1994.* IFLA APL Project report 3. Uppsala, Uppsala University Library, 1995.

Jegede, O.J. From talking drums to electronic networking: Africa's snail-mobile through cyberspace. *FID News Bulletin*, 45, 1995. 218–24.

Kabadiki, K. Rural African women and development. *Social Development Issues*, 16, 1994. 23–35.

Kamba, A.S. Archives and national development in the Third World. *Information Development*, 3, 1987. 108–13.

Kaniki, A.M. Exploratory study of information needs in the Kwa-Ngwanase (Natal) and Qumbu (Transkei) communities of South Africa. *South African Journal of Library and Information Science*, 63, 1995. 9–18.

Kaniki, A.M. Information seeking and information providers among Zambian farmers. *Libri*, 41, 1991. 147–64.

Kantumoya, A. Public libraries and community information services in Africa. *African Journal of Library, Archives and Information Science*, 2, 1992. 33–8.

Kaungamno, E.E. and Ilomo, C.S. *Books Build Nations*. 2 vols. London, Transafrica, 1979.

Kedem, K.A. Libraries as partners in the fight to eradicate illiteracy in sub-Saharan Africa. *Journal of Library and Information Science*, 16, 1991. 87–101.

Kishindo, P. The Functional Literacy Programme in Malawi: educating adults for improved standards of living. *Journal of Social Development in Africa*, 9, 1994. 19–26.

Kohnert, D. and Weber, P.G. The new mission of agricultural research and extension in African agriculture. *Sociologia Ruralis*, 31, 1991. 162–8.

Kotei, S.I.A. *The Book Today in Africa*. Paris, Unesco, 1981.

Kotei, S.I.A. Some variables and comparison between developed and developing library systems. *International Library Review*, 9, 1977. 249–67.

Linney, B. *Pictures, People and Power: People-centred Visual Aids for Development.* London, Macmillan, 1995.

Lippman, M.J. The library as information producer: the case of the Ministry of Health Library and Documentation Centre in Malawi. *Journal of Documentation*, 49, 1993. 55–9.

Lor, P.J. Africanisation of South African libraries: a response to some recent literature. Paper delivered at the Info Africa Nova Conference, Pretoria, 4 May 1993.

Louw, A. Survival information services in South African public libraries. *African Journal of Libraries, Archives and Information Science*, 4, 1994. 91–8.

Lundu, M.C. Library education and training: at home or abroad? *International Library Review*, 14, 1982. 363–78.

Lundu, M.C. and Lungu, C.B.M. Acquisition of scientific literature in developing countries: Zambia. *Information Development*, 5, 1989. 99–106.

Maack, M.N. *Libraries in Senegal: Continuity and Change in an Emerging Nation.* Chicago, American Library Association, 1981.

Maack, M.N. The role of external aid in West African library development. *Library Quarterly,* 56, 1986. 1–16.

Made, S. *Made in Zimbabwe.* Gweru, Mambo Press, 1980.

Mchombu, K.J. *Information Needs and Seeking Patterns for Rural People's Development in Africa.* Gaborone, University of Botswana, 1993.

Mchombu, K.J. Information needs for rural development: the case study of Malawi. *African Journal of Librarianship, Archives and Information Science,* 2, 1992. 17–32.

Mchombu, K.J. Information support for democratization in Africa. In: Feather, J.P. (ed.) *Transforming Libraries and Educating Librarians: Essays in Memory of Peter Havard-Williams.* London, Taylor Graham, 1997. 41–56.

Mchombu, K.J. On the librarianship of poverty. *Libri,* 32, 1982. 241–50.

Mchombu, K.J. and Miti, K. Formulation of National Information Policies in Africa: some unlearnt lessons. *International Information and Library Review,* 24, 1992. 139–71.

Morris, M.L. and Stavrou, S.E. Telecommunication needs and provision to underdeveloped black areas in South Africa. *Telecommunications Policy,* 1993. 529–39.

Moyo, M. Development through radio. *Community Development Journal,* 26, 1991. 227–32.

Mupedziwa, R. The challenge of economic development in an African developing country: social work in Zimbabwe. *International Social Work,* 39, 1996. 41–54.

Mutanyatta, J.N.S. and Mchombu, K.J. *The Village Reading Room Services in Botswana: Final Report of an Evaluative Study.* Gaborone, Botswana National Library Service, 1995.

Namponya, C.R. Agricultural development and library services. *International Library Review,* 18, 1986. 267–74.

Ndiaye, A.R. *Communication à la base: enraciner et épanouir.* Dakar, ENDA, 1994.

Ndiaye, R. Oral culture and libraries. *IFLA Journal,* 14, 1988. 40–6.

Neill, J.R. Library manpower planning in Southern, Central and Eastern Africa. In: Huttemann, L. (ed.) *Manpower Training Needs. Proceedings and Papers of the Information Experts Meeting, Harare, Zimbabwe, 1985.* Bonn, DSE, 1985. 19–28.

Nkhata, B.W.M. CD ROM in developing countries: is it a technology for the distribution of information? *Electronic Library,* 11, 1993. 295–7.

Nzotta, B.C. The administration of branch libraries in a developing country: a case study. *Public Library Quarterly,* 9, 1989. 47–60.

Obasi, J.U. Bibliographical control of Nigerian publications: social science primary materials. *Journal of Documentation,* 38, 1982. 107–24.

Obiagwu, M.C. Foreign exchange and library collections in Nigeria. *Information Development,* 3, 1987. 154–60.

Obiechina, E. *An African Popular Literature: A Study of Onitsha Market Pamphlets.* London, Cambridge University Press, 1973.

Ocholla, D.N. Essentials for school library development. *New Library World*, 93, 1992. 9–15.

O'Connor, B. and Roman, S. Building bridges with books: the British Council's sixty-year record. *Logos*, 5, 1994. 133–8.

Odi, A. Library and information dissemination in a traditional society: the Igbo of eastern Nigeria. *International Information and Library Review*, 26, 1994. 1–9.

Ogunsheye, F.A. Education and training for library and information service to rural communities. In: Aboyade, B.O. (ed.) *Education and Training for Library and Information Services in a Predominantly Non-literate Society*. The Hague, FID, 1981. 87–103.

Ojiambo, J.B. School library services in sub-Saharan Africa. *International Library Review*, 20, 1988. 143–55.

Oladele, B.A. Toward an integrated agricultural information consolidation scheme for farmers in the Nigerian rural areas. *Quarterly Bulletin of the International Association of Agricultural Librarians and Documentalists*, 32, 1987. 98–101.

Olden, A. Constraints on the development of public library service in Nigeria. *Library Quarterly*, 55, 1985. 398–423.

Olden, A. *Libraries in Africa: Pioneers, Policies, Problems*. Lanham, MD, Scarecrow Press, 1995.

Olden, A. Sub-Saharan Africa and the paperless society. *Journal of the American Society for Information Science*, 38, 1987. 298–304.

Parker, J.S. *Unesco and Library Development Planning*. London, Library Association, 1985.

Pretty, J. Alternative systems of inquiry for a sustainable agriculture. *IDS Bulletin*, 25, 1994. 37–48.

Priestley, C. The difficult art of book aid: an African survey. *Logos*, 4, 1993. 215–21.

Rahnema, M. The sound library, a simple but revolutionary tool for development. *UNESCO Journal of Information Science, Librarianship and Archives Administration*, 4, 1982. 151–8.

Raseroka, K.H. Relevant library services in developing countries. *IFLA Journal*, 12, 1986. 288–91.

Richards, P. Community environmental knowledge in African rural development. In: Brokensha, D., Warren, D.M. and Werner, O. *Indigenous Knowledge Systems and Development*. Lanham, MD, University Press of America, 1980. 181–94.

Rolls, M.J., Jones, G.E. and Garforth, C. The dimensions of rural extension. In: Jones, G.E. (ed.) *Investing in Rural Extension: Strategies and Goals*. Amsterdam, Elsevier, 1986. 5–18.

Rosenberg, D. Can libraries in Africa ever be sustainable? *Information Development*, 10, 1994. 247–51.

Rosenberg, D. A review of university libraries in Africa. *Development in Practice*, 6, 1996. 77–80.

Rosenberg, D. Rural community resources centres: a sustainable option for Africa? *Information Development*, 9, 1993. 29–35.

Saracevic, T. Consolidation of information: a concept of needed information products and services for developing countries. In: *Proceedings of the*

48th Annual Meeting of the American Society for Information Science. Medford, NJ, ASIS, 1985. 150–4.

Saracevic, T. Experiences with providing a low-cost high-quality collection of journals in medicine for developing countries. *INSPEL,* 25, 1991. 69–98.

Saracevic, T. Progress in documentation: perception of the needs for scientific and technical information in less developed countries. *Journal of Documentation,* 36, 1980. 214–67.

Scoones, I. and Thompson, J. (eds) *Beyond Farmer First: Rural People's Knowledge, Agricultural Research and Extension Practice.* London, Intermediate Technology Publications, 1994.

Singh, K. Managing science and technology development in Africa: policy tasks ahead. *Africa Quarterly,* 30, 1990. 65–88.

Sitzman, G.L. *African Libraries.* Metuchen, NJ, Scarecrow Press, 1988.

Stilwell, C. Towards transformation? An update on the Resource Centre Fora of South Africa. *International Information and Library Review,* 26, 1994. 303–13.

Sturges, P. International transfer of information and national self-sufficiency: the case of Botswana. In: *Proceedings of the 49th Annual Meeting of the American Society for Information Science.* Medford, NJ, ASIS, 1986. 320–5.

Sturges, P. The political economy of information: Malawi under Kamuzu Banda 1964–1994. In: Feather, J.P. (ed.) *Transforming Libraries and Educating Librarians: Essays in Memory of Peter Havard-Williams.* London, Taylor Graham, 1997. 57–73.

Sturges, P. What librarians feel about their careers: a survey of diploma and certificate holders. *Botswana Library Association Journal,* 7, 1985. 9–21.

Sturges, P. Using grey literature in informal information services in Africa. *Journal of Documentation,* 50, 1994. 273–90.

Sturges, P. and Chimseu, G. The chain of information provision in the villages of Malawi: a rapid rural appraisal. *International Information and Library Review,* 28, 1996. 135–56.

Sturges, P. and Chimseu, G. Information repackaging in Malawi. *African Journal of Library Archives and Information Science,* 6, 1996. 85–93.

Sturges, P. and Chimseu, G. Qualitative research in information studies: a Malawian study. *Education for Information,* 14, 1996. 117–26.

Tali, M. Libraries in Luanda, Angola, problems and prospects. *Cadernos BAD,* 2, 1993. 29–53.

Tallman, J.I. and Ojiambo, J.B. *Translating an International Education to a National Environment.* Metuchen, NJ, Scarecrow Press, 1990.

Thairu, R.W. Cataloguing policies and problems in Kenyan Libraries. *African Research and Documentation,* 40, 1986. 8–15.

Tiamiyu, M.A. Sub-Saharan Africa and the paperless society: a comment and a counterpoint. *Journal of the American Society for Information Science,* 40, 1989. 325–8.

Ugboajah, F.O. Oramedia in Africa. In: Ugboajah, F.O. (ed.) *Mass Communication, Culture and Society in West Africa.* London, Hans Zell, 1985. 165–76.

Unesco. *Development of Public Libraries in Africa: the Ibadan Seminar.* Paris, Unesco, 1954.

Vaughan, O. Assessing grassroots politics and community development in Nigeria. *African Affairs,* 94, 1995. 501–18.

Wiggins, S. Agricultural policy and agricultural extension: the African experience. In: Jones, G.E. (ed.) *Investing in Rural Extension: Strategies and Goals.* Amsterdam, Elsevier, 1986. 99–105.

Woherem, E.E. *Information Technology in Africa.* Nairobi, ACTS Press, 1993.

Zaaiman, R.B., Roux, P.J.A. and Rykheer, J.H. *The Use of Libraries for the Development of South Africa* (Final report on an investigation for the South African Institute for Librarianship and Information Science). Pretoria, Unisa, 1988.

Zulu, S.F.C. Africa's survival plan for meeting the challenges of technology in the 1990s and beyond. *Libri,* 44, 1994. 77–94.

Index